The People of
DEVON
1918 – 1930
From War to Peace

To Pamela, Cheryl and Neil

Published in 2021

Copyright © 2021 David Parker

All rights reserved. Apart from any fair dealing for the purpose of private study, research, criticism or review, as permitted under the Copyright, Designs and Patents Act, 1988, no part of this publication may be reproduced, stored in a retrieval system, or transmitted in any form or by any means, electronic, electrical, chemical, mechanical, optical, photocopying, recording or otherwise, without the prior written permission of the copyright owner. Enquiries should be addressed to the Publishers.

Every attempt has been made by the author and publisher to secure the appropriate permissions for materials reproduced in this book. If there has been any oversight we will be happy to rectify the situation in future editions.

A CIP catalogue record for this book is available from the British Library.

ISBN: 978 0 85704 353 5

Halsgrove
Halsgrove House,
Ryelands Business Park,
Bagley Road, Wellington,
Somerset TA21 9PZ
Tel: 01823 653777
Fax: 01823 216796
email: sales@halsgrove.com

Part of the Halsgrove group of companies
Information on all Halsgrove titles is available at: www.halsgrove.com

Printed and bound in India by Parksons Graphics

Opposite: Daisy Blackmore and her father from Hatherleigh at Woolacombe in 1923.
(Courtesy Beaford Old Archive images: © Beaford Arts).

The People of DEVON
1918–1930
From War to Peace

David Parker

HALSGROVE

CONTENTS

ACKNOWLEDGEMENTS		6
CHAPTER 1	**1918: THE ARMISTICE AND CHRISTMAS**	7
CHAPTER 2	**THE MEN RETURN & COMMUNITIES REMEMBER**	10
	Demobilisation: welcome home	
	The men still fighting: Russia, Ireland and the Middle East	
	Peace celebrations and Armistice Days	
	The missing and the post-war casualties	
	Medals and trophies	
	Comrades of the Great War	
	The memorials	
CHAPTER 3	**REALIGNMENTS**	36
	Running down the war effort	
	Patriots and rebels	
	Clergy and congregations	
	Women in public life	
CHAPTER 4	**THE RECOVERY: TOWNS, TOURISM & TRANSPORT**	60
	Towns and tourism	
	Home for Heroes: the problem of housing	
	Sport: the widening appeal	
	Transport by air, sea and land	

Dolton Carnival. (Author's collection).

Historical tableaux: Victory pageant at Collipr near Tiverton 1919. (Courtesy of Tiverton Museum)

CHAPTER 5   **RURAL RELATIONSHIPS: THE CHANGING PATTERN OF LIFE**   85
                        Breaking up the great estates
                        The survival of patrician influence
                        Village life
                        Farmers and farming

CHAPTER 6   **HEALTH & WELFARE: WORKING TOWARDS A SYSTEM**   108
                        The 1918-19 influenza pandemic
                        Hospitals: voluntarism and the battle to survive and expand
                        Mothers and babies: the recognition of need
                        Those on the edge
                        Workhouses and their infirmaries: the end in sight

CHAPTER 7   **CHILDREN & SCHOOLS: STRENGTHENING THE DIVIDE**   128
                        The 1918 Education Act: opportunities and omissions
                        Devon's response
                        The 1919-21 depression and the battle for progress
                        Later troubles and advances
                        Teaching and learning: the age of competition
                        The secondary grammar schools: diverging paths.

BIBLIOGRAPHY   150

INDEX   156

Unveiling Black Torrington's war memorial.
(Boniface Old Archive images © Boniface AHS).

ACKNOWLEDGEMENTS

This book owes much to the curators, librarians and volunteers who care for the many records I consulted – newspapers and council records, charity files and brochures, diaries and memoirs, logbooks and letters, brochures and photographs. For their time and expertise I remain grateful to Naomi Ayre and colleagues at the Atheneum and North Devon Heritage Centre in Barnstaple, Katherine Burrell at Beaford Old Archive, Sara Charman at Colyton Heritage Centre, Emma Laws and Margaret Knight at the Devon & Exeter Institution (DEI), Scott Pettitt and colleagues at the Devon Heritage Centre in Exeter, Lin Watson and colleagues at Teignmouth Museum, Pippa Griffith, Bernard Swain and Pam Sampson at Tiverton Museum of Mid Devon Life, Catriona Batty and Rosemary Hatch at Topsham Museum, and Katy McBean at Torquay Library. Staff and volunteers at Dawlish Museum, Exmouth Museum, Ilfracombe Museum, Plymouth Library, and Tavistock Library and Museum were also welcoming and ever ready with help. I appreciate, too, the help of archive staff mentioned above, and also Derek Payne in Torquay, John Street of Exeter City Council, Natalie Jones of Reach PLC Licensing, Deborah Gray of the *Bone & Joint Journal*, and Ron Cosens of the Victorian Image Collection in clarifying copyright.

My thanks, too, are given to Tony Ovens for his photographs of Exeter City's war memorial. And once again I remain grateful for the expertise of Mark Ware who photographed many period illustrations for me, and skilfully rendered them suitable for printing.

MONEY VALUES

Throughout this book money amounts remain in pounds, shillings and pence, and are written as £12:10s:6d for pounds, shillings and pence, 7/6d or 2/- for shillings and pence, and 9½d for pence. 10s equates to 50p, 1/- to 5p, and 6d to 2.5d in decimal currency. However inflation and changes in income levels and prices make realistic comparisons difficult between then and now. For example, property was relatively cheaper and new clothing dearer in the 1920s.

As an approximate guide, if an entry in the text refers to commodity prices then 1/- in 1920 is comparable to about £2 today rising gradually to £2.80 for 1923 and then flattening out. Thus £1 in 1920 equates to £39.50 today, and £1 in 1923 to £56. A land sale of £1,000 in 1920 equates to about £40,000 today.

If an entry refers to wages then a 1/- rise in 1920 is comparable to £5.70 today rising to around £9.60 for 1923 and afterwards. Thus a £2 weekly wage in 1920 equates to about £230 today rising to around £380 in 1923.
(www.measuringworth.com/calculators/ukcompare)

CITATION & REFERENCE ABBREVIATIONS

CC	*Crediton Chronicle*
DG	*Dawlish Gazette*
DEI	Devon & Exeter Institution
D&SN	*Devon & Somerset News*
DEVON HDB	Snell, F.J., *Devonshire: Historical, Descriptive, Biographical* (Wm Mates, 1907)
DHC	Devon Heritage Centre, Exeter
MDA	*Mid Devon Advertiser*
NDH	*North Devon Herald*
NDJ	*North Devon Journal*
PLU	Poor Law Union
PO	*Paignton Observer*
SMG	*South Molton Gazette*
TG	*Tavistock Gazette*
TT	*Torquay Times*
WEH	*Western Evening Herald*
WO	*Western Observer*
WT	*Western Times*

1
1918: THE ARMISTICE & CHRISTMAS

Introduction

Devon remained frantically busy as October 1918 turned into November. Men in uniform were everywhere. The reasonably healthy ones were briefly on leave, or in training camps, or in transit in trucks and trains. Those wounded physically or mentally were being assessed, treated, or convalescing in the dozens of war emergency hospitals scattered across the county. And across the county thousands of families were coping with the death of their menfolk, or hoping for their recovery from wounds, or worrying about them in prisoner of war camps, or just endlessly and anxiously waiting for news.[1]

After four years of appalling warfare many of these families, often grouped in local working parties, were still contributing money and food, tobacco and cigarettes, books and magazines, and knitted gloves, jumpers, scarves and balaclavas to the war hospitals and to the thousands of parcels sent to Devonians in prison camps, and serving on warships, air stations and in army units across France, the Balkans and the Middle East. Their efforts were co-ordinated through the highly efficient Mayoress of Exeter's Depot.[2] And hundreds of women, and also men unable for various reasons to join the armed forces, had joined the hundred or so Voluntary Aid Detachments (VADs) across the county. Many women trained as nurses but some were orderlies, clerks or drivers as were some male volunteers, while others were responsible for transport and the maintenance of equipment, furniture and buildings. All were essential for the running of the vast system of war hospitals.

Twyford School 'Peace Float', Kingsbridge 1919.
(Courtesy Kingsbridge Museum).

The People of Devon 1918–1930

In 1918 the government controlled nearly every aspect of life through the draconian Defence of the Realm Act, including newspaper reports, train timetables, hotel registrations and licensing hours. Numerous directives related to identifying likely spies and saboteurs were particularly relevant to a coastal county such as Devon, and recruiting drives and newspaper articles ensured Germany was seen, in the Bishop of Crediton's words, as the Anti-Christ. Few had any sympathy with the views of conscientious objectors. Devonport and other yards turned out warships, Devon's foundries manufactured armaments and its textile mills wove uniforms. Farms were increasingly closely supervised by the government through its county war agricultural committee, and farmers, whether willing or not, were required to produce an ever increasing tonnage of cereals at the expense of beef and mutton. And the Allied offensive earlier in 1918 meant many of the young men previously excused military service because they could prove they were essential to the survival of farms and businesses had been conscripted.[3]

After years of frustrated hopes that the next big campaign would bring victory and peace, the blunting of a major German attack along the Western Front in Spring 1918 followed by determined and successful counter-attacks by British, French and American forces during the summer months gave a hint, and an increasingly strong one, that the tide was turning in the Allies favour. German moral among its armed forces and its civilian population began withering away under the pressure of the determined Allied onslaught and the chronic shortages of food caused by the Allied naval blockade. After defeats in Central Europe and the Balkans the vast polygot Austro-Hungarian Empire began to implode as its subsidiary states of Romania and Galicia, Bohemia and Slovakia, Slovenia and Croatia, abandoned its cause and asserted their independence, as they had long wanted to do. News trickled through in September that both Germany and Austria-Hungary had put out peace feelers, but they were rejected as inadequate.[4]

The Allied advance and blockade continued, and in October a German civilian government replaced the generals as the arbiters of Germany's fate. By now influenza and its corollary, pneumonia, were killing soldiers as well as civilians in their thousands on all sides, but the fighting and slaughter continued. At last mutinies in the German fleet and German and Austro-Hungarian army units, along with Bolshevik inspired riots in German streets, and the sullen admission of the German High Command that the war was lost, led to renewed peace negotiations early in November. The abdication of the almost uncomprehending Kaiser was announced on 9 November, the day before the German government accepted the Allied armistice terms that included evacuating all occupied territory and virtually disarming. The fighting went on, though, and men were killed right up to the 11.00am deadline the following day when suddenly, many survivors recalled, a tense eery silence fell – to be followed after a minute or two by the rippling sound of cheering.

News of the Armistice was greeted with relief and instant celebration born of years of pent-up anxiety. In Exeter thousand gathered in front of the cathedral to sing hymns and be blessed by the bishop, and then marched with civic dignitaries and army units to General Buller's statue to be addressed by Sir James Owen, the mayor. In Brixham and Ilfracombe trawlers, patrol boats and minesweepers sounded their sirens and let off rockets, and in Tavistock railway locomotives whistled, factory sirens hooted and schools closed early. Bampton Quarry workers had a half day holiday, and in Hatherleigh rockets were fired and crowds gathered in the market square where the schoolchildren sang hymns and patriotic songs. In Barnstaple several works bands gathered to play in the main streets, and in Uffculme Fox Brothers' textile factory closed for the day in celebration. People in Okehampton gathered in the Arcade, and in Tiverton they filled the Electric Theatre, to take part in *ad hoc* thanksgivings and sing the National Anthem.[5]

Later in the day people flocked to hastily compiled church services. In some places, but far from all, unity of purpose transcended sectarianism. In Tiverton, for example, there was an interdenominational service in St Peter's Church but in Honiton each denomination hurriedly arranged its own service of thanksgiving. Wherever the services were held, though, the churches and chapels were packed as relief overflowed briefly into overwhelming gratitude. In Exmouth hundreds of people were obliged to stand outside Holy Trinity Church and partake of the service as best they could.[6] Everywhere lay and clerical speakers highlighted the sacrifices of those who died along with thanks to God for giving the nation and its Empire such a stunning victory. They hoped, as the vicar of Barnstaple exemplified, that they were 'at the beginning of a new and glorious era in the history of the world – days when peace would flow like a river, a peace based upon righteousness.'[7]

The following days saw the mood change again. The casualty lists continued to be published, but now there was the added poignancy that so many men had died so close to the Armistice. Vengeance remained a powerful emotion, and bonfires burning effigies of the Kaiser lit up evening skies. There was no let up for the hospitals, the VADs, the working parties,, or the Mayoress of Exeter's Depot. In December the donations of money and goods were still flowing into the Depot and the parcels of 'comforts' still flowing out to servicemen in local hospitals or overseas. And while the huge cost of the war meant the wartime campaign promoting War Bonds had not slackened, the cries for the government to honour its promises to reform education, invest in child health care, and build thousands of comfortable new homes were rapidly getting louder.[8]

On 27 December the *Western Times* devoted three pages to celebrations of the first post-war Christmas across the county. There was a determination that people should enjoy themselves as much as possible, and more than a hint of striving to turn the clock back to Christmases before the war. Shops were well-stocked and busy. More donations than ever before flowed in to charities giving Christmas dinners and presents to hospital patients, to the inmates of workhouses, and to pauper children living in the Boards of Guardians 'Scattered Homes'. Mayors, councillors, senior officers and other local dignitaries visited all manner of institutions to bring seasonal greetings and distribute gifts. Nurses and choirs toured wards singing carols. Foreign seamen were fed and entertained in the Seamen's Missions in coastal ports. Christmas Day services were packed, and the churches aglow with candles, flowers and greenery. However no-one, and not least the *Western Times*, could ignore the increasing number of returning service personnel in widely varying degrees of health and fitness. 'They are to be seen here, there, and everywhere. All branches of the service seem to be represented – naval officers, bluejackets, infantrymen, and artillerymen, cavalrymen, and the airmen. There are also to be seen flitting about numerous young women in the uniforms of the auxiliary services – the 'Waacs", the 'Wrens', and the 'Penguins'.[9]

The derogatory use of females 'flitting about' was not surprising, but certainly ill-considered. A month earlier the headmistress of Cheltenham Ladies College, Miss Lilian Faithfull, had roused the girls of Exeter's Maynard School by saying the war had taught women 'resource, initiative, patience, perseverance, and powers of endurance' and they, too, must be ready soon 'to take part in the work of reconstruction.[10] The world had changed, whether people wished it or not.

REFERENCES

1. *WT* 15 October 1918, 2 November 1918

2. *WT* 3, 7, 15 & 24 October 1918, 1 & 11 November 1918

3. Details taken from Parker, D., *The People of Devon in the First World War*

4. Details in this and next paragraph from Gilbert, M., *First World War*, pp431-504

5. *WT* 12 & 14 November 1918, *D&SN* 14 November 1918, TG 15 November 1918

6. *WT* 12 November 1918

7. *WT* 14 November 1918

8. *SMG* 23 November 1918, *WT* 16, 17, 19, 26 & 27 November 1918, 6 & 13 December 1918

9. *WT* 27 December 1918

10. *WT* 16 November 1918

2
THE MEN RETURN & COMMUNITIES REMEMBER

Demobilisation: welcome home

The government's carefully laid plan to demobilise 3,750,000 service personnel did not work. It was predicated on the need to avoid two potential catastrophes – mass unemployment if too many men returned home without the security of a job, and rampant inflation if industry could not switch production quickly to domestic needs. Therefore initial demobilisation favoured key civil servants and industrial personnel first, then those with guaranteed jobs, and finally everyone else. The scheme was sensible but manifestly unfair as those called up in 1917 and 1918 were far more likely to have kept links with employers than an early volunteer who had survived four years of war.

Demobilisation began on 9 December but by early January 1919 thousand of soldiers were staging protests in major camps and ports at home and abroad. Fearing trouble with so many troops in the vicinity, the mayors of Exeter and Torquay asked Brigadier Sir Hugh Stewart, the District Director from the Ministry of Labour, to address public meetings on the situation. The newspaper reports intimated that local businessmen and trades unions were united in giving him a rough time.[1] Local builders and engineering works, for example, were crying out for the release of skilled men.[2] In addition, 300 uniformed staff of the Army Pay Corps based in Exeter protested to the War Office about their poor wages and billets but, above all,

The men from Shaldon who returned from the war photographed outside Fonthill House. (Courtesy of Teignmouth Museum).

their delayed demobilisation due to their continuing heavy workload.[3] After the 1918 general election Winston Churchill became Minister of War and quickly amended the regulations so that those enlisting before 31 December 1915, or aged over 37, or had three wound stripes, were released at once. By the end of 1919 the army's strength had shrunk to under 400,000 men, most of whom were volunteers. Unemployment did not soar, remaining at roughly its pre-war figure of 2.7%, and domestic production quickly rose to meet the pent-up demand.[4] However, as we shall see, it was a very different story in 1920.

Most prisoners of war (POWs) from Germany started the journey home within days of the Armistice, but those from the Devonshire Regiment held by the Turks often took longer because of their ill-treatment and poor health in captivity. The first POWs to return received enthusiastic welcomes. On 26 November Lieutenant Halford of the Royal Flying Corps was greeted at Crediton station by the Boy Scouts, Grammar School Cadets, hospital nursing staff and convalescing soldiers who between them pulled his carriage home.[5] Throughout December the *Western Times* was full of stories of other communities – from Clovelly and Holsworthy in the north and west to Brixham and Cullompton in the south and east – cheering POWs home. Many public houses organised collections and rousing receptions for the returnees.[6]

In early 1919 many towns staged more formal receptions for ex-POWs, often complete, as at Torquay, with roast beef dinners, plentiful cigarettes and alcohol, fulsome speeches of welcome, and ending with dances.[7] In January 200 POWs home from Germany, Austria, Bulgaria and Turkey were entertained by music, songs and games in Exeter's Guildhall in the presence of the mayor (Thomas Bradley Rowe), the Bishop of Exeter (The Rt Rev. Lord William Cecil), the Lord Lieutenant (Earl Fortescue) and the city's MP (Sir Robert Newman) and their families. The report admitted 'It was a difficult thing to know just how to entertain such a mixed party, but after the first few minutes the strangeness of the situation wore off, and the guests unthawed.' The following month Exeter's Guildhall twice entertained further groups of POWs. At the first the star turn was Lieutenant Sidney, an Australian acrobat badly wounded in action who had learnt to play the cornet during his recovery, while the second was attended by the cast of 'Bubbly', currently at the Theatre Royal.[8] Villages were equally welcoming. Typical among the events were the tea parties were organised by Miss Kennaway at Escot and the vicar and his wife at Parkham.[9]

Contrary to assumptions about the silence of returning servicemen, local newspapers were adept at persuading POWs to speak of their experiences, and no doubt their anti-German stories were very welcome. Lieutenant Halford was a clergyman's son from Crediton. Shot down in 1916 he experienced relentlessly brutal treatment in several prison camps where, he said, officers were beaten, locked in cells and refused food for the slightest infringement of regulations. Their food parcels were stolen, and two officers who escaped had been shot after recapture.[10] Private Warren of Tiverton, Private Jackson of Budleigh Salterton and Lance Corporal Rhodes and Corporal Walter, both of Totnes, were among the many who recalled the mindless beatings, solitary confinement, freezing cold, appalling food, labouring 16 hours a day in dangerous mines or muddy fields, and enduring bouts of dysentery.[11] Others spoke of their long forced marches to camps, rations consisting of bad horseflesh and boiled mangolds, and witnessing POWs starving or worked to death.[12] Private Tucker and Sergeant Kendall, both from Exeter, were two of many POWs who believed their survival depended on the food and clothing parcels from the Mayoress of Exeter's Depot. Boots falling apart was a particular hardship, and new ones appreciated more than tobacco. Kendall, and Lance Corporal Dunn from Dawlish, were two POWs who had also witnessed the appalling conditions endured by many German civilians in 1918 when every commodity was in short supply.[13]

Communities welcomed other discharged servicemen home equally enthusiastically. In March 1919 'the ladies of Teignmouth' provided three 'sumptuous' teas followed by smoking concerts and musical entertainments for the home-comers.[14] In August Hemyock's streets were decorated and its bells rang as ex-servicemen marched to church and then enjoyed games and tea on the village field. In the evening they were given dinner at Culm Davey House with 'twenty young ladies, attired in white, with tri-coloured rosettes and ribbons, acting as waitresses.'[15] In November the men from Bovey Tracey were given a salmon supper and smoking concert, with moving speeches of gratitude and also sad references to those who died.[16] Such contrasting emotions which were mirrored in every similar event. However, worries about post-war national stability were ever present. In December Dawlish ex-servicemen enjoyed a lavish Christmas supper, and as so often at these events speakers highlighted their hopes that the battle-weary men would now turn their hands to peacefully rebuilding the nation's greatness – as one officer remarked, let us 'meet together in a social way. It was far better than Socialism.'[17]

Relief and gratitude took many forms. During a day of both celebration and remembrance in Barnstaple 600 'heroes of the borough' were presented with certificates of gratitude. The families of the men killed were remembered and entertained in another hall.[18] In December 1919 the parish of Starcross on the Exe estuary presented 95 ex-servicemen with inscribed electro-plated loving cups. Nearby Kenton did the same the following March.[19] On Boxing Day the men from Black Torrington were treated to 'a bountiful tea' and then presented with silver pendants for their watch chains.[20] Some larger firms publicly honoured their employees who served. The Southwood family who owned Exeter's Dynamo Printing Works entertained their returnees at the city's renowned Dellars' Cafe. Deep gratitude was expressed to all 70 men who donned uniforms, 'some of whom now lay silently overseas.'[21]

A few places staged full-scale welcoming pageants. Bridwell Park hosted the one at Halberton in early June 1919. Eight thousand people attended; some came by train to nearby Tiverton Junction and the roads witnessed 'an unbroken procession of char-a-bancs, cars, cycles, traps, wagons and pedestrians.' With most villagers taking part, the pageant celebrated local events within a national setting from Saxon and Viking times (culminating in the defeated Vikings becoming Christians), through the Middle Ages (centring on the Crusades and chivalry) and Tudors (highlighting Merry England and the defeat of the Spanish Armada), to the nineteenth century (with rural feasts, dancing and poetry celebrating the defeat of Napoleon). The Grand Finale featured Britannia flanked by the

The inscribed Loving Cups presented to Starcross ex-servicemen. (Mark Ware: WT 2 January 1920. Courtesy of Devon & Exeter Institution Trustees).

The historic costumes forming part of the 1919 Victory Pageant at Collipriest near Tiverton. (Courtesy of Tiverton Museum).

costumed villagers presenting each ex-serviceman with a silver cigarette case and a framed photograph of the pageant. Written by a clergyman relation of the influential Lovett family who were the prime movers of the pageant, the theme caught the patriotic mood of the moment and also provided an antidote to more revolutionary thoughts crossing Europe from Bolshevik Russia.[22] A similar pageant was organised by Mrs Bond, the rector's wife at Ashburton. Here the highlight was St George declaring the people free from the dragons of evil, poverty and unemployment, and confidently assuring Britannia that the nation's future was bright.[23]

Not every man was welcomed back. When Mr Guard returned to teaching at Bideford Old Town Boys' School the 'very hostile reception' by parents and children turned into a well-publicised strike by more than 60 pupils. Guard had been a conscientious objector refusing to bear arms and spent the war working on farms. The boys booed and threw old potatoes at him and the police had to escort him to and from school. The school managers had been divided on the issue of his return, but nevertheless Guard stood his ground with the support of the headmaster and gradually the absentees returned. The situation had not been helped by newspapers citing the strident criticisms of Guard – as a 'coward' and someone 'who could not be called a man' – by a minority of County Education Committee members. Others, though, had defended him as a man of deep religious faith.[24] Budleigh Salterton Council discussed the rumour that a conscientious objector might become a local tax collector but with opinions divided – primarily on whether or not the war was fought for individual liberty – it was decided not to register a formal objection.[25] Plymouth Council acted differently and voted by a large majority to bar a conscientious objector from returning to teaching in the town.[26] And as late as October 1920 an aggressive public meeting in Seaton sought to hound a conscientious objector out of his post as secretary of a local charity dedicated to relieving starving children in post-war Europe.[27]

The men still fighting: Russia, Ireland and the Middle East

Not every man left the armed forces. In August 1919 Devonians in the Devonshire Regiment's 6th Battalion were welcomed home to Barnstaple after five years in India and Mesopotamia just as the 2nd Battalion, recently restored to strength after suffering heavy casualties in France, was seen off from Devonport for a three year tour of duty in

India. Many '2nd Devons' men were 'Regulars', and it seems new recruits had not been difficult to find.[28]

From time to time in 1919 news trickled through about Devonians fighting in Russia. In March 1919 local newspapers published an account by Petty Officer Albert Chudley, who served in the British 15th destroyer flotilla fighting along the Baltic coast, of the corpses and burnt out villages resulting, he claimed, from Bolshevik atrocities. He added, 'I used to be a bit off a Socialist myself before I went abroad but since I have seen a little of what Bolshevikism means I should be sorry to see anything like it here in England.'[29] Chudley lived in Newton Abbot where several Bolshevik sympathisers were active among the railway and clay workers, and Exeter, too, had a few Communist agitators. Devon's newspapers were hostile to all thoughts of Russian inspired unrest, but most industrial centres across the country possessed their coterie of Communist sympathisers, and there was widespread opposition among the Labour movement as a whole to British involvement in Russian affairs.

Overall 20,000 British and Imperial soldiers were part of the Allied force assisting the Imperialist 'White Russian' attempts to defeat Lenin's 'Red Army'. More than 200 men from the Devonshire Regiment served in Russia in 1919, some volunteering from the 2nd Battalion recouping in Devonport and others drafted, rather than volunteering, from units still in France.[30] After a short period of home leave the men were dispatched from Devon camps to become 'C' Company of the Oxford & Buckinghamshire Light Infantry. They sailed from Southampton to Archangel in May along with several large boxes of clothing and medical equipment supplied by the Mayoress of Exeter's Depot. From Archangel they sailed upriver to Ust Vaga, a straggling collection of wooden houses along the Northern Dvina River, a few miles from the battle zone. The region was covered in forests and swamps with, unnervingly, no clear front line. Bolshevik units could easily steal close to attack outposts, and supposedly friendly civilians were adept at thieving and liaising with the enemy. Skirmishes were confused amidst the trees and gullies, with enemy forces disappearing as fast as they had arrived, and in the desultory campaign several Russian villages and towns were taken, evacuated and retaken by both sides.[31] Lieutenant Ronald Gould from Exeter was a pilot responsible for bombing and staffing enemy river barges and shot down at least one Russian aeroplane.[32] 'C' Company took part in a major attack on a Bolshevik held town – Kitsa in the far north – but the assault was defeated with several casualties.

Long before the end of 1919 the Allies found the warfare costly and fruitless, without any chance of ultimate success. After participating in a hopeless cause the men arrived back in Plymouth on 4 October 1919, and immediately many broke ranks, flooded into the city, sought out the public houses, became riotous, and had to be rounded up under armed guard.[33] However in January 1920 the awards of a Distinguished Service Order, a Military Cross, a Distinguished Conduct Medal and two Military Medals were made to ex-Devonshire Regiment men serving in Russia for their determined repulsion of a Bolshevik assault on their headquarters at Ust Vaga.[34]

After decades of controversy and violence Parliament granted Ireland Home Rule in 1914 only for its implementation to be suspended until after the war. However in 1916 Irish republicans staged the famous Easter Rising, and after its defeat the execution of its leaders and on-going British repression created a surge in Irish support for Sinn Fein which won 73 of the Irish 105 seats in the 1918 general election. On 21 January Sinn Fein unilaterally created the Dail Eireaan, declared Ireland independent and made the Irish Republican Army (IRA) its official military force. It began a vicious war of independence, making the Royal Irish Constabulary (RIC) and British army its main targets. In September Lloyd George outlawed the Dail and increased British forces while pondering a new Home Rule Act. In January 1920 many unemployed ex-servicemen, Devonians among them, were attracted by British government offers to join the RIC. With uniforms in short supply they wore a mix of army khaki trousers and RIC dark green or British police dark blue jackets, and became known as 'the Black and Tans'. Their role was to act as defensive back-ups to the RIC. The government also recruited ex-army officers as

RIC Auxiliaries; their role, however, was offensive, namely destroying IRA units. One Devonian Auxiliary was Major John Kirkwood who owned Yeo Vale in north Devon as well as an estate in Ireland. He commanded a company based in Woodstock House in Kilkenny where its presence was bitterly resented.[35] The Devonshire Regiment's 1st Battalion (The '1st Devons'), comprising mainly new recruits led by few seasoned veterans, had been stationed in the district since 1919 to supplement the RIC.[36]

As the war intensified both sides engaged in assassinations, ambushes and arson attacks, and showed little mercy to suspected sympathisers.[37] In November 1920 Lieutenant Henry Hambleton was buried with full military honours at Exminster. He was an Intelligence Officer with the Northamptonshire Regiment in Ireland and was shot while riding a motor cycle near Nenagh. He had been a ward of the Kekewich family at Peamore.[38] In December 1920 Lieutenant Ernest Lucas was buried in Shaldon where he had settled with his wife in 1918. He had joined the RIC as a cadet and been killed on 28 November with 16 other cadets and officers in a IRA ambush not far from Cork.[39] In March 1921 Captain Roger Peek, the younger son of Sir Cuthbert Peek of Rousdon, was killed when his party's lorry was ambushed at Scramoge in County Roscommon. He was buried near his home in Loddiswell with full military honours and among the mourners were many of the Peek's aristocratic connections.[40] That June Lieutenant Robert Betteridge, Royal Field Artillery, from Totnes was one of three officers found blindfolded and shot several hours after leaving their barracks in County Tipperary.[41]

Between 1920 and 1922 the Chief of Police in Ireland was Lieut-General Sir Henry Tudor. He was born in Newton Abbot, and his father was Prebendary Henry Tudor of Exeter Cathedral. In 1922 Sir Henry became Director of Public Safety in Palestine, soon after Great Britain was mandated to govern the region on behalf of the League of Nations. Many Auxiliaries transferred to his new command where their skills were considered entirely appropriate for combatting the endemic highway robberies and murderous tribal vendettas.[42]

Elsewhere across the Empire two officers from Devon died in action suppressing the Iraqi revolt of 1919-20 against British rule. They were Lieutenant Arthur Whittome, 123rd Outram's Rifles, from Tavistock and Captain Arthur Lewis, 52nd Sikh Regiment, from Goodleigh.[43]

Peace celebrations and Armistice Days

The signing of the peace treaty in the Palace of Versailles on Saturday 28 June 1919 was celebrated across the county. Typically, in Bampton the church bells rang out, houses were bedecked with flags and bunting, the brass band played 'pleasing national and patriotic music' in the main streets, and on Sunday the services in the parish church included 'suitable hymns' and 'an impressive sermon' on the treaty.[44] The following Sunday, 6 July, was deemed a day of national thanksgiving and in Exeter city dignitaries, county councillors and the Board of Guardians processed to the cathedral where Bishop Cecil preached from the psalmist's words 'Remember the marvellous works that He hath done' and emphasised that 'the bravest troops and the most skilful generals would have been useless to us in the war if we had not had God's Blessing.'[45] In Sidmouth each church had its own service in the morning and in the afternoon 2,000 people flocked to the cricket ground for an interdenominational thanksgiving backed by the town's massed choirs. Here, as elsewhere, the sermons and hymns – notably 'O God, our help in ages past', 'For all the saints who from their labours rest', and 'Praise the Lord, the King of Heaven' – were held to reflect the greatness of God in the victory He had secured for the British Empire, and the rightness, and indeed, the righteousness, of the national cause.[46]

The government designated Saturday 19 July 1919 as 'Peace Day'. In London 15,000 Allied troops marched down Whitehall past a temporary representation of Sir Edwin Lutyens' Cenotaph, and across the capital major parks hosted patriotic concerts. In Devon local councils and voluntary committees had wrestled with various celebratory ideas, and ways to finance them, and sometimes found themselves mired in controversy. Sometimes, as at public meetings in Broadclyst, Brampford Speke, Cheriton Bishop, Dawlish and Woodbury everyone agreed that tea and sports for servicemen and their families were the way forward, and committees were duly appointed to raise funds. However divisions quickly appeared at Exeter City Council meetings over whether celebrations were appropriate when several European countries were still at war over disputed territory, when Devon men were fighting in Russia, when bereaved families might feel bitterly insulted, and when riotous crowds could bring the city into disrepute. The Council voted that no ratepayers' money should underwrite the events, and similar arguments triumphed in other towns such as Crediton, Newton Abbot, Tavistock and Torquay.[47]

In the end voluntary efforts and local subscriptions ensured communities, if not the weather, rose to the occasion. Exeter's shop windows and main streets were lavishly decorated with the flags of the Allies, coloured lamps, red, white and blue streamers, and banners featuring patriotic slogans. While the rain poured down crowds sheltered as best they could to cheer the bands and troops splashing through the gloomy streets. The children's afternoon sports had to be postponed and after watching the Victory Parade 9,000 wet pupils returned to their various schools for their promised teas. At the County Ground 500 elderly people were fortunate that the Salvation Army provided their tea in a marquee, but in the city's hospitals and workhouses everyone had the celebratory teas in their wards, not spread out on the lawns.[48]

Elsewhere the processions went ahead, and at least local dignitaries and ex-servicemen had their celebratory meals under cover, mainly in assembly rooms and marquees. However most afternoon sports were postponed, and schoolrooms (as at Dawlish and Whimple) covered markets (as at Newton Abbot, Okehampton and South Molton) and even barns (as at Feniton) hurriedly replaced sodden fields and parks for the free tea parties. By all accounts tens of thousands Devon children got soaking wet marching to and from town centres. In north Devon, though, the children of Ilfracombe, Barnstaple, Appledore and Bideford were lucky that the weather cleared in the afternoon. And in general the evening firework displays triumphed over the weather.[49]

The ex-servicemen's Peace Day reception at Newton Abbot.
(Mark Ware: WT 25 July 1919: Courtesy of Devon & Exeter Institution Trustees).

The Men Return & Communities Remember

The human PEACE display at Ilfracombe. (Author's collection).

The Mayor of Exeter asked for the city's church bells to ring from 10.55am to 11.00am on 11 November 1919 to remind everyone to remain still and silent for two minutes as a personal act of remembrance. A factory siren in Barnstaple, rockets in Ilfracombe and Tiverton, and church bells across Torquay gave similar signals. In Exeter civic dignitaries gathered with the Salvation Army band outside the Guildhall to honour the moment, and in many other towns leading citizens did the same. Probably Juliet Nicolson's comment in *The Great Silence* on the ceremony at the Cenotaph was apposite everywhere. 'It was a silence designed for the common man, and brimming over with pain.'[50] That evening many towns organised far more festive events; in Exeter thousands of families enjoyed public displays of fireworks, in Torquay bands marched in a torchlight procession, in Seaton there was a charity carnival, and in Dawlish an Armistice Ball.[51] However, the *Western Times* reported fewer evening events the following year, and probably the vicar of St Leonard's in Newton Abbot was not the only one decrying the amusements as inappropriate, although the lingering fashion for bonfires probably stemmed from joyously burning the Kaiser in effigy at the Armistice.[52] And as more communities erected war memorials so the 11.00am parades, prayers and wreath laying centred around these sombre sites. For a few years some newspapers listed all the messages on the wreaths laid by families – over 70 at Tavistock in 1923.[53] The eleventh hour ceremony became the main community act of remembrance, and services in churches and chapels ensured the day increasingly centred on remembrance, not celebration. Increasingly successful efforts were made to ensure war memorial parades began or ended with church services, as for example at Axminster, Bampton, Buckfastleigh, Crediton, Moretonhampstead and North Tawton in 1929 and 1930.[54] In many towns ceremonies around the memorials evolved to entwine civic theatre with religious ceremony with mayors and councillors, servicemen and relatives of the fallen, Scouts and Guides, schoolchildren, and clergy from all denominations playing a part.[55] Within a year of the Armistice companies were offering families guided tours of the deserted and haunting Western Front and Italian battlefields. The Touring Guild of London, for example, charged £9 for a week's motor tour around Ypres and Bruges.[56]

Territorials in uniform, ex-servicemen in civilian attire and Girl Guides assemble for an Armistice Day parade at Topsham in the 1920s. (Courtesy of Topsham Museum).

The missing and the post-war casualties

When the Armistice was announced not every family knew where their menfolk were serving or even if they were alive. Agonisingly, later that month news reached homes that Lance Corporal Mingo of Topsham had died in a German hospital on 8 November, that Able Seaman William Birch of Dawlish had died when a German submarine sunk the battleship HMS *Britannia* off Cape Trafalgar on 9 November, and that Sergeant Fred Hunt from Exeter had died from dysentery in Gaza just as the war ended. In January 1919 Lance Corporal Daniells family in Bradninch finally found out he had died in a prison camp the previous June.[57]

In the same month, in the desperate hope of eliciting news from regimental colleagues, the *Western Times* published photographs and details of Lance Corporal Harvey-Endacott of Denbury, Private Perkins of Exeter, Private Murch of Cullompton and Lance Corporal Martin of Milton Damerell, all of whom had been missing for many months, mainly in the last great Allied offensive of the war.[58] The Devonshire Red Cross Association made great efforts to find out news but sometimes there was none. In July 1919 the Lane family of Broadclyst were informed that the last news of their son, a corporal in the '8th Devons', was when the battalion made an unsuccessful attack during the great battle for Passchendale Ridge on 26 October 1917. Any wounded had had to be left behind in the retreat.[59]

Wounded men continued to die, some before they could travel home such as Rifleman Arnold from Exeter who died at Tooting Hospital in London on 16 November, and Lieutenant Ashton from Bradworthy who died in Egypt on 4 December 1918.[60] Influenza was a killer, especially if its victims were already weak. In January 1919 Lance Corporal Shapland was buried at Sandford after succumbing to influenza having survived four years of war and being wounded twice. In February

The Men Return & Communities Remember

Sergeant Fred Hunt.
(Mark Ware: WT 22 November 1918: Courtesy of Devon & Exeter Institution Trustees).

Private W.J.Perkins.
(Mark Ware: WT 31 January 1919: Courtesy of Devon & Exeter Institution Trustees).

Corporal Street died in Exeter of post-influenza pneumonia after active service in Mesopotamia, and in March it killed Sergeant Major Bulley who was home in St Thomas after four years in the Middle East.[61] The debilitating effects of malaria and dysentery picked up overseas finally killed other servicemen after they arrived home. Among the former was Sergeant Major Lockyer of Exmouth who died in July 1920; among the latter was Lance Corporal Cudmore who arrived home in Torrington just in time to be sent to hospital in Exeter where he died.[62]

The delayed effects of injuries and stress killed many others. Private Venn of Tiverton died from the effects of wounds and gas poisoning in March 1919, as did Gunner Jack Lethaby of North Molton in June 1920.[63] Richard Giles returned to teaching in Holsworthy after serving in India, Mesopotamia and Palestine but was beset with constant headaches, chest pains and sleepless nights, and died suddenly in a violent convulsion one night in May 1922. The coroner had no hesitation in blaming the war.[64] Later that year Lieutenant Frederick Rowcroft's injuries finally killed him just as he was taking possession of a county council smallholding.[65] When Nurse Olive Rice of Newton Abbot died aged 25 in May 1919, the cause was reported as sheer mental and physical exhaustion after years caring for casualties in Plymouth's Southern General Hospital.[66]

Sometimes death was self-inflicted, and sometimes occurred many years after the war. In January 1920 a soldier's cap was found on Londonderry Quay with a postcard addressed to a girl saying 'Thank God I am gone.' The body was recovered and discovered to be Corporal A. J. Copp from Exeter.[67] Inquests concluded war wounds, mental instability and depression led to the drowning of Lieutenant Harold Hatt near Tiverton in 1919, and of Frederick Poole in Exeter Canal in 1924.[68] In January 1920 Charles Pike who had been wounded in France and later served with the '8th Devons' in Egypt cut his throat in an Exmouth orchard leaving a wife and two young children. His wife said he had been depressed since his discharge, and the coroner agreed that many men were dying due to 'what they had seen and gone through.'[69] In February the body of Arthur Vicary who had suffered from malaria contracted in Palestine and subsequent memory loss and depression, was found under the cliffs at Beer.[70] In 1922 'war insanity' and delusions were given as the reasons Frank Restorick threw himself off the same cliffs.[71] And after years of suffering from shrapnel wounds and reduced to walking painfully on crutches with a foot in a sling, in February 1929 Charles Weeks, formerly of the Devonshire Regiment, hung himself from a tree near Tavistock.[72]

In September 1919 Albert Hedges appeared before Exeter magistrates for 'wandering abroad and sleeping on a seat without visible means of subsistence.' An ex-soldier with one leg, he had previously appeared twice on charges of drunkenness. Now he said he had spent his pension and was homeless. The magistrates levied a small 2/6d fine and directed him to the war pensions officer in Southernhay.[73] William West was another ex-serviceman unable to hold a job or manage his war pension and was repeatedly drunk and violent. The best Exeter's exasperated magistrates could do was to hold him in custody and seek his admission to a certified institution.[74] Barnstaple's magistrates delivered the same judgement when faced with William Dark, another ex-serviceman suffering from malaria, gassing and shell-shock whose estranged behaviour included demanding credit in shops and banks with the cry that the Royal Family would settle the debt.[75] In October 1920 Exeter magistrates accepted the assurance that Captain George Williams's brother and family would care for him. He had had a nervous breakdown serving in Gallipoli, and then enteric fever in Egypt, and in a delusional state he was now embarrassing women in the city's streets by dropping notes in front of them.⁷⁶ Not every ex-serviceman convinced magistrates the war was responsible for their crimes. In 1920 and 1921 several cases across the county concerned with demanding money with menaces, arson, bigamy and indecent assault were dealt with severely.⁷⁷ Probably Lieut-Colonel Sydney Rumbold, formerly employed in drapers' stores in Exeter and Torquay, endured the most humiliation. Rising steadily through the ranks, he had won a DSO and bar and an MC on active service, but also suffered grievous nervous strain, and ended up court-martialled and cashiered, complete with the forfeiture of his medals, for indecent behaviour in 1920.⁷⁸

In December 1919 a bedraggled man was found lying in Paris Street in Exeter. He was taken to the Royal Devon & Exeter Hospital (RD&E) and then vanished until found lying in a fit in Rolle Street in Exmouth. He remembered nothing but said he was Lieutenant Michael O'Leary VC. He was taken to Exeter's Palace Gate Hospital for treatment for shell-shock, and amazingly his claim was found to be true. On 30 January 1915 Lance Corporal O'Leary had won the VC for single-handedly charging and capturing two machine gun posts, killing or capturing their crews, thereby enabling a key hill post near Cuinchy in northern France to be recaptured. After his award he was much fêted across London, and as a commissioned officer he served in Salonika where he caught malaria which probably accounted for much of his recurrent ill-health.⁷⁹ In December 1921 Gilbert Auton, fined £2 for stealing bales of hay in Broadclyst, was found to have risen from the ranks to Acting Captain and won the DCM and MC in France, and a bar to his MC in Russia. It seems that the senior magistrate, Sir James Owen, the wartime mayor of Exeter, had viewed his case sympathetically.⁸⁰

The neurological specialists at Exeter's Palace Gate Hospital had a spectaculars success with Gunner C. E. Norton who had been hit in the chest by shrapnel in the Ypres salient in May 1916 and subsequently lost the use of his left arm. Amputation had been recommended, but the surgeon designated to carry out the operation suggested shell-shock might be the cause and recommended Palace Gate. Within three weeks his previously wasted arm regained both its strength and movement.⁸¹ In 1919 the *Western Times* celebrated this almost miraculous outcome, and also featured James Miller who had returned to his pre-war post in Exeter's General Post Office 'after lying helpless from shell shock for over two years' before being 'cured by suggestion' in Chepstow's Mount Pleasant neurological hospital.⁸²

In 1918-19 300 soldiers believed to be suffering disorders associated with shell-shock were accommodated in Seale-Hayne Agricultural College outside Newton Abbot under the care of Dr Arthur Hurst. He achieved similar remarkable results. Indeed they were so remarkable that his claims remain suspect to this day, largely because a film showing men before and after treatment – with jerking bodies, twitching faces, twisted limbs and incoherent speech rendered completely normal – was deemed fraudulent. Nevertheless Lieutenant Hall from the Royal Army Medical

Ex-Lance Corporal James Miller back at work.
(Mark Ware: WT 7 November 1919: Courtesy of Devon & Exeter Institution Trustees).

Seale-Hayne Agricultural College (and emergency war hospital). (Author's collection).

Corps witnessed many rapid cures there and in September 1918 the War Pensions Gazette published his findings. An officer struck dumb for five months was soon speaking loudly and coherently, another officer with three limbs and part of his face paralysed was suddenly up and about and making and eating his own tea, and Hall saw many others cured within days, even hours, of arriving.[83] Hurst had abandoned his early approaches with electric shocks and hypnosis, and now prioritised psychotherapy. The men were treated as though they were normal both mentally and physically, and certainly not as cowards, deserters or freaks deserving contempt, incarceration or execution as so often occurred earlier in the war. In December 1918 a lengthy report in the *Mid Devon Advertiser* cited an article by Hurst in which he discussed how a disturbed mind could exaggerate the effect of a bodily injury. He argued that in such cases, even when everyone else seems to have confirmed the victim's own pessimistic view of his condition, the use of positive 'persuasion', 're-education' and 'suggestion' was often effective. Hurst believed that if the problems were purely 'functional' they could be cured, and quickly. He added that occupational therapy – in Seale-Hayne's fields or workshops – was important in securing a long-lasting recovery. On occasion he pretended to operate on patients and when they came round he said they could now hear, see and move normally – and they did. His professional critics argued that the removal of symptoms ignored their underlying causes, but Hurst replied that the men he 'cured' were able to withstand experiencing mock battle conditions in the college grounds.[84]

Sometimes ex-servicemen were reduced to seeking admission to workhouses. Such humiliating cases caused considerable embarrassment to local Poor Law Boards of Guardians, and sometimes outrage to local communities, but the question inevitably arose of whether these men had received, or should receive, war pensions, possibly because they were disabled. Often the men themselves were mentally confused or physically ill, or both, and professed no knowledge of their entitlements. This meant a time consuming investigation had to be followed through, and to everyone's embarrassment the ex-serviceman had to stay in the workhouse until his situation was clarified. And if the relevant ministry thought a man's current disability was not caused by the war, no payment would be forthcoming and his fate lay in the hands of the Guardians.[85]

Medals and trophies

During the war several major award ceremonies were held in Northernhay Gardens in Exeter. In October 1918 Major General Sir Henry Sclater presented two dozen men, or their mourning families, with the Distinguished Conduct Medal (DCM) or its junior companion, the Military Medal (MM).[86] Many wartime acts of bravery, though, only received public recognition after the Armistice. In December 1918 40 Devonians were awarded Military Medals, and Lieutenant Jordain from Brixham received a Military Cross (MC).[87] It was not until January 1919 that the London Gazette published the names of Devonians awarded gallantry crosses and medals for the campaigns in Italy, Egypt and Salonika. One was Corporal Gush, a Royal Engineer from Beer, who received a posthumous bar to his MM for reconnoitring and then rallying his men to face the bullet strewn crossing of the River Monticano in Italy on 29 October 1918. He had died from influenza the following month.[88] In January 1919, too, the Exeter Diocesan Gazette recorded the MCs awarded to three Torbay curates – the Revs. J.G.Lane Davies of Babbacombe, H.R. Cooke of Torquay and W.E. Trelawny-Ross of Paignton – who had enlisted as forces' chaplains.[89] In June Earl Fortescue flanked by South Molton's civic dignitaries and military figures presented DCMs to two local men, Sergeant Major George Pearce and Sergeant George Rivers. With justification Fortescue said that in any previous war their exploits in the face of enemy fire might well have won them VCs.[90] Formal ceremonies continued, but times and interests began to change; the 15 Devonian officers and men receiving medals in Devonport's Raglan Barracks in December 1919 merited only a short back page entry in the *Western Times*.[91]

However as late as April 1920 Exeter City Council held a civic ceremony for the award of a DCM to Sergeant (now Police Constable) Charles Hooper at Bois-des-Buttes. This was a wooded hill occupied by the '2nd Devons' during the third battle of the River Aisne in May 1918. Here the battalion repelled repeated German attacks, and successfully held up the enemy advance, but at terrible cost. No more than 80 men finally struggled back to Allied lines, leaving 29 officers and 552 men dead or captured. The heroic action had justifiably caught the public imagination.[92] In May 1922 another civic and military ceremony in Exeter's Guildhall marked the French award of the Croix de Guerre to Devon's 24th Field Ambulance for its valour in evacuating 2,000 people, many of them wounded, sick or infirm, from the village of St Amand during the bombardment launched by the Germans prior to their final retreat in October 1918.[93]

There were, of course, men who wore medals without ever earning them, usually to gain money from sympathisers. In May 1919 Maurice Pickholt received two months imprisonment for theft and wearing unauthorised DCM and MM medals around Torquay, and in September 1920 Ottery St Mary magistrates sentenced Robert Hall, an habitual fraudster, to three months in goal for a similar offence. A few years later James Stephens, a hotel chauffeur in Sidmouth, was lucky merely to be fined for wearing unauthorised gallantry medals. The leniency was due to evidence of his war service.[94]

A number of towns received war relics for their patriotic efforts. In this respect patriotism was generally defined as what percentage of the population donned uniform and how much the community had invested in War Bonds. In general small villages were visited by a team of soldiers who exhibited a German gun there for a short time before moving on, as occurred around south-east Devon as early as December 1918. However towns expected permanent displays. In late June 1919 Teignmouth seemed pleased with the German field gun sited near the sea front, and later that year similar guns were presented to Tavistock and Totnes.[95]

The top trophy was a complete tank, usually a battle-stained British Mark IV. The one presented to Exmouth let everyone down by first getting lost around Yeovil Junction on its train journey and then completely breaking down skewed across the Esplanade 300 feet from its designated site. It was in this embarrassing position that the 32 ton tank was presented to the town by Earl Fortescue himself.[96] Another tank found its way to Tiverton

The Men Return & Communities Remember

The arrival of Tiverton's tank. (Courtesy of Tiverton Museum).

for a successful drive through the crowded streets. Here it was the VC won by a local man, Private Thomas Sage, as well as the borough's impressive £600,000 War Bond record that earned it this prize. Several people, though, were heard to say how 'ugly' the tank looked.[97]

In September 1919 a Mark IV tank arrived in Torquay, but possibly families were equally pleased, and maybe more so, by the flag presented to the town by the departing New Zealanders in gratitude for local hospitality.[98] That summer General Sir William Birdwood, wartime commander of the combined Australian and New Zealand forces, had visited Exeter to present the city with a German field gun captured by his men. The presentation was a token of gratitude for the Mayoress of Exeter's Depot providing no less than 328,000 Australians with meals when their trains had stopped at the city's stations.[99]

Not everyone welcomed having a trophy, and not everyone was pleased with the one they were granted. In February 1919 Crediton felt insulted when it was offered only a machine gun and a belt of ammunition. 'Hand them to the Boy Scouts', said a disgruntled councillor.[100] In Paignton the council was riven with controversy when a minority group of councillors opposed accepting a German gun.[101] Their reasons were the same as the vocal minority opposed to accepting a tank at Newton Abbot – that the trophy represented arrogant militarism and would morally deface the town. Newton Abbot's tank ended up well away from the town centre in Baker's Park and by June 1920 its critics were complaining it looked derelict, was a danger to children, and should be sold for scrap.[102] Most relics were quietly dismantled long before the next war.

Comrades of the Great War

The Comrades of the Great War was the main ex-servicemen's association. It was founded in 1917 by the Earl of Derby and Wilfrid Ashley, a strongly anti-Socialist Tory MP, as a right wing alternative to the more militant National Federation of Discharged & Demobilised Sailors & Soldiers (NFDSS) and National Association of Discharged Soldiers & Sailors. The number of Comrades of the Great War 'Posts' (branches) grew steadily. By January 1919 there were 20 across Devon with 2,500 members, and they were actively engaged in securing ex-servicemen's pension rights, raising funds for club houses and destitute colleagues, and contributing their views on possible war memorials.[103] Branches of the rival NFDSS were established in Exeter and Torquay where they condemned all charitable collections on behalf of ex-servicemen as providing the government with an excuse for not paying satisfactory pensions and family allowances.[104] And during 1919 Bideford's NFDSS branch drew swords with the local council over its failure to reinstate returning servicemen to their pre-war jobs.[105] However neither the Federation nor the Association seriously rivalled the Comrades within the county – possibly because despite all the fears of Bolshevism the vast majority of local ex-servicemen, while seeking fair wages and pensions, preferred peace and companionship to politics and conflict.[106]

Support from local councils and dignitaries for the Comrades' Posts was usually readily forthcoming, no doubt from a combination of genuine sympathy and the desire to exercise influence over them. In Barnstaple the mayor and corporation actively supported its flag days, and in Newton Abbot a Concert Party called 'The Trunk Cats' raised funds for the local Post.[107] As early as November 1918 Teignmouth's Comrades settled into their new clubroom with its library and billiard tables donated by local well-wishers. Its president was Vice Admiral Archibald Stoddart who, as Rear Admiral, had been Vice Admiral Sir Doveton Sturdee's second in command at the much celebrated sinking of four German cruisers off the Falkland Islands in December 1914.[108] That December the Commandant (chairman) of Exeter's Post highlighted the non-party clause in its constitution, and directed members' attention to securing and fitting out permanent premises, and, significantly, to identifying prominent senior officers to become their president and vice president.[109]

Comrade of the Great War lapel badge.
(Mark Ware: author's collection).

Activities expanded to include supporting war widows and their children, finding jobs for members, building and fitting out clubhouses, and organising charity whist drives, dances and sports days for the locality. In January 1920 Torquay's Post had 1,350 members and proudly celebrated the 53 members of the Ladies Section, the 584 pensions gained for members or widows, the 78 jobs obtained, and the 17 war service medals secured.[110] Unusually, in 1920 Barnstaple Comrades opened up its own Cabinet & Joinery Works where members constructed numerous items including poultry houses, beach huts and small wooden bungalows, and through their contacts secured numerous orders.[111] Sometimes, though, national decisions were hard to accept, and Torquay's Post protested publicly at the gross discrepancy between ordinary soldiers' gratuity of 2/6d for each week of uniformed service and the tens of thousands of pounds given to generals and admirals, peaking at £100,000 each for Admiral Beatty and Field Marshal Haig.[112]

In 1920 ideas were raised at a national level about amalgamating all ex-servicemen's organisation, including the Officers Association. Devon's Posts were sympathetic, but wanted reassurance that the new organisation would remain non-sectarian and non-political.[113] In December amalgamation was agreed, and helped by the popular Prince of Wales agreeing to be patron and the widely admired Haig (despite his gratuity) becoming president.[114] The British Legion was born on 15 May 1921 and the first Poppy Day held that year. Each Post had to decide whether to cooperate or not; across Devon some, notably Newton Abbot and Tavistock, were doubtful and long delayed a decision but eventually all agreed that unity brought strength.[115] In a largely celebratory public meeting in Exeter in April 1922 Earl Fortescue, Major General Sir Louis Bols (Colonel of the Devonshire Regiment) and Philip Foale Rowsell (the city's mayor) hammered home that the Legion's aims were to promote unity among the classes, to instil loyalty to the Legion and the country, to help restore national confidence, to avoid the 'machinations of agitators', and to wait for 'the dark days to pass'.[116]

When the Prince of Wales toured the West Country in May 1921 groups of ex-servicemen along with Boy Scouts, Girls Guides and schoolchildren were part of the welcoming parades in towns and villages as the royal party hurried through its itinerary. The Prince unveiled the county's war memorial on the Cathedral Green during his visit to Exeter, and a group of ex-servicemen were selected to attend. The *Western Times* took a particular interest in the time he spent with a group of blinded and severely disabled ex-servicemen in Plymouth. 'He stayed some time talking to them, and, as he left, reached out and placed his hand in those of the sightless men.' In a rare act he signed the autograph album of Miss Mary Matthews, a wartime VAD nurse who had lost the use of her right arm due to sceptic poisoning contracted in a wartime operating theatre.[117]

The Legion was not to everyone's taste though. Several branches lamented that membership remained modest, climbing only slowly. In mid-decade both Sir Frederick de la Pole in Colyton and Francis Acland in Broadclyst urged local men to join and begged families to support the branches.[118] At the Legion's annual supper in Ottery St Mary in 1930 the female section outnumbered the men.[119] Perhaps some men felt they did not need the help and support of the Legion, and perhaps suspicions around the impersonal nature of the national organisation, the motives of the Establishment figures leading it, and the repeated messages hammering home patriotism, class unity and moderation were to blame. In 1930 several branches across Devon complained that the non-sectarian principle was

The Prince of Wales visits Cullompton, May 1921. (Courtesy of Tiverton Museum).

being broken by some local Anglican and Nonconformist clergy refusing to attend united religious services. At the same time there were thoughts that notwithstanding the Legion's non-political stance it should protest at the government's lamentable failure to tackled unemployment.[120] Perhaps some men loathed all reminders of wartime army life. In 1930 delegates to a Legion conference in north Devon protested at donning full uniforms for formal inspection before attending acts of remembrance, including the County Rally in November. Several speakers, including officers, argued that 'militarism' was inappropriate, that many men hated army uniforms, and that most members thought more relaxed events, including family sports days, were more enticing signs of peace, freedom, equality and remembrance – which, they asserted, was what they had been told the war was all about. Not surprisingly ex-servicemen's associations fully supported the establishment of League of Nations branches across the county.[121]

The memorials

Celtic crosses were the most common war memorials, but they were not always a community's first choice. Within a few weeks of the Armistice towns and villages started to hold public meetings, often chaired by clergy or prominent councillors, where ideas were generally readily forthcoming and an organising committee proposed and elected. Typically, at Bampton suggestions included a reading room, recreation ground, swimming baths, allotments, and a public clock.[122] However, often a duplication of effort complicated things. The most popular choice at Honiton was a memorial hall, and in Brixham it was a clock tower topped with a statue of liberty, but in both towns problems arose when churches and chapels went ahead with their own memorials to the detriment of wider community funds. In the end Brixham had to settle on a community cross overlooking the sea, and Honiton on a cross by the parish church but outside Church of England land.[123] The civic memorial committee in Bampton, and also in Barnstaple, had to abandon plans for major public facilities and settle for crosses. In June 1920 the ex-wartime mayor of Barnstaple expressed disgust that only £500 had been subscribed to the borough fund, declaring its memorial would be 'the object of scorn and derision.' The parish of St Mary Magdalene already had set about raising its own funds for an ornate chancel screen remembering the 96 parishioners killed.[124] Elsewhere, too, enthusiastically agreed ideas never materialised because they were out of financial reach. South Molton's committee wanted new public baths, Chulmleigh a memorial lych gate and public hall, and West Hill a clock tower on the village green, but all three eventually opted for much cheaper crosses.[125] Uffculme, though, acted differently. After initial controversy it rejected a cross in favour of a recreation field. £2,000 was raised to buy an eight acre field, six acres of which were sold for housing, and then everyone settled down to create a bowling green, tennis courts, playground and club house.[126]

Sometimes successful compromises were reached. After long discussions Cullompton decided upon a wall tablet in the parish church and a memorial cross in the High Street. Suggestions that ex-servicemen would prefer two new cottages were rejected as too expensive, aesthetically unpleasing and, strangely, as not obviously a war memorial.[127] Discussions in Colyton regarding a cross or a social institute also ended with hopes of both as £200 had been collected specifically for a cross leaving £350 in hand towards the £850 needed to purchase the vacant Drill Hall.[128] By 1920 Whimple had secured its two memorials – a YMCA hut as a village hall for £721 and a churchyard cross for £165. The Anglican vicar shared the dedication of the cross with the Congregational minister – whose two sons were named on it.[129]

Some projects were completed quickly. At Kennford a combination of donations, the sale of £1 shares and volunteer building parties meant its brick built memorial hall could open in September 1920.[130] At Halberton in December 1918 the vicar's suggestion of a new lady chapel was overridden when the village decided to raise £800 to purchase the vacant Swan Inn and then turn it into a memorial hall. It was duly opened in April 1919 with just a memorial tablet being placed in the church.[131] Conversely, by January 1919 the villagers of Chagford had funded the refurbishment of an ancient side chapel of their parish church complete with panels naming the fallen.[132]

Wealthy donors sometimes hastened things along. Lord Clinton's gift of a site, together with a series of dances and whist drives, and several large donations meant by the end of 1919 Beer was on its way to achieving £4,000 for a village hall.[133] The stimulus of the Acland family's gift of a site and £500 helped Broadclyst fund its Victory Hall, although another £900 was needed.[134] (Some villages opted for Victory Halls, others for Memorial or just Village Halls.) Exminster's Victory Hall was helped by free timber from the Earl of Devon and the Kekewich family, and cheap stone from local quarries.[135]

Occasionally no fund raising was necessary. Kenton's memorial obelisk was paid for by Mr J.J.Neale in gratitude for all five of his sons surviving the war, Broadhembury's memorial hall was a gift by Mrs Gundry in memory of her husband Lieutenant Colonel Henry Gundry, and North Tawton's memorial park and column was the gift of Frank Gibbings, a local man who moved away and prospered.[136]

Sometimes projects took time. Tiverton was particularly ambitious in seeking £10,000 to buy and largely demolish the rambling old Angel Hotel and build a multi-use social centre. Energised by the long-serving mayor, Alfred Gregory, and supported by an influential committee, the enterprise was never seriously questioned and the memorials financed by local churches and chapels were seen to complement, not rival, the civic project. The fund raising was intense, including a massive historical Peace Pageant in August 1919. Miss Katherine Lazenby, a noted Tiverton benefactor, laid the foundation stone (see picture, page 56) and Lord Mildmay, Lord Fortescue's successor as Lord Lieutenant, opened the fully completed memorial hall in April 1929. It was hoped the edifying volumes in the library, including those specifically given by the Heathcoat-Amory family on horses and hunting, would help turn young people away from 'frivolous pleasures'.[137]

In 1919 Crediton embarked on an unusual project. After endless anxiety and fund raising, in 1923 enough subscriptions – around £1,800 – were forthcoming for a meadow to be purchase and converted into a public garden. Near its entrance a cenotaph was built, attractively reminiscent of a small medieval market place with a tall pointed roof supported by eight substantial oak posts. Within it a stone centre piece was inscribed with the names of the fallen. In addition a new organ and a memorial tablet were dedicated to the fallen in the parish church.[138]

Many Devon churchyards became the site of tall memorial crosses rising from steps and plinths. The one at Chudleigh Knighton's was eye-catchingly different as it stood above an inscribed stone entrance arch to the churchyard.[139] However other communally funded crosses were built on

Crediton's public war memorial. (Author's collection).

entirely secular sites, often clearly visible at road junctions as at Sidbury, or village greens as at Morchard Bishop, or in public parks as at Barnstaple, although their dedications customarily included prayers and blessings by local clergy.[140] After prolonged wrangling Newton Abbot decided to fell a venerable oak tree, revered by some as representing the spirit of the town, in the centre of a major crossroads and replace it with a tall Tuscan column surmounted by a female figure, variously described as Victory or Freedom, holding broken chains. Its defenders countered its secular imagery by pointing out it stood close to several different churches and chapels.[141] And while many memorials contained Christian dedications others, such as Newton Abbot's, did not. Shobrooke's granite cross funded by 200 subscribers and listing 25 names was placed at the junction of five roads. Although dedicated by the vicar, it stated solely that it was erected by parishioners in remembrance of the dead. At Churston Ferrers the cross erected high on the Common had a similar inscription, and so did Oakford's cross with the poignant addition 'In sorrow, in gratitude, in hope'.[142] The diversity of decisions clearly reflected the post-war divergence of views on social hierarchies and religious beliefs.

As the photographs of outdoor dedication ceremonies show, civic dignitaries, senior military figures and local clergy occupied centre stage with local families and ex-servicemen surrounding them. Sometimes church choirs or school children, or both, augmented the hymn singing, and often a local band accompanied them. After the prayers and dedication by the clergy, the names of the fallen were read out, and a senior officer from the locality, or specially invited, gave a tribute. Finally families laid their wreaths.

As early as 26 November 1918 Earl Fortescue, Devon's Lord Lieutenant, proposed a county war memorial to be placed in Exeter, the county town, and suggested two German guns, without carriages, placed muzzle upward on a suitably inscribed granite plinth. The idea was readily accepted, but not the earl's design. Some wanted a monument, perhaps sited high on Dartmoor, but others preferred completing the cathedral cloisters or adding a ward to the RD&E Hospital.[143] However by August 1919 it was clear that Exeter's City Council was planning its own memorial, and that many villages, towns, churches and chapels were busy with their own collections. Reluctantly, Fortescue's county committee decided upon a simple and relatively cheap cross on the Cathedral

Newton Abbot's public war memorial. (Author's collection).

The Men Return & Communities Remember

Combe Martin's public war memorial. (Author's collection).

Green together with as full a list as possible of Devon's war dead – estimated between ten and eleven thousand – and a donation of £200 to the Devonshire Regiment's memorial at the scene of its 2nd Battalion's stand at Bois des Buttes. All this was against the wishes of the NFDSS which much preferred building houses for servicemen's families.[144] And there had been significant acrimony between Sir James Owen, the city's wartime mayor, and Lord Fortescue over what the latter thought was Exeter's pre-emptory decision and lack of cooperation. The mayor claimed the city had been snubbed.[145]

Both parties went their own way. For Exeter the sculptor John Angel produced a striking, and completely secular, memorial topped by a statue of Victory holding aloft a wreath. Her foot was on a dragon and below her on the four sides of a tall plinth were large dynamic figures commemorating the bravery, dedication and endurance of the city's sailors, soldiers, female workers and prisoners of war – 958 of whom had given their lives. The cost of £6,000 was quickly raised by collections and special events. A high central site in Northernhay Gardens was chosen and the inscription deliberately embraced both the county and city saying:

IN PROUD AND MEMORY OF ALL MEN AND WOMEN OF EXETER AND OF DEVON WHO GAVE THEIR LIVES FOR ENGLAND DURING THE GREAT WAR, 1914-1918.

It was unveiled on 24 July 1923 by the national hero Admiral of the Fleet Earl Beatty and dedicated by the Bishop of Crediton.[146] A separate memorial was erected in Higher Cemetery, initially under the auspices of the Exeter War Hospital's

Unveiling Tavistock's public war memorial. (Author collection).

The 4th Earl Fortescue. (Mark Ware: Devon HDB: Courtesy of Devon & Exeter Institution Trustees).

Organisation, for all the servicemen across the world who died in the city's hospitals.[147] Fortescue's committee raised around £1,500 to commission Sir Edwin Lutyens to design a simple but elegant cross from Haytor granite. The Lord Lieutenant secured a coup as the county memorial was completed in time for its unveiling in the Cathedral Close to be included in the West Country tour of the Prince of Wales in May 1921.[148]

In May 1924 a memorial to the 180 dead of the North Devon Yeomanry (NDY) was dedicated in Barnstaple parish church. Their names were inscribed on two panels, one each side of a central panel featuring the figure of Victory. During the war the NDY had amalgamated with the southern Royal 1st Devon Yeomanry to become the 16th Yeomanry Battalion of the Devonshire Regiment. They fought at Gallipoli, in Egypt and in France.[149]

The vastly expanded wartime Devonshire Regiment had a memorial in Exeter Cathedral funded by several hundred families primarily linked to the regiment's three regular battalions. It was a large bronze relief figure of a soldier lying prone, and although his arm is bandaged, he clutches his rifle ready for imminent action. He defends the nearby figure of Christ Crucified.[150] In a packed civic and naval ceremony in 1929 the two sons of Archdeacon Ernest Sandford of Exeter – Captain Francis Sandford RN DSO and Lieutenant Richard Sandford RN VC – were given a permanent memorial in Exeter Cathedral. The VC was awarded to Richard for ramming his explosive laden submarine under heavy fire between the piers of a bridge to deny German defenders access to the Mole during the British attack on Zeebrugge Harbour in April 1918. He survived the raid only to die of enteric fever shortly after the Armistice. Francis also survived the war, but died of blood poisoning in 1926.[151]

The soldier and the female war worker: two of the dramatic panels on the City of Exeter's war memorial in Northernhay Gardens. (Courtesy of Tony Ovens).

The Devonshire Regiment's war memorial in Exeter Cathedral. (Author's collection).

Most interior church memorials were brass tablets with the names of all worshippers who served, or just those who died, etched in black. However stained glass windows presenting opportunities for more elaborate expressions of feeling proved popular, although far more costly. They represented the entwining of Christianity with militant patriotism, and the assertion that the sacrifices had been worthwhile. At Wolborough in Newton Abbot a window featured St Nicholas and St George, patrons of the sea and England, together with St Edmund and St Alban, two English martyrs.[152] At Pilton a window also portrayed St Nicholas and St Alban but alongside the Crucifixion with accompanying angels holding the Heraldic Arms of the Devon Regiment and North Devon Hussars.[153] At Uplowman a window pictured St Dennis of France and St George of England with the Archangel Michael holding a sword and scales of justice, and in Pyworthy's window St Adrian, the patron saint of soldiers, is flanked by a tank and aeroplane and St Nicholas holds a modern battleship with an airship hovering overhead.[154] The window in Bovey Tracey's parish church was particularly crowded with symbolism. King Alfred and his longship recalled the Royal Navy, St Oswald (King of Northumbria) the Christian fight against heathens, St Martin the nation's self-sacrifice, St Joan of Arc supreme patriotism, and St Boniface (of Crediton) the role of Devonians. Each of the 55 men who died had his initials, the badge of his regiment or ship, and the date of his death engrave in a small diamond lozenge.[155]

Sometimes communal memorials were accompanied by separate ones dedicated to particular figures, usually from wealthier families. In Sowton parish church three tablets were dedicated at the same time – two family memorials to a major and a lieutenant, and a communal one to six NCOs and private soldiers.[156] At Withycombe and Broadclyst the sons of the vicars were listed in the communal memorials but further remembered by their families alongside representations of God and His saints in stained glass windows.[157] At Newton St Cyres, the vicar gave an inscribed lectern in memory of his son alongside the village roll of honour and tablet and the window from the Quicke family, the local squires.[158]

Other institutions honoured colleagues who served. Schools dedicated memorials to the 'Old Boys' who died – such as the 35 from Bideford Grammar School, 37 from Totnes Grammar

School, 64 from All Hallows in Honiton, and 74 from Hele's School, Exeter.[159] Some firms did the same, and so did major Post Offices, and football clubs.[160] At a Trusham quarry eleven servicemen who returned safely from the war created a war memorial to their five colleagues who died. The ruins of a medieval house provided the two broken granite pillars that flanked a further block of granite for the names.[161]

The naming of the fallen was important, and revealed communities' views on social class and military hierarchies. Were the names to be accompanied by ranks and gallantry awards, and listed in order of rank – or not? Most were alphabetical, irrespective of whether or not they included ranks, but a minority such as Huntsham, Littlehempston and Kentisbury listed the fallen in order of rank, officers first.[162] And communities had to decide whether or not to include those who died of war wounds in the days and weeks after the Armistice or were killed in Russia. For these reasons some committees decided to date their memorials 1919 rather than 1918. And on occasion women were included. For example, Sidmouth's churchyard cross names Nurse Mary Gertrude Tindall who died while serving in an Exeter hospital in 1917; Heavitree's memorial includes Sister Annie Broster who served in Exmouth's VAD Hospital and died in 1916, and Exmouth's includes Nurse Doris Page who died in 1917 and Nurse Olive Willey who died in 1918.

Clerical and lay speakers at early dedication ceremonies in 1919 and 1920 trusted that the sacrifices of the fallen and overall gratitude for the Empire's God-given victory would suffice to keep the social classes united in the struggle for national reconstruction. However in 1921, after the depression struck home, the tone changed and speakers increasingly condemned the unrest as subversive and a slur to the memory of the fallen. That April Lieut-Colonel N. R. Radcliffe, commanding officer of the '6th Devons' had no hesitation at the dedication of Great Torrington's memorial in saying 'When they looked around they saw nothing but unrest, strife, distress ands selfishness, and they began to wonder whether the example that these brave lads set them and the great sacrifices they had made had not been made in vain.'[163] At the dedication of Horwood's marble tablet General Kelham equated the current 'dissensions' with a negation of the dead warriors' sacrifices. Constant strikes, he asserted, will ruin the country and bring it to the same state as Russia.[164] The Colonel and General made it clear that the spirit of the war needed to return. One wonders who else agreed.

REFERENCES

1. *WT* 20 December 1918, 6 January 1919
2. *WT* 23 January 1919
3. *ibid*
4. DeGroot, G.J., *Blighty: British Society in the Era of the Great War*, pp253-258
5. *WT* 27 November 1918
6. *WT* 13 & 28 December 1918
7. *WT* 28 January 1919
8. *WT* 3 January 1919, 22 & 28 February 1919
9. *WT* 10 January 1919, 7 February 1919
10. *CC* 30 November 1918
11. *WT* 29 November 1918
12. *DG* 23 November 1918, 30 December 1918, *WT* 27 December 1918, 17 January 1919, *NDJ* 5 December 1918
13. *DG* 14 December 1918, *WT* 17 December 1918, 18 & 21 February 1919
14. *WT* 25 March 1919
15. *WT* 8 August 1919
16. *WT* 4 November 1919
17. *DG* 21 December 1918
18. *NDJ* 2 October 1919
19. *WT* 6 December 1919, 22 March 1920
20. *WT* 2 January 1920
21. *WT* 5 February 1920
22. *D&SN* 12 June 1919
23. *MDA* 28 June 1919
24. *NDJ* 13 February 1919, *NDH* 6 March 1919, *WT* 10 January 1919, 11 & 28 February 1919
25 *WT* 20 February 1920
26. *WT* 14 February 1919
27. *WT* 9 October 1920
28. *WT* 6, 18, 20 & 28 August 1919
29. *WT* 15 March 1919

30. *TG* 18 April 1919, *WT* 15 October 1919

31. *TG* 7 February 1919, *WT* 15 October 1919

32. *WT* 18 August 1919

33. *SMG* 11 October 1919, *WT* 15 October 1919

34. Atkinson, C.T., *The Devonshire Regiment 1914-1919*, pp465-469, *WT* 24 January 1920

35. *WT* 14 March 1924, Walsh, E. S., *Kilkenny: In Time of Revolution 1900-23*. Kirkwood had risen to lieutenant-colonel during the First world War, and he also survived the conflict in Ireland.

36. *WT* 25 February 1921

37. *WT* 10 September 1919, 3, 17 & 24 August 1920

38. *WT* 12 November 1920, www.cairogang.com

39. *WT* 10 December 1920, www.theirishrevolution.ie/1920, www.theauxiliaries.com/men-alphabetical

40. *WT* 1 April 1921

41. *WT* 24 June 1921

42. www.policehistory.com/tudor, Heath, A.J.K., 'The Palestine Police Force under the Mandate' in *Police Journal* 1928.78-88

43. *WT* 13 November 1920, *NDJ* 26 April 1923

44. *WT* 1 July 1919

45. *WT* 8 July 1919

46. *ibid*.

47. *TG* 11 July 1919, *DG* 5 July 1919, *TT* 18 July 1919, *MDA* 5 July 1919, *WT* 9 & 11 July 1919

48. *WT* 21, 25 & 29 July 1919

49. *ibid*., *DG* 26 July 1919; *NDJ* 24 July 1919

50. *WT* 11 & 12 November 1919; Nicolson, J., *The Great Silence*, pp144-148

51. *TT* 14 November 1919, *WT* 12 & 14 November 1919

52. *MDA* 13 November 1920

53. *TG* 16 November 1923

54. *WT* 15 November 1929, 14 November 1930

55. *WT* 12 November 1926; *NDJ* 15 November 1928

56. *WT* 16 July 1920

57. *DG* 16 November 1918, *WT* 22 November 1918, 6 December 1918, 24 January 1919

58. *WT* 31 January 1919, 21 February 1919

59. *WT* 11 July 1919

60. *WT* 20 & 27 December 1918

61. *CC* 1 February 1919, *WT* 14 & 18 February 1919, 18 March 1919

62. *WT* 3 July 1920, 28 February 1919

63. *SMG* 12 June 1920, *WT* 25 March 1919

64. *WT* 26 May 1922

65. *WO* 30 November 1922

66. *MDA* 31 May 1919

67. *WT* 23 January 1920

68. *D&SN* 13 February 1919, 27 March 1919, *WT* 21 March 1924

69. *WT* 3 January 1920

70. *WT* 6 February 1920

71. *WT* 3 January 1922

72. *TG* 8 February 1929

73. *WT* 6 September 1919

74. *WT* 5 December 1919

75. *NDJ* 5 February 1920, *WT* 3 February 1920

76. *WT* 30 October 1920

77. *WT* 29 January 1920, 19 June 1920, 9 & 24 August 1921, *NDH* 12 June 1929

78. *London Gazette* 2 March 1920, *TT* 12 March 1920

79. *London Gazette* 16 February 1915, *WT* 4 December 1919

80. *Edinburgh Gazette* 11/12/19, *WT* 16 December 1921

81. *WT* 5 December 1919

82. *WT* 7 November 1919

83. DHC 1262M/0/0/LD/113 Lord Lieutenancy Files

84. *MDA* 28 December 1918, Loughlin, T., *Shell-Shock & Medical Culture in First World War Britain*, pp79-114. On 24 December 1920 the *Western Times* suggested shell-shock caused a repatriated horse to panic and bolt in Exmouth when the bit its driver had removed scraped a pan of water it was about to drink.

85. DHC Tiverton PLU/1 25 July 1922, 6 February 1923, Honiton PLU/4 7 September 1918, *NDJ* 29 May 1919, *NDH* 20 January 1921, *WT* 29 November 1919, *TG* 23 July 1920; de Groot cites the bitterness caused by widespread stories of unfair ministry decisions – op.cit., pp257-261.

86. *WT* 8 October 1918

87. *WT* 13 & 17 December 1918

88. *WT* 6 January 1919, *NDJ* 30 January 1919

89. *WT* 10 January 1919

90. *NDJ* 26 June 1919

91. *WT* 5 December 1919

92. *WT* 28 April 1920

93. *WT* 3 May 22

94. *TT* 23 May 1919, *WT* 7 September 1920, 21 January 1927

95. *WT* 18 December 1918, 2 July 1919, 11 November 1919, *TG* 10 October 1919

96. *WT* 10 September 1919

97. *D&SN* 21 November 1918, 25 December 1919. Sage won the VC by throwing himself on a live hand grenade to save colleagues from the blast.

98. *WT* 18 September 1919, 13 October 1919

99. *WT* 26 & 29 August 1919

100. *WT* 28 February 1919

101. *WT* 18 November 1919

102. *MDA* 10 May 1919, 23 & 30 August 1919, 26 June 1920

103. *WT* 11, 14 & 21 October 1918, 6 January 1919

104. *WT* 8 October 1918, *TT* 20 February 1920

105. *WT* 21 January 1919

106. *WT* 14 October 1918, 21 January 1919; for a different view see www.jacobinmag.com/2018/11/remembrance-day

107. *WT* 3 & 21 October 1918, 20 September 1919

108. *WT* 5 & 11 November 1918

109. *WT* 18 December 1918

110. *WT* 9 & 16 January 1920. See also Culmstock *D&SN* 15 July 1926, Combe Martin *NDH* 9 September 1920, Axminster and Exeter *WT* 3 February 1920

111. *NDH* 23 September 1930

112. *WT* 6 August 1919

113. *WT* 30 October 1920, 2 November 1920

114. *WT* 14 December 1920

115. *MDA* 12 January 1923, *TG* 6 April 1923

116. *WT* 8 April 1922

117. *WT* 17, 20 & 21 May 21

118. *WT* 8 April 1922, 26 January 1923, 18 December 1925

119. *WT* 28 February 1930

120. *ibid*.

121. *WT* 26 September 1930, 2 August 1919, 18 December 1919, *MDA* 16 February 1924, Hanna, E., *Veterans' Associations: GB & Ireland*

122. *WT* 17 & 20 January 1919

123. *WT* 29 November 1918, 14 February 1919, 3 & 25 March 1919, 23 January 1920

124. Barnstaple eventually raised £1,000 for a fine granite cross. *NDJ* 10 June 1920, *WT* 17 January 1919, 1 & 28 July 1919, 13 & 20 October 1919, 1 December 1919, 17 December 1920, 20 October 1922, 6 November 1925

125. *WT* 28 October 1919, 28 November 1919, 7 May 1920, 1 February 1921

126. *D&SN* 25 May 1922

127. *D&SN* 20 February 1919

128. *WT* 27 November 1919, 13 July 1920, 2 November 1920, Colyton Heritage Centre paper on Memorial Social Club

129. *WT* 26 March 1920, 8 April 1920

130. *WT* 24 September 1920

131. *WT* 27 December 1918, 20 January 1919, *D&SN* 24 April 1919

132. *WT* 31 January 1919. Other parishes were equally idiosyncratic. At Northam a chapel in the parish church became the main war memorial but at Lustleigh the idea was rejected – *WT* 22 September 1922, DHC 1987A/PR Lustleigh Parish Magazines 1918-19

133. *WT* 20 November 1919

134. *WT* 19 July 1921

135. *WT* 8 November 1921

136. *WT* 16 March 1920, 2 November 1920, 18 July 1921

137. *D&SN* 17 April 1919, 10 January 1921, 10 March 1927, 4 & 11 April 1929, WO 30 November 1922, 21 December 1922

138. *CC* 10 May 1919, 19 May 1923; *WT* 8 & 14 February 1919, 9 February 1920, 17 November 1921

139. *WT* 27 October 1922

140. *WT* 14 May 1920, 12 July 1920

141. *MDA* 8 & 31 March 1922, 1 April 1922

142. *WT* 26 September 1919, 9 March 1920, 23 April 1920

143. *WT* 26 November 1918, 17 January 1919, *TT* 13 June 1919

144. *WT* 3 July 1919, 4 August 1919

145. DHC 1262/M/O/O/LD 130/154 & 157 Owen/Fortescue letters, *WT* 8, 18 & 19 August 1919, *NDH* 21 August 1919

146. *WT* 21 January 1919, *CC* 28 July 1923

147. *WT* 22 November 1919, 11 July 1922

148. *WT* 17 & 20 May 1921

149. *WT* 2 May 1924, Freeman, B., *The Yeomanry of Devon 1794-1927* pp168-248. After the war the Yeomanry faced disbandment but after much lobbying, especially by Lord Fortescue, they were amalgamated in the 96th Brigade, Royal Field Artillery.

150. *WT* 21 & 27 July 1921

151. *WT* 1 November 1929, www.msubs.co.uk/crew/vc-winners/sandford, www.dreadnoughtproject.org/tfs/index.php/Francis_Hugh_Sandford

152. *WT* 10 September 1919

153. *NDJ* 27 May 1920

154. *WT* 20 February 1920, 29 October 1920

155. *WT* 17 November 1922

156. *WT* 10 August 1920

157. *WT* 14 January 1919

158. *WT* 22 March 1920, 29 October 1920

159. *WT* 4 & 5 December 1919, 26 July 1921, 25 May 22

160. Viz Exeter Post Office *WT* 17 April 1920, Exmouth FC *WT* 6 April 1920

161. *MDA* 28 August 1926

162. *WO* 7 October 1920, *WT* 15 October 1920, *NDJ* 5 May 1921

163. *WT* 11 April 1921

164. *NDH* 23 June 1921

3

REALIGNMENTS

Running down the war effort

The Armistice heralded another campaign, this time to run down the vast network of emergency war hospitals and their supply depots. For the remainder of the year fund raising continued apace for extra 'comforts' for patients, and local communities still entertained wounded soldiers with whist drives, teas and concerts.[1] The extensive voluntary supply chain for the celebrated Mayoress of Exeter's Depot ensured that many hundreds of parcels of food and clothing were sent to Holland for prisoners-of-war gathering there prior to embarkation home.[2] At Christmas 1918 300 wounded soldiers still in Exeter were regaled with dinner, tea, carols and gifts, and '75 young ladies took the greatest pleasure in attending to their every need'.[3] In January 1919 sick and injured soldiers were among the patients enjoying a concert at Barnstaple's North Devon Infirmary, and as usual love songs and comedy sketches dominated the repertoire.[4] In the same month local working parties were asked to continue to collect, mend and make items of clothing for Belgian and French refugees to take home with them.[5] And gathering sphagnum moss from local wetlands for drying into antiseptic dressings for wounds continued well after the Armistice. A final letter from the secretary of Devon's Central Sphagnum Moss Depot in Exeter in February 1919 recorded that over 830,000 dressings had been sent to hospitals at home and abroad.[6]

In December 1918 a formal farewell ceremony marked the closure of Torquay War Hospital Depot after 3½ years work raising £4,000 and providing 315,000 assorted articles. Presentations were made to Miss Purvis who had run the depot and her heads of departments – Mrs Biddell (bandages) Miss Tucker (sphagnum moss), Miss Eales (splints), Miss Latchford (commissariat) and Miss Tucker (pneumonia jackets).[7] The Mayoress of Exeter's Depot did not close until October 1919. Among its last acts were the refreshments given to hundreds of Belgian refugees on their homeward train journeys and to 2,000 men from the Devonshire Regiment when they met for the Peace March through Exeter. During the war the Depot had dispatched two million parcels of food, clothing, toiletries, books and games to servicemen across the world, and each worker received a certificate of thanks from Lady Owen, the wartime mayoress.[8]

One by one the three dozen war emergency hospitals across Devon were emptied of patients, and at farewell ceremonies thanks were given to the VAD auxiliary nurses and domestic staff, and to local families for their regular gifts of extra equipment, clothing and food.[9] Exmouth Red Cross Hospital closed in March 1919 with a farewell whist drive and dance 'for Tommies and Nurses'.[10] The following month the two war hospitals in Crediton closed and the speech of thanks to staff by the County VAD Director, Major J.S.C. Davis, celebrated the unique absence of disputes he was called upon to resolve there. Elsewhere, he added cryptically, this was far from the case.[11] The buildings returned to their pre-war owners, and the equipment, or the proceeds of its sale, shared among local hospitals and health services. When Torquay's War Hospital returned to being the Town Hall, the beneficiaries included the Open Air School, Rosehill children's hospital, the town and local TB hospitals, Ockendon convalescent home, and the Voluntary Nursing Association.[12]

However things were different in Exeter where several buildings requisitioned as war hospitals and controlled directly by the Army were not handed back despite complaints. They housed serious neurological and orthopaedic cases, and the many soldiers suffering from venereal diseases. As late as January 1921 around 100 sick servicemen remained in Streatham Hall, the Bishop's Palace and the Children's Home in Heavitree.[13] For much of 1919 the Army Pay Corps still occupied St Luke's Teachers' Training College and much of Topsham Road Barracks. That summer the female staff were the first to be dismissed once numbers could be reduced, while disabled ex-servicemen were deliberately retained in employment until last.[14]

In mid-January 1919 Miss Mary Calmady-Hamlyn, the indefatigable secretary of the women's branch of Devon's Food Production Department, reported the 'happy position' that the women's wartime Land Army had been reduced from around 700 to 130 'tried and good girls' that farmers were keen to keep. She said they could stay as long as they were needed, but she fully understood why women wanted to quit such arduous low paid work now the war had ended.[15] A fortnight later the final batch of 60 Good Service Ribbons were awarded, with employers' testimonials paying tribute to the women's skills managing milking parlours, driving tractors, caring for flocks of sheep, felling trees and mending roads. During Miss Calmady-Hamlyn's speech she could not resist referring to the women's long and hard fight to win grudging acceptance from Devon's farmers as proficient workers. However it seems farmers' wives had been as opposed to the women's daily presence as their husbands – and perhaps more so.[16]

As early as December 1918 the *Western Times* helped promote alternative employment for

J.S.C. Davis, CBE. (Mark Ware: Devon HDB: Courtesy of Devon & Exeter Institution Trustees).

middle class women war workers. It recognised that many would not be content with returning to their 'leisured lives' and cited the various 'useful' training courses on offer for would-be health visitors, infant welfare workers, sanitary inspectors and teachers in girls' secondary schools. As several speakers across the county said, these expanding professions, along with the array of hospital and school nursing posts, were vitally necessary in the post-war world, and especially suitable for women.[17] More circumscribed attention was paid to working class women. In February 1919 a WEA speaker in Exeter urged the creation of training institutions for domestic servants to help restore interest, even pride, in this increasingly unpopular occupation.[18] At that time around 130 women in Barnstaple were unemployed, and in an unusual move the town's Derby Lace Factory sought approval to employ some on its night shift.[19]

In January 1919 Sir James and Lady Owen, together with Earl and Countess Fortescue, hosted a farewell gathering for the Belgian refugees living in the city. After fulsome speeches, gifts were exchanged, but although the tributes harked back to 1914 no-one mentioned Miss Clara Andrew, the initial organiser of the county's refugee reception and housing scheme. Although she had worked tirelessly to secure homes for several thousand refugees fleeing the German invasion, in 1916 she was sidelined by Earl Fortescue. He thought she was 'brittle' and getting out of her depth, and preferred Miss Bannatyne and her sister, Mrs Ludovic Amory, who were the better connected daughters of the wealthy owner of Haldon House. Fortescue's memoirs reveal he had little liking for the refugees, many of whom he thought ill-bred and even criminal, and privately he welcomed their departure.[20] Similar farewells were held across the county, and soon afterwards the refugee families boarded special trains taking them to Tilbury Docks.[21] There were some tearful departures. Among them, the impoverished van der Putte family from devastated Antwerp had been taken to heart by their hosts in Crediton, and they departed overwhelmed by a purse of money to help restore their shop.[22] During 1919 other trains repatriated the German and Austrian prisoners of war who had been employed on Devon's farms. The last camp, at South Molton, closed in October 1919.[23]

The vase presented to Teignmouth by the Belgian refugees lodged in the town. Restored, it is displayed on Teignmouth seafront. (Mark Ware).

In July 1919 religious and civic ceremonies in Exeter marked the end of the wartime services of Devon's Voluntary Aid Detachments and their 2,735 members. Cohorts gathered from across the county to process in uniform from Rougemont Castle to the Cathedral where the Dean's sermon blended thanks for past services with socially conscious thoughts that 'no life of merely selfish pleasure can entirely satisfy you now' and 'among the poor, among the children, and among the falling or the fallen' there will be work to do. Outside the Cathedral Lord Fortescue inspected the VADs, and cited the 3,900 hospital beds and 45,000 patients they had served. In conclusion ex-Major Davis was presented with an inscribed silver platter and a motor car.[24] Surplus Red Cross funds were allocated to the County Nursing Association, and to hospitals that had or were still treating ex-servicemen. The sums were substantial, with, for example, the Royal Devon & Exeter Hospital receiving £10,000, the County TB Sanitorium £18,000, the Nursing Association £3,000, and Torbay and Bideford Hospitals £500 each.[25]

Davis stayed VAD County Director after the war and was instrumental in establishing several medical supply depots, notably in Exeter and Plymouth, 'from which poor people would be able to hire, for a nominal weekly sum, sick-room requisites which would be too expensive for them to buy.'[26] To the delight of Davis and Lady Fortescue, early in 1925 Devon's Number 42 VAD was reformed in Barnstaple with Lady Baird of Fremington House as commandant, assisted by Lieut-Colonel Harper. Nearby, Instow VAD was also revived, and both detachments declared that just as Devon was ready for the last war it must be ready for the next one.[27]

In January 1920 an influential group including the Earl of Portsmouth, Sir Ian Amory, Sir William Ferguson-Davie, Sir John Shelley, Sir Edward Chaning Wills (Chairman of the RD&E's Governors), Mrs Mildmay (Devon Red Cross Vice-President), and the mayor of Exeter (Mr Bradley Rowe) met to discuss how best to mark Georgiana Buller's wartime work as commandant of Exeter's array of First Line military hospitals that received casualties straight from the Front. They were supported by Earl and Countess Fortescue and Lady Florence Cecil, wife of the Bishop of Exeter. In a letter Sir Henry Davy, who had held the post of Southern Command's consulting physician, highlighted the efficiency of the hospitals, the respect senior officers had for Miss Buller, and the warmth patients felt towards her.[28] His daughter had been her chief of staff.

No-one, of course, mentioned the interminable problems the army had caused to relations with Devon's VADs and Red Cross from 1916 by unilaterally transferring all Exeter's First Line war hospitals from Major Davis's sphere of responsibility to that of the Army Medical Service at Southern Command's Headquarters in Plymouth – and then placing Georgiana Buller in complete administrative command of them. Until then she had been Devon's VAD deputy director under Davis, although with responsibility for Exeter. Her appointment – as a young woman with no medical qualification – was unique and far from universally popular. However, as Lord Fortescue wrote in his memoirs, Miss Buller's powerful personality, tirelessness, and detailed command of regulations ensured she largely got her way and the complicated system ran efficiently. He added that she worked 'her staff unsparingly and herself so remorselessly that in 1919 her health completely broke down.'[29]

A few months later, in August 1920, the county branch of the Red Cross decided to publish its view of events. It asserted that the highhanded attitude of the Army, and by strong implication, Miss Buller herself, made life extremely difficult for the VAD and Red Cross running the Second Line hospitals that received patients from the First Line ones once they were deemed ready for convalescence care. It added that there was little coordination of effort which meant some Second Line hospitals were either overcrowded or half empty, that there were constant carping criticisms from visiting army medical staff, a succession of empty promises of change, and the Army cared nothing that the vast majority of VAD and Red Cross staff were hardworking unpaid volunteers. As County Director, Davis found his authority consistently undermined by the Army and Miss Buller, and in 1917 he, all nine Assistant VAD Directors, and several Exeter war hospital doctors came dangerously close to resigning.[30] Only patriotism stopped them. For all her positive qualities Lord Fortescue thought Georgiana Buller had inherited the 'obstinacy' of her father, General Sir Redvers Buller, while he described Davis as 'methodical and business-like, but a little slow and precise'. He recorded his frequent intervention in their rows.[31]

Between late 1918 and 1921 a flurry of awards honoured the work of civilians across Devon. In 1920 Georgiana Buller was made a Dame Commander of the Order of the British Empire (DBE), and whether it was perceived as an honour or a slight the indefatigable Davis became a Commander of the British Empire (CBE) which fell short of a knighthood. CBEs also went to Countess Fortescue as County President of the Red Cross, Mrs Penn Curzon, owner and commandant of Watermouth Castle near Ilfracombe which became an officers' hospital, Dr Sylvia Payne, commandant and medical officer at Torquay Red Cross Hospital, and Lady Layland Barratt, commandant of the Auxiliary Hospital for Officers at her home in Torquay. Several dozen men and women heavily involved in the auxiliary war hospitals, war savings movement, and food control programmes were awarded the lower grades of Officers or Members of the British Empire (OBE or MBE). They included Dr Muriel Morris OBE, the commandant and medical officer at Paignton's war hospital, the Hon Mrs Burn OBE, owner and Commandant at Stoodley Knowle Officers' Hospital in Torquay, Major G. S. Strode JP, OBE, Commandant of Plymouth VAD Hospital, and James Clark Tozer JP, OBE, Chairman of Plymouth's Appeal Tribunal.[32] In addition Red Cross war service medals featuring a Geneva Cross hung by a white ribbon were awarded to many VAD personnel. A final gathering of 140 men and women received them in Exeter Guildhall in June

Dame Georgiana Buller (in later decades). (Mark Ware: Courtesy of Bone & Joint Journal).

1922.[33] In addition to a DBE, Georgiana Buller herself received the far more prestigious Royal Red Cross (RRC) 'for exceptional service'.

One wartime institution most people were pleased to see disbanded was the array of district appeal tribunals set up to determine whether or not applicants had sufficient reason – such as being the only wage earner in a large dependant family – not to be drafted into the armed forces. Widely criticised for being either too harsh or too lenient on applicants, they faced their greatest challenges when confronted with conscientious objectors and had to decide whether their convictions were deeply held or merely arguments of convenience. And conscientious objectors were only too aware that most tribunal members – often civic dignitaries, magistrates, ex-officers, and businessmen – had little sympathy with them.

When Tavistock's tribunal ceased, its Clerk recorded it had dealt with 1,702 cases, and admitted 'It was work which was not congenial to anyone, work which would tend to increase the number of one's enemies rather than to multiply the number of one's friends.' He claimed 'that although possibly mistakes had been made in some instances, in the bulk the work had been well done and generally to the satisfaction of the neighbourhood.'[34] In Exeter Sir James Owen, the mayor, had chaired the tribunal and after the war he professed pride that only 477 of the 6,028 decisions had gone to appeal where 379 of the original decisions had been upheld. He was particularly pleased that only 18 conscientious objectors had been exempted from taking up arms.[35]

The discharge with honour of most Special Constables was another welcome relief. Typically, in December 1919 300 Special Constables in Exeter were presented with certificates acknowledging their wartime services. This had included regular street patrols to deter criminals, spot saboteurs and spies, and find billets for troops, but among the general public their more unwelcome activities included ensuring a host of intrusive wartime restrictions and food controls were obeyed.[36]

Patriots and rebels

Hailed as heroes when in uniform and at war, attitudes towards servicemen were more ambiguous when they donned civilian clothes and took up peacetime occupations. At ex-servicemen's functions they remained honoured as saviours of the country, but when strikes occurred it was easy for commentators to lump them together with all other workers and accuse them of disloyalty, Bolshevism, and revolution. Indeed as early as May 1919 one ex-servicemen lamented to the *North Devon Herald* that those unemployed colleagues 'who a short time ago were 'our gallant lads,' 'our brave boys', etc, but now, when they've got their uniforms off, and there is no further use for them, they are designated 'loafers', 'loungers', 'won't works', etc.'[37]

The widely quoted wartime class unity tended to mask the distinct lack of it in the decade before the war when bitter strikes across docks, mines and railways had threatened to bring the country to a standstill. And strikes returned in abundance in 1919. The government tried to face down a series of stoppages, again by dockers, miners and railway workers, and even the police in various regions. Extreme positions were taken. The Coalition government of 1918 to 1922 led by the Liberal Lloyd George but dominated by the Conservatives sought to avoid concessions and tar the strikers as revolutionary Socialists, while the strikers portrayed the government's response as merciless class oppression. By and large, though, behind all the bluster compromises were reached that gave workers slightly better wages and conditions, but fundamentally satisfied no-one. However the brief postwar boom collapsed in 1920. Industrial output dramatically fell, and the gulf between employers and workers grew even greater as men were laid off and those remaining in work were pressurised to take lower wages.[38]

As 1919 progressed a flurry of strikes hit Devon just at the time servicemen were returning home seeking re-employment. At various times Exeter's carters and Dartmouth's shipbuilders and painters struck, as did building workers in Okehampton and the employees of Barnstaple Cabinet Works.[39]

Local newspapers reported the strikes in lurid terms. STRIKE FEVER SPREADS shouted the *Western Times* as early as 3 February 1919, and a few days later when a brief national railway strike reached Devon, which merely resulted in a few trains not running, the stoppages were termed an 'epidemic'.[40] By the summer the wave of strikes was inciting angry responses from the likes of Colonel Charles Burn, the right wing Conservative MP for Torquay, who envisaged workers' gross self-interest and slack working practices coupled with creeping Bolshevism bringing chaos to the country. Such speeches drew loud applause across Torbay. And no doubt this hostility was stoked by the railwaymen's demonstration in Newton Abbot that August full of speeches, including one by a self-professed Bolshevik, condemning British intervention in Russia, urging unions to flex their muscles, and prophesying the end of capitalism.[41]

For a few days straddling September and October 1919 another national rail strike caused confusion across Devon, not least to many holidaymakers, but some staff, including managers, turned up to handle restricted local services, and civilian volunteers took over several routes operated by railway company lorries. However the mail was badly disrupted, milk that could not be sent to London had to be hurriedly turned into butter and cheese, and grocers were told to conserve supplies and ration sales.[42] Colonel Mildmay, Conservative MP for Totnes, called the strikers 'heartless' and 'callous'.[43] Across Devon the railway workers had little popular support. Hostile crowds tended to gather around union speakers and wreck the meeting with catcalls, constant questions and raucous singing. At Cullompton the crowd's anger was fuelled by accusations that the strikers were delaying the soldiers' homecoming.[44]

However the uncertain prospects for returning 'heroes' could not be easily ignored. By summer 1920 Lord Fortescue calculated that 2,000 ex-servicemen were unemployed in Devon – about 1% of the workforce – and he urged employers and employment exchanges to find them jobs.[45] There was resentment against thousands of women holding onto their posts, especially as shop assistants.[46] Local councils wrestled with the embarrassing plight of returning servicemen on the poverty line, but the situation was complex and the opportunities for remedial action were severely limited when the 1920 depression struck, jobs disappeared, and the aggressive campaigns to reduce public expenditure got into their stride. The County Council established several training

Strikers return to work at Barnstaple Cabinet Works after a 14 week lockout. (Mark Ware: WT 7 November 1919: Courtesy of Devon & Exeter Institution Trustees).

Training ex-servicemen at Barnstaple School of Art & Technology. (Mark Ware: WT 1 July 1921: Courtesy of Devon & Exeter Institution Trustees).

centres for ex-servicemen. Barnstaple and Torquay Schools of Art and Technology provided practical courses, and groups of ex-servicemen were housed and trained at Holcombe County Farm near Dawlish. A few specially arranged road improvement schemes across the county absorbed some of the unemployed, but County Council meetings reveal the reluctance to spend public money at this time.[47] 'Distress funds' were launched for out-of-work families, and charities prepared to open soup kitchens.[48] Such were the vagaries of the economy that Barnstaple's Derby Lace Factory contributed £43 to the local distress fund but in 1921, barely a year later, its workers ended up temporarily joining the hundreds of unemployed.[49] Ominous reports flowed in of Torquay and Paignton's building workers, Dartmouth's shipbuilders and coal heavers, Brixham's builders and seamen, and Totnes and Ashburton's millworkers being under dire threat of unemployment.[50]

In April 1921 a national strike by the 'Triple Alliance' of mining, railway and transport unions seemed imminent over the imposition of wage reductions on miners. An interdenominational service in Exeter Cathedral prayed for an end to 'angry hatred' and 'tumultuous passion'.[51] On the same day, and later the following week, a few demonstrators led by two railwaymen claiming to be Bolsheviks, and derisively called 'Comrade Lucy' and 'Comrade Porter', attempted to hold meetings in Exeter's Bedford Circus. Each time they were jeered, jostled and chased away by a hostile crowd, many of them, said the equally hostile *Western Times*, ex-servicemen.[52] To many people's surprise and relief, the crisis subsided a few days later when the other unions abandoned the miners in a confused disagreement over settlement aims and union solidarity.[53] Despite all the protests, however, wages were reduced nearly everywhere, and by up to 15% in Devon for workers in engineering, building, tailoring, road transport and shipping.[54]

In February 1921 Exeter alone had 370 women and 1,086 'non-disabled' and 56 disabled men on its unemployed register. They evoked sympathy and criticism in about equal measure. A city meeting of employers and councillors despaired of women scorning the numerous advertisements for domestic servants, and agreed, with little firm evidence, that many men were content to draw pensions of £2 and unemployment benefit of 29/- and avoid all work.[55] And not long afterwards the the recession hit government reminded councils – who were already keen to economise – that all claims had to be thoroughly investigated.[56] That September over 150 unemployed men and women marched peacefully through the city, doffed their hats at the Cathedral Green war memorial, and gathered in Bedford Square. They asked for jobs, not charity, and the City Council offered sympathy but little more than vague hopes of future road schemes and a suggestion that the new Halwill to Great Torrington railway line under construction might need labourers.[57] The city's soup kitchens, supported by donations and flag days, remained busy, serving 300 gallons a day at a 1d a pint well into 1922.[58] Up in north Devon the Barnstaple and Bideford shipyards on the River Taw that within the last year or two had launched and completed half a dozen steel-hulled steam powered coasters amidst general celebration were reduced to laying off workers in 1921, along with the glove factories at Torrington and Pilton. In January 1922 897 men and women in and around Bideford were on the unemployed register and a further 195 on short time. And Barnstaple's Derby Lace Factory remained in a perilous state – occasionally busy but often slack – throughout the early 1920s.[59]

By mid-decade the general economy was more buoyant, but union anger across the outdated iron and steel industry, and especially in coal mines, at the owners' persistent refusal to agree to better working conditions and wages steadily grew into the General Strike of May 1926. Seeing a new trial of strength with the unions looming, early that year the government ensured each region had created detailed contingency plans with official co-ordinators, local authorities and volunteer groups to withstand the likely disruption. When the General Strike finally occurred, between 3 and 12 May that year, most Devon rail services ceased, but civilian volunteers helped non-strikers run a skeleton train service run between Newton Abbot and Moretonhampstead, Exeter, Torquay and Plymouth, between Tavistock and Plymouth and Exeter, and between Exeter and Ilfracombe, Exmouth and Honiton. In addition a few meat, dairy and fish trains succeeded in getting out of the county, although some lucky shoppers found stocks of butter and eggs that missed the trains

Road widening at Lydford in early 1920s. (Beaford Old Archive images: © Beaford Arts).

being sold cheaply. Most Exeter and Plymouth trams stopped working, but some transport companies, and notably Hardy-Colwill and the Devon Motor Transport Company, ran extra passenger and goods services throughout the county, and even to London. Many car owners volunteered to deliver mail, and most local newspapers managed to publish reduced editions using volunteers and non-striking print workers. As coal supplies had been built up satisfactorily, the plans to ration or cut gas supplies and switch off street lights were not needed, even though the miners stayed out on strike long after the other unions had acknowledged defeat.[60]

At least one one bout of violence occurred when strikers in Plymouth attacked several tramcars at work and running battles erupted with the police. Tram windows were smashed, and there were several injuries and arrests, including an irate women who threw eggs from her shopping basket at the police. Bizarrely on the same day in the same town 10,000 people watched a football match between strikers and the police. There was no trouble and the strikers won 2-1.[61]

Several clergy, notably in the railway centre of Newton Abbot, held services for strikers, and counselled conciliation. The Rev. W. Rushby of Torquay pointedly reminded his parishioners that the strikers were the same men who were hailed as heroes in the war.[62] The Rev. R.C.L. Lamplugh of Barnstaple said his sympathies lay with the miners threatened with 'grinding poverty', while conversely the Rev. H.M.Drake of Paignton feared the country would 'go like Russia.'[63] When it was all over, and even though the strike had failed to achieve its aims, many railwaymen and other unionists at Okehampton, Tavistock, Teignmouth and Tiverton attended special church services while they negotiated their return to work. At Tavistock the hymn chosen by the men was 'Lead, Kindly Light amidst the encircling gloom', a favourite of troops on the Western Front.[64]

Although the vast majority of Devonians had jobs, the varying levels of demand for such locally made goods as lace and textiles, leather goods, pottery and baskets meant unemployment remained a constant sore throughout the later 1920s with Exeter consistently hovering around 550,

A vital trade: a collier and steam delivery lorries at Pilton Quay.
(Beaford Old Archive images © Beaford Arts).

The Rt Rev. . Lord William Cecil, Lord Bishop of Exeter, 1916-36, at the laying of the foundation stone of the new Torbay Hospital, the gift of Mrs Ella Rowcroft who is sitting next to him, 23 June 1926.
(Mark Ware: Courtesy of F.J. Payne's History of Torbay Hospital).

Barnstaple around 450 and Bideford around 350.[65] There were a few 'star' moments though. Three special pieces of Barnstaple's Brannam pottery were shown at the 1924-25 Wembley Exhibition, and the Derby Lace Factory secured a contract to help fit out new carriages for the prestigious Golden Arrow express train.[66]

Clergy and congregations

At Tavistock's packed thanksgiving service for the Armistice in 1918, the vicar, the Rev. H. L. Bickersteth, pointed out that people had come to the ancient church over the centuries to thank God for our victories at Agincourt, over the Armada, and against Napoleon. He had no hesitation in claiming the Armistice as another victory but, he added presciently, 'They were there that night also to ask guidance for the days ahead.'[67] The mood was briefly celebratory but it was overshadowed by grief and exhaustion, anxiety about the future, and the dreadful question – was it all worthwhile?

The vast majority of Devon's clergy from all denominations had ended up actively supporting the Allies whatever their initial doubts may have been as war approached in 1914. A few clergy retained muted sympathy with conscientious objectors, but others openly scorned them. Some clergy became forces' chaplains, and they suffered their share of wounds, a few fatal, and, as we have seen, several were awarded medals for bravery. Some clergy families, including both Bishop Cecil and his suffragan, the Right Rev. Robert Trefusis, Bishop of Crediton, grieved the deaths of their sons just like their parishioners, and pulpits resounded with patriotic assertions of the virtues of Great Britain's struggle against unprovoked German aggression and brutality. Thus armed, local clergy supported the county's recruitment drives, held special services for departing men, and urged upon them the ideals of the courageous and virtuous Christian soldier. However by 1917 when the horrifying war of attrition seemed endless, most clergy, just like the Bishop of Exeter, ended up promulgating the argument that man's descent into sin and selfishness had led to the bloodshed, and God would bring victory in His own time but only when people had repented and renewed their faith.[68]

In November 1918 much of the wrestling with ways Christians could come to terms with total war was superseded by the questions posed by the Christian engagement in national reconstruction and international peace. The answers clergy gave were many and varied, and frequently far from optimistic. It was as though the turmoil of war had thrown them out of kilter with a nation deeply divided between those seeking to preserve the pre-war social order with all its inequalities and those determined to bring about, one way or another, radical welfare reforms and a fairer division of wealth. Nevertheless whether through conviction, custom or familiarity, or a combination of factors, the number of Easter communicants in the Diocese of Exeter remained constant at 65,045 in 1911, 65,508 in 1921 and 70,304 in 1931, but they represented only around 10% of the slowly rising population.[69] (On Easter Sunday all confirmed Anglicans were expected to receive communion).

However churches remained important institutional symbols of national life, and often were full at weddings, funerals, Easter, Harvest, Christmas, 'Hospital Sundays' – and 'Remembrance Sundays'. Tourist guide books still listed all the places of worship, and many clergy retained some authority over people's lives as school managers, Poor Law Guardians, trustees of charities, and a few still sat as magistrates. Some also endured obloquy as the beneficiaries of tithe money reluctantly paid by farmers and landowners. Although the ancient 'gifts' of produce to the parish priest had been long replaced by cash, such payments at a time of rural recession, and often forced upon Nonconformist farmers, were an unwelcome and embarrassing symbol of social and religious divisions.[70] Interestingly, in 1921 the vicar of the country parish of Burlescombe thought most vast old rectories should be burnt down as too costly to maintain and symbolising an unfortunate separation between priest and parishioners.[71] Not far removed from this view, the historian David Cannadine scarifies the Church of England at this time as 'the landed establishment

The Rt Rev. Robert Trefusis, Suffragan Bishop of Crediton, 1897-1930. (Mark Ware: Devon DHB: Courtesy of Devon & Exeter Institution Trustees).

at prayer; rural, propertied, privileged and suffused by an aristocratic social authority.'[72] Indeed, Bishops Cecil and Trefusis were scions of the aristocratic Salisbury and Clinton families, and the 15th and 16th Earls of Devon, grandsons of the 13th Earl had been ordained long before they inherited the title. They served as local parish priests – of Powderham and Honiton respectively.

However, in February 1919 the Bishop of Lichfield, the Rt Rev. John Kempthorne, joined a Chapter House meeting at Exeter Cathedral on the Church of England's National Mission of Repentance & Hope which had started in the darkest days of the war in 1916. He was a key figure attempting to stoke the Mission's local fires, and possibly found plenty of talk about Repentance but new ideas, and perhaps Hope itself, in short supply. Although Exeter's Diocesan Missioner said he had visited 500 parishes to inspire some enthusiasm, Dr Kempthorne stressed the need for church services and parochial activities to be the result of greater lay and clergy dialogue and agreement. He came dangerously close to saying lay disinterest in parish affairs, and of Christianity itself, could be laid directly at the feet of stand-offish clergy. He gave notice that direct lay intervention in parochial matters through the establishment of mandatory church councils was on the way.[73] That March Canon Robinson of Canterbury gave an address in Exeter on the National Mission, and openly acknowledged 'the

Church must be the first to repent' – notably, he added, of being too much the church of the rich and too little in sympathy 'with certain movements, both social and intellectual.'[74] These 'movements' were not specified, but no doubt he meant those leaning towards the Left not the Right.

There was some movement in the diocese, and it consisted largely of blaming others for the state of the nation and its spiritual health. In January 1920 the Dean of Exeter, Dr Henry Gamble, publicly stated 'it was quite clear now that socially, economically, morally and spiritually, the country was in a worse condition than before the war.' He itemised the spiralling wage demands, the disinclination to do a good day's work, 'the wave of lust' and immorality, the shameless profiteering of businessmen, the threat of Bolshevism, and the unrest across the British Empire. He believed 'the prospects of civilisation had never been so dark since the beginning of the middle ages.'[75] Such arguments had been building up for some time. In March 1919 the Exeter Diocesan Conference had resounded to complaints that teachers in council schools, and many parents, were failing to instil Christian convictions into children.[76] And at the annual meeting of the Diocesan Association for the Care of Friendless Girls that month Mrs Gamble, the Dean's wife, asserted that many single girls who became pregnant did so because of their apathetic and neglectful mothers.[77] In May 1919 Bishop Cecil himself used the *Diocesan Gazette* to remind Anglicans that sloth was a cardinal sin, and all too apparent.[78] Clearly some clergy found the laity depressing. The Rev. W. Gabriel Harris, vicar of Walkhampton, thought the phrase 'I love Christ: I hate Christians' summed up many people's views, and he blamed the laity rather than the clergy for this dismal state of affairs as many churchgoers failed to behave as Christians in their daily lives. He thought business owners were particularly culpable.[79]

The Haldon Races Fancy Dress Ball at Peamore House. At the far right is Dean Gamble of Exeter in clerical black with his wife seated by him. Lady Kekewich of Peamore is seated left.
(Mark Ware: WT 6 September 1929: Courtesy of Devon & Exeter Institution Trustees).

Nevertheless change was imminent. In 1919 the new Enabling Act created the Anglican Church Assembly comprising laity as well as clergy, and its formation was heralded as a major step forward in achieving unity across the Church of England. The Assembly was a forum for discussing major questions and advising Parliament on future legislation. It was welcomed by the Diocese of Exeter, and Bishop Trefusis urged laity and clergy at a parochial level to cooperate more fully in supporting church schools, Sunday Schools, Scouts and Guides, social clubs, bell-ringing and 'popular lectures and instructive entertainments'. Thereby they would enliven parochial life, replenish congregations, and encourage Christian behaviour. He did not hesitate to acknowledge some clergy needed to be stirred out of their isolated 'grooves', and that laity should do some of the stirring.[80] Speaking in South Molton, Mr Clifton Kelway of the Church Reform League, was even more direct when he hoped the new initiative would remove 'the powerlessness of the faithful laity to prevent an improper appointment or to obtain the removal of one who is no pastor but an incubus.'[81] No doubt he had in mind St Winifred's Church in Manaton where the Rev. John Sanders had been ejected in January 1920 by the Diocesan Consistory Court after 20 years of bitter conflict with parishioners.[82] However the 1921 Diocesan Conference voted to ensure the diocesan bishop retained the final say in all liturgical disagreements between incumbents and laity.[83]

The 1921 Diocesan Conference endorsed the wider Anglican Lambeth Conference's view that Christians 'must show the Gospel everywhere in action' and also voted for an explanatory rider saying 'it is the duty of all Churchpeople to study and to take an active part in improving the social conditions of our country.' The implication was that the Church of England should adopt a more vigorous and far more visible social mission. However several Conference speeches and comments revealed the deep divisions behind the vote, notably how far down the path of social equality the Anglican Church would go in its new 'applied Christianity' programme. Fundamentally delegates worried to what extent the Church would become the Labour Party rather than the Conservative Party at prayer, and views varied widely with some speakers fearing a Bolshevik style revolution if the Church veered too far to the Left, and others fearing a similar upsurge of discontent if the Church did nothing to help repair the broken social order. Several Conference contributors followed the 'social control' argument and thought part of the solution lay in parishes providing instructive and elevating activities to ensure families knew how best to spend any increased wages and leisure time they might be 'awarded' in industrial settlements.[84]

Dean Gamble made his views clear on St George's Day that year when he ennobled patriotism as a Christian virtue in the battle against Bolshevism. He cited the famous words of Nurse Edith Cavell just before the Germans executed her as a spy that 'Patriotism is not enough' to strengthen his argument that patriotism and Christianity were inextricably intertwined in the defence of the nation. In 1925 the Dean once again used the St George's Day symbol of the Christian knight slaying the dragon to condemn the current monster, Bolshevism, as 'the power of chaos and darkness'.[85] A year later when some some clergy held special services of gratitude to God for ending the 1926 General Strike their sermons portrayed the strikers as misguided innocents in the hands of a minority of revolutionaries, and greatly in need of Christian re-direction.[86] And yet, as we have seen, many strikers were church-goers.

In June 1923 a diocesan conference debated 'The Church & Social Problems', and in doing so revealed a strange mix of mild concern and dull complacency. No-one disagreed with the Dean when he suggested, without citing his evidence, that intemperance was declining, church attendances were rising again and that families were restoring discipline. The Dean approved that 'whacking' children was still in vogue. The issue of sexual 'impurity' faded away in vague agreement that mixed schools were now acceptable and that church schools remained bastions of moral instruction. Although some delegates demurred, the conference as a whole accepted that healthy recreational activities on Sundays – after attending divine worship – were preferable to idleness which so easily could turn to vice in villages as much as towns. Even parish dances were deemed acceptable, but not on Sundays, as long as they were 'guided' – although 'guided' was not defined. The conference's main item, however, was the progress of the much disputed revised Prayer Book through the National Assembly. It caused the conference to turn in on itself and highlighted the schism between traditionalists and modernists, and also between Anglo-Catholic and Evangelical liturgical devotees. The latter strongly suspected the former of foisting the Roman mass on parishes, but whatever the worth of the arguments it made the diocese's call for unity look somewhat hollow.[87]

As a postscript to this conference, in 1925 Tavistock Rural Deanery finally decided local Bands of Hope had done their work and agreed that now their youthful members had become adults the 'drink problem' had subsided. Most other deaneries were less optimistic, and the Anglican Temperance crusade, like the Nonconformist one, was far from over – particularly, it seems, across north Devon.[88]

Individual clergy continued to promote their own sometimes extreme positions. On Armistice Sunday in 1923 the Rev. T. C. Walters, vicar of Highweek, Newton Abbot, itemised the 'anger and suspicion between class and class, strife and bickering between party and party, a want of discipline and seriousness, and a throwing overboard of restraint and morality in social and business life.' Noting the significance of the day, he added, 'England at war was a better place than England at peace.' The solution, he claimed, was a return to Christian living 'so that God who brought us victory in war will bring us victory in our troubled peace'.[89] The vicar, like many others, sought to return to an illusory pre-war world where Christian standards reigned supreme over a generally accepted social order, forgetting that all the 'evils' he had itemised were readily apparent then. A few other clergy thought very differently and in doing do helped to confuse the situation, notably regarding what exactly the Church of England stood for at this critical time. In 1925 the radical Cornish priest, the Rev. Jack Bucknall, hit the local headlines with a speech in Tavistock when he condemned the British Empire as nothing less than the commercial exploitation of conquered

A Sunday School parade at Hatherleigh in 1922 highlighting the virtues taught to its members. (Beaford Old Archive images © Beaford Arts).

nations, and denigrated the established domestic social order as barely fettered exploitation of the working class. He rejected all thoughts that deaths from disease and hunger should be tainted with the words 'Thy Will Be Done', and asserted that 'God's will was health, justice, freedom, and a splendid life' despite most clergy failing to preach this essential truth. Until they did, he said, Communism would remain a threat. Although a member of the tiny Catholic Crusade of Christian Socialist clergy, Bucknall's professed sympathy with Communist (rather than aggressive Bolshevik) ideals rendered him an isolated and much criticised figure.[90]

Not surprisingly moral crusades abounded, all of them with strong nationalist overtones. Devon's Anglican and Nonconformist clergy, Salvation Army officers and Young Men's Christian Association (YMCA) officials actively promoted the All-Round-England Campaign of the Alliance of Honour. Begun in 1904, with Major General Baden-Powell (of later Scouting fame) and William Bramwell Booth (later the Salvation Army's General) among its founders, the highly nationalist Alliance exhorted young people to lead morally upright lives and pledge themselves to the service of 'religion, home and empire.'[91] It remained active amongst church groups throughout the inter-war decades. In 1922 the Rev. Cyril Edgington from the Church Army made his organisation's view of post-war society clear in Tavistock by asserting, 'The morals of the younger generation, probably as a result of recoil from the war, seemed to have absolutely run wild … The trouble was not only among uneducated girls. They had terrible cases in other classes of Society.' To ram home his partisan point he asserted 'he had never seen at a Police Court, Bolsheviks, Communists, or Extremists give a home to the boy or girl who had got into trouble. There were no good Samaritans of that kind.'[92] In 1929 the Diocesan Conference spent much time trying to differentiate between 'legitimate speculating' and gambling, and finally decided both were evil as they relied heavily on chance and were a misuse of money. The conference also condemned 'extravagant expenditure upon recreation and amusements', but in an interesting moral postscript found it most reprehensible in those who could not really afford it.[93] Gambling and extravagance joined drinking as activities to be vigorously challenged.

Devon's Free Churches were Anglican but outside diocesan authority. Each one, as in Exeter, Exmouth, Totnes and Bideford, had been established in the previous century by groups of worshippers objecting to 'Popish' liturgical practices introduced by the incumbent. After the war, they wrestled with declining numbers and sought to define their separatism from the 'established' Church of England by criticising its alleged apathy and weakness. Thus, in 1919 the Rev. James Ellis of Exmouth's Free Church thought the decay of Sunday Observance exemplified the failure of clergy to stem the tide of irreligion, and expressed disgust at the Sunday queues for tickets at Devon's railway stations.[94] The Free Churches sought to make their presence felt with open-air meetings and vocal opposition to the sale of alcohol, sports on Sundays and dancing licences. Significantly, in 1929, a decade later, Exeter's Free Church Council openly acknowledged the negativity of its campaigns, but its members decided they remained vital to make 'our city an even more wholesome place.'[95]

Nonconformists seemed equally perplexed by the post-war world and the place their faith occupied in it. In February 1919 the Rev. J. W. Bowler of Exeter's Providence Chapel bemoaned the 'uncertainty of religious feeling in men – no-one seems to know what to do for the best, and to help Christianity'. At the Wesleyan Convention in Exeter in February 1919 the Rev. Samuel Chadwick lamented the schisms blighting the Methodist movement that antagonised the faithful and confused potential converts.[96] However at least some of the self-imposed wounds created by Methodist splinter movements were healing after the Bible Christians, Methodist New Connexion and United Methodist Free Churches had come together in 1907. The differences between Primitive, United and Wesleyan Methodists were also gradually fading, but the pleas for unity were as much the result of shrinking numbers as the theological arguments supporting reconciliation.[97]

In 1922 the Rev. H. G. Classey, a Congregational minister at Plymtree, analysed the testing times for all churches when the men 'who had looked into Hell in Flanders' and now hoped for a better world were tormented instead by 'the transition into a petulant, peevish, and by no means permanent peace.' He added ominously, 'The war had had its effect within the Church itself; there was the horrible feeling that some earlier ideals had faded; here, too, the haunting questions whether the championing of this war in particular had not weakened the force of their protest against war in general, and whether habits, such as that of regular worship, suspended during wartime, remained in abeyance in the days of peace.'[98] The Rev. E. W. Coltman, chairman of the Devon Congregational Union, added a lament about the return of class warfare. He feared 'the world seemed to be beset with the spirit of selfishness; so that there was a mad rush for pleasure and excitement and self-gratification.'[99]

In 1922 the East Devon Congregational Union was faced with closing or amalgamating struggling churches.[100] The North Devon Congregational Union was equally glum, its president stating, 'Whether or not the churches have failed to justify their existence, they certainly have failed, as we know, to maintain that place and potency in the lives of men which was theirs a generation ago.'[101] In 1924 the Rev. J. Morley Davies from Braunton, said, 'Converts had to be found, and Congregationalists had to engage with the modern world whether they liked that world or not.' As a primary focus, he thought they must voice even more widely their opposition to the drink trade and the denigration of Sundays with sports and amusements.[102] Negativity rather than a positive message of faith seemed to dominate conferences and meetings.

Other Nonconformists felt much the same, and perhaps they felt strengthened by their opposition to much of the post-war world. As early as 1922 a Methodist minister in Tiverton had thundered that the dwindling influence of all churches lay in their failure to insist on keeping the Sabbath Day holy. 'Things were certainly bad', he concluded, 'and they would be infinitely worse when Sunday became a second Saturday.'[103] In 1924 the county president lamented 'it was a despiritualised age' and although, he claimed, connecting the Christian message to contemporary issues for worshippers was easy, making that connection relevant to 'outsiders' was difficult.[104] Another Methodist clergyman felt the same in 1926, asking, 'The

Buckfast Abbey under construction 1929. (Author's collection).

The People of Devon 1918–1930

question that should concern them most was had they a message to proclaim in the modern age just as Wesley had a message to proclaim in his age.'[105] By the end of the decade Exeter's Methodists acknowledged they were losing the battle for membership against the mounting tide of films, day trips and sports fixtures. However much numbers dwindled, the remaining members expressed pride in their faith, and perhaps also in their exclusivity, while the world appeared to ignore their message.[106]

Although comparatively small in numbers Devon's Roman Catholics continued to build congregations, and churches, across Devon. Freed from legal constraints in the previous century, several churches had been built in Plymouth, a major centre of Roman Catholicism, and also one in Exeter and several smaller towns – notably coastal resorts such as Sidmouth, Teignmouth, Bideford and Barnstaple. Private chapels such as the one protected by Lord Clifford of Chudleigh within his mansion at Ugbrooke came into the open, several dozen schools were opened, and closed orders came to the county such as the Bridgettine nuns to Chudleigh, and later Marley House near Rattery. Expansion was steady but quiet, with the greatest prominence reserved for the Benedictine monks who had returned to the site of the pre-Reformation abbey at Buckfast in the 1880s and in the 1920s were well on the way to building a new abbey.[107]

Women in public life

Women had risen to prominence in various fields long before the Franchise Act of 1918, and carved successful, if hard won, careers in art, literature, education, medicine and science. Locally, in 1895 Dr Rosa Bale had become the first female medical practitioner in Plymouth, and, indeed, west of Bristol. She was also a prominent supporter of the Liberal Party and the non-militant suffragist movement.[108] And two successive teacher representatives on Exeter's Education Committee were women elected by their peers, with Miss Bidwell replacing Mrs Chinnick in 1918.[109] Alongside them, of course, thousands of women were in modestly paid employment, from office clerks, nurses and teachers (and headteachers) to textile workers, seamstresses and domestic servants. And Devon's censuses and street directories show that a significant minority of farms and shops were run by women.[110] As David Cannadine has written, the ideology of 'separate spheres' between wage-earning men and domesticated women was never as common as contemporary prescriptive literature, mostly written by men, had suggested.[111] In addition, women from more socially and politically influential families had customarily involved themselves in giving speeches in support of local parliamentary candidates, hosting political garden

Lady Kekewich distributes prizes at Exminster Sports Day. (Mark Ware: WT 16 September 1921: Courtesy of Devon & Exeter Institution Trustees).

parties and dinners, actively supporting charitable fund raising and taking a patrician interest in community affairs. However no women, whatever their social status, could have been more in the public eye in the decade before the war than the those campaigning for the vote, some peacefully, some militantly. And without a doubt the sterling wartime work and qualities of leadership shown by many women helped secure their post-war posts of public responsibility.

Civic affairs had offered some opportunities to women before the war. Miss Katherine Penrose Hammond was the daughter of an Anglican clergyman, and educated at Lady Margaret Hall, Oxford. Later in life she settled in Ilfracombe where she devoted herself to church and civic affairs. She served on the church council, and became a school manager and Sunday School teacher. In 1914 she was elected a district councillor and served on the Hospital, Allotment, Highways, Lighting & Licensing, Housing, and Pleasure Ground & Entertainments Committees. In addition, during the war she held office on the local War Savings and Food Control Committees. In August 1920 her obituarist said, 'Miss Hammond was a fine example of a woman who could work on equal terms with men in municipal and other public life without losing an atom of womanliness.'[112] Another was Miss Jessie Montgomery who died in October 1918. A pioneer of the University Extension movement she arranged several series of public lectures at Exeter's Royal Albert Memorial Museum, and became a promoter and governor of Exeter University College, and a co-opted member of Exeter Education Committee. An advocate of women's education and social clubs, she was also a lead figure in the city's non-militant National Union of Women's Suffrage Societies.[113]

However only in February 1918 were women over the age of thirty who met a minimal property qualification given the vote in parliamentary elections. This enfranchised about two thirds of women. Equality with men only came about in 1928 when all women over the age of 21 could vote without any property restrictions. In February 1919 the keynote speaker at Exmouth Women's Citizens' Association exemplified the new post-war mood, asserting, 'A great many women liked to adopt and act on their husbands ideas on public affairs, and not to think individually. Were women to be slaves, and do what they were bidden? Were they to ask to be allowed to have opinions? Were they really such a set of ninnies?' She enumerated all the problems deserving women's attention and action – the 'strikes, child welfare, and the condition of moral life' and the threat posed by Bolshevism to 'the ideal of family life as they knew it.'[114] Stuck in an earlier age, Bishop Cecil was less sure about women's wider role in post-war society. Visiting north Devon in June 1919 he thought men and women had different parts to play, and women should limit themselves to working with and influencing other women – notably the 'foolish girl, with vanity as her failing and folly her characteristic.'[115]

Miss Jessie Montgomery. (Mark Ware: WT 18 October 1918: Courtesy of Devon & Exeter Institution Trustees).

However positions of political power now beckoned. In March 1919 Miss Katherine Anson Cartwright was welcomed home by the Ladies Committee of Teignmouth Liberal Club after four years working for the YMCA, mainly in camps in France. She asserted that 'They were now faced with problems to make life worth living, and to make the world a better place to live in' and she believed the traditional Liberal values of 'peace, retrenchment and reform' remained paramount.

She became Teignmouth Urban District Council's first female councillor in 1919, and its first female chair in 1925.[116] She was also Secretary of the Devon Union of Women's Liberal Associations, and in a wide-ranging speech in February 1920 she argued for Home Rule for all of Ireland, for the maintenance of Free Trade and rejection of import tariffs, for the strongest possible League of Nations and against the Versailles Peace Treaty as unacceptably vengeful towards Germany. County wide, the Association had several thousand members, and from 1918 all women's political associations assumed far greater importance in constituency affairs.[117] Although disappointed at the performance of Asquith's rump of the Liberal Party at the 1922 election – a mere 63 seats, with just one in Devon held by George Lambert in South Molton – she asserted, optimistically if ultimately vainly, that its principles of international peace, individual freedom and welfare reform would triumph once again.[118] Mrs Frances Acland of Killerton was another forceful speaker on behalf of the Asquithian section of the Liberal Party. Speaking to Exeter's Women's Liberal Association in March 1920 she praised Asquith as a great reforming prime minister (1908-16) and utterly condemned Lloyd George's hopeless war in Russia when he should be concentrating on domestic reconstruction.[119]

In January 1920 Mrs Jewell, the ex-wartime mayoress of Barnstaple, was elected its first female borough councillor on a wide programme of better schools, more houses and industrial expansion.[120] In November 1920 Mrs Juanita Maxwell Phillips was elected mayor of Honiton. Born in South America of Anglo-Scottish parents, and married to a local solicitor, she was described 'as thoroughly British in spite of her rather 'foreign' vivacity and charm of manner.' She was involved in everything at a senior level – the town council, Board of Guardians, secondary school, welfare clinic, Women's Institute, swimming club, and relief fund. On election she said the council's priorities must be housing, pure water supplies and better drainage.[121] In another key sector, in 1924 Mrs Harry Bazeley MBE became the first 'lady chairman' (sic) of Bideford Hospital Committee. This was partly in recognition of her wartime efficiency in charge of Westward Ho! Hospital.[122]

Mrs Juanita Phillips. (Mark Ware: WT 12 November 1920: Courtesy of Devon & Exeter Institution Trustees).

In 1922 Exeter hosted the county conference of the Women's Local Government Society during which the mayor, not surprisingly, urged the greater involvement of women in public affairs, primarily to advance welfare reforms. In full support, the *Western Times* editorial thundered that 'Face to face with the ravages of disease which have their origin in bad housing, untrained motherhood, drink, poverty, vice, uncleanliness and ignorance, it is to its enlightened women that the County must turn for salvation.' Several local campaigners, including Alice Vlieland and Clara Andrew, had already argued much the same as conference speakers.[123] Although Clara Andrew had been eased out of her leading role in receiving and housing Belgian refugees in 1916, this able and determined woman had turned her attention to destitute children and the means through which responsible couples could adopt them. She founded the National Child Adoption Association in Exeter in February 1918, and that summer established its headquarters in Sloane Street in London. In June 1919 two London hostels were opened to receive children awaiting adoption, and Miss Andrew secured high profile patrons for her work, notably HRH Princess Alice, Countess of Athlone. Within two years 500 children had been placed with carefully investigated and monitored families, and several other countries were copying her painstaking methods.[124]

Alice Vlieland was an ex-mayoress of Exeter, and a foremost figure in the city's Women's Citizenship Association supporting local hospitals, lying-in charities and infant welfare clinics, urging greater house building, and promoting the League of Nations. She showed little hesitation in publicly condemning much of Exeter's ancient housing and castigating its inspectors for failing to report some of the appalling properties she herself had visited. In October 1919 Mrs Vlieland was pleased that Edith Splatt, well known for her Labour sympathies, had offered herself as an Independent candidate for an Exeter City Council ward, and she urged women to vote for her.[125] Although Miss Splatt was defeated in 1919 and again in 1920, she was successful in 1921 when she decided to swim with the popular tide as a Ratepayers' Association candidate campaigning against profligate city expenditure. Juanita Phillips, the mayor of Honiton, lent her a car for her successful campaign. Later in the decade Miss Splatt appeared openly as a Labour Party speaker on local platforms vigorously campaigning against parsimonious public bodies.[126]

Local branches of the Labour Party worked hard across Devon to wrestle voters away from the traditional Liberal and Conservative camps. Although their candidates usually came in poor thirds in Devon's rural constituency elections, in Exeter they pushed the Liberal candidates into third place in 1924 and 1929, and in Plymouth Sutton they seriously eroded Lady Astor's Conservative majority as the decade wore on. Kate Spurrell, a Plymouth schoolteacher and former president of the National Union of Teachers, was the Labour candidate at Totnes in 1924 and 1929 but although she more than doubled her vote from 2,240 to 5,828 both elections were effectively 'two horse races' between the Liberal and (winning) Conservative candidates.[127] Nevertheless, despite electoral statistics showing most of Devon's rural voters remained Liberal or Conservative their candidates' pre-election speeches revealed that Labour's growing national support was a significant worry. This meant that a great deal of time was spent tarring Labour candidates such as Miss Spurrell as dangerously Socialist with pronounced Bolshevik tendencies. She in turn had no hesitation in condemning the capitalists who thought they were 'doing the workers a favour by owning land, keeping retinues of servants, buying expensive clothes, and over-feeding themselves.'[128]

Throughout the decade Nancy Astor was MP for Plymouth Sutton, and renowned for being the first woman to take her seat in the Commons – in 1919. However, Tavistock nearly provided Devon with a second one in 1929. Standing as a Liberal, Mrs Hilda Runciman had won the Cornish seat of St Ives in a 1928 by-election, but in the 1929 general election she agreed to let her husband, Walter (later Viscount) Runciman contest it and she stood

Nancy, Lady Astor, on the campaign trail in 1919 with her recently ennobled husband whom she succeeded as MP for Plymouth Sutton. (Author's collection).

in Tavistock where the Conservatives had a tiny majority. 1929 was the first election in which women below the age of 30 could vote, and the campaigning was vigorous, with Mrs Runciman promoting temperance, cutbacks, Free Trade, house building, and a meritocratic education system, while her Conservative opponent, Brigadier Wallace Wright VC, presented the election as one between Socialism and Conservatism with the shattered Liberals hopelessly see-sawing between the two. However local Conservatives felt it necessary to strengthen their case by bringing in Dame Caroline Bridgeman, who with her husband, the First Lord of the Admiralty, was a close friend of Stanley Baldwin, the Prime Minister. In public meetings she took apart Liberal claims, deriding cutbacks as wrecking the navy and weakening welfare services, and condemning Free Trade as punishing home producers. In the end the Labour candidate came a poor third, but Mrs Runciman lost by only 62 votes to Brigadier Wright.[129]

The free-speaking Mrs Gamble, wife of the Dean of Exeter, was President of the Exeter Branch of the National Council of Women, and in 1919 she urged members to accept the City and County Council invitations to stand as councillors, rather than wait for co-option. She thought women should become magistrates now this had been legalised 'as they would certainly give different decisions in some cases to those of men.'[130] She did not explain how or why. In October 1920 the first female Justices of the Peace (JPs) were appointed in Devon. All had impeccable credentials as key, and well-connected, personnel in the wartime Red Cross, VADs and Agricultural Committees. They were Mrs Jean Baker of Budleigh Salterton, Mrs Frances Acland of Killerton, the Hon Mrs Eva Trefusis of Exeter, Miss Katherine Cartwright of Teignmouth, Miss Mary Calmady-Hamlyn of Bridestowe, and Mrs Alice Mildmay (soon to be Lady Mildmay) of Flete.[131]

In 1921 Mrs Malcom Patton and Miss Florence Skirrow MBE became Torquay's first JPs. Mrs Patton was Dame President of Torquay's Conservative Primrose League and a town councillor, and Miss Skirrow had been influential in the War Savings and War Bonds campaigns and promotion of child welfare clinics. Earlier in her life she had been a friend of the social reformer Emily Rowntree and run a working girls' club in York.[132] In the same year Miss Kathleen Lazenby, a wealthy benefactor of Tiverton, and a co-opted member of the County Education Committee since 1903, became Tiverton's first female JP. Other influential appointees that year, all with appropriate social standing and welfare credentials, included Lady Peek of Widworthy Court near Honiton, Mrs Anna Griggs of Cann House in Tamerton Folliot, and Mrs Mary Hancock of Ryll Manor, East Anstey.[133] In 1922 Barnstaple's magistrates were joined by Miss Sophia Adams, a well-connected school manager and welfare worker, and Mrs Mary Brannam from the local pottery family possessing close links with the corporation, parish church, war charities and infirmary.[134] Later that year 'Whispers for Women' in the *Devon & Somerset News* pontificated that female JPs were already learning the lessons of justice tinged with mercy and hopes of reform, especially for 'that unfortunate class known as street walkers, so often more sinned against than sinning' that marked a good magistrate.[135]

Miss Kathleen Lazenby laying the foundation stone of Tiverton Library/Memorial Hall. (Courtesy of Tiverton Museum).

The list grew steadily longer during the decade. Appointees such as Mrs H. W. Fulford of Bideford, Miss Elsie Batten of Holsworthy, Miss Elizabeth Bayly of Plymouth, Miss Frances Dickinson of Ottery St Mary and Miss Eleanor Vicary of Newton Abbot all had shared social, legal and organisational backgrounds as Poor Law Guardians, Red Cross workers, school managers and rescue workers. Miss Eleanor Vicary was a particularly notable appointment in 1928. She had been a wartime VAD telephone operator, cook and quartermaster in France before a transfer to Red Cross headquarters. She became a senior figure in Devon's Nursing Association, YMCA, and Women's Section of the British Legion, and a co-opted member of the County Council's Education and Mental Hospital Committees.[136]

Mrs H. W. Fulford, JP. (Mark Ware: WT 23 May 1930: Courtesy of Devon & Exeter Institution Trustees).

In contrast, although a few women joined the special constabulary in Plymouth, the Devon county force steadfastly rejected female officers. The County Standing Joint Committee heavily supported this view in 1923, although only narrowly in 1927. Most members agreed the idea was an expensive 'fad' and not enough work would be found for them. It was sufficient, they said, for the police to liaise with female rescue workers and hostels around the time cases came before the magistrates. A minority argued in vain that women police were far better suited than men to deal with family cases and with vulnerable girls descending into criminal ways.[137]

REFERENCES

1. *CC* 30 November 1918, *WT* 14 December 1918

2. *WT* 14 November 1918

3. *WT* 6 January 1919

4. *WT* 31 January 1919

5. *NDJ* 30 January 1919

6. *DG* 25 January 1919, *WT* 21 February 1919

7. *WT* 17 December 1918

8. *SMG* 9 November 1918, *WT* 29 October 1919, 8 November 1919

9. *MDA* 11 January 1919, NDH 16 January 1919

10. *WT* 22 March 1919

11. *CC* 5 April 1919

12. *DHC* 1262M/L112 Booklet Red Cross and VA in Devonshire during the war 1914 to 1918 and after 1919 & 1920, pp52-53

13. *WT* 15 & 23 December 1919, 18 February 1920, *D&SN* 6 January 1921. Bishop Cecil disliked the Palace and never lived there.

14. *WT* 4 August 1919

15. *WT* 18 January 1919, 2 February 1919

16. *WT* 1 February 1919, Parker, D., *The People of Devon in the First World War*, pp213-222

17. *WT* 18 December 1918, 4 January 1919, 2 July 1919

18. *WT* 6 February 1919

19. *WT* 6 February 1919, 14 March 1919

20. *WT* 4 January 1919, DHC 1262M/L117 + L139 Exeter/Devon War Refugee Committee, 1262M/FH42 Fortescue Memoirs

21. *DG* 1 February 1919, *WT* 6 January 1919, 24 February 1919, *NDJ* 23 January 1919, 27 February 1919

22. *CC* 5 April 1919, and in Barnstaple, see *NDH* 27 February 1919

23. *CC* 11 October 1919

24. *WT* 12 July 1919, *CC* 19 July 1919. The later Red Cross report cited 4,287 beds and 45,475 patients in VAD hospitals and 12,725 in civil and

private hospitals partially staffed by VADs, see *DHC* 1262M/L112 Booklet

25. *DHC* 1262M/L112 Booklet; *WT* 15 September 1919

26. *WT* 2 February 1923

27. *NDJ* 5 February 1925

28. *SMG* 7 February 1920, *WT* 31 January 1920

29. *DHC* 1262M/FH42 Earl Fortescue's memoirs, pp27-39

30. *DHC* 1262M/L112 Booklet

31. *DHC* 1262M/FH42 Earl Fortescue's memoirs, pp27-39

32. *NDJ* 17 June 1919, *WT* 1 April 1920, 17 March 1921

33. *WT* 27 June 1922

34. *TG* 22 November 1918

35. Parker, D., *Exeter: Remembering 1914-18*, p109

36. *WT* 3 December 1919

37. *NDH* 22 May 1919

38. Seaman, L.B.C., *Post-Victorian Britain 1902-1951*, pp105-120

39. *WT* 11 January 1919, 18 March 1919, 4 August 1919, 2 & 8 September 1919, 20 October 1919,

7 November 1919

40. *WT* 3 & 7 February 1919

41. *WT* 4 & 11 August 1919

42. *SMG* 4 October 1919, *WT* 29 September 1919, 1 & 10 October 1919

43. *WT* 2 October 1919

44. *D&SN* 9 October 1919

45. *WT* 7 June 1920

46. *TT* 23 April 1920

47. *WT* 18 June 1920, 2 & 9 July 1920, 31 December 1920, 1 & 25 January 1921, 12 & 26 March 1921

48. *NDJ* 30 December 1920, *WT* 18 October 1920, 14 December 1920, *NDH* 3 March 1921

49. *NDJ* 16 & 30 December 1920, 17 March 1921, 30 June 1921

50. *MDA* 24 September 1920

51. *WT* 9 & 11 April 1921

52. *WT* 12 & 19 April 1921

53. *WT* 13 April 1921. Seaman, L.C.B., op.cit., pp113-115

54. *CC* 5 March 1921, *D&SN* 19 May 1921

55. *WT* 2 & 5 February 1921

56. *WT* 17 September 1921, 21 February 1922

57. *WT* 8 & 21 September 1921

58. *WT* 29 November 1921, 17 February 1922, 13 May 1922

59. *NDJ* 3 & 17 March 1921, *WT* 7 October 1921, 13 January 1921, 29 November 1921, 4 January 1922

60. *D&SN* 6 & 13 May 1926, *NDJ* 6 & 13 May 1926, *NDH* 13 & 27 May 1926, *TG* 7 & 14 May 1926, Porter, J. H., (1978) 'Devon and the General Strike, 1926' in *International Review of Social History*, Vol 23.3 pp333-356

61. *WT* 6 & 14 May 1926

62. *TT* 21 May 1926

63. *NDJ* 29 April 1926, *PO* 13 May 1926

64. *D&SN* 6, 13 & 20 May 1926, *TG* 14 May 1926, *WT* 14 May 1926, *MDA* 15 May 1926

65. *NDH* 29 April 1926, *NDJ* 15 November 1928, *WT* 23 December 1926, 12 July 1929

66. *NDJ* 11 September 1924, 21 November 1929

67. *TG* 15 November 1918

68. *WT* 4/11/18, Parker, D., *The People of Devon in the First World War*, pp74-77

69. Orme, N., (ed.) *Unity & Variety*, p184.

70. *WT* 24 April 1925. Tithe Acts in 1925 and 1936 reduced payments but the situation was not fully resolved until the 1977 Finances Act.

71. *WT* 12 August 1921

72. Cannadine, D., *The Decline & Fall of the British Aristocracy*, p255

73. *WT* 20 February 1919

74. *WT* 28 March 1919

75. *WT* 6 January 1920

76. *WT* 12 March 1919

77. *WT* 18 March 1919

78. *CC* 10 May 1919

79. *TG* 20 November 1925

80. *SMG* 17 April 1920, *WT* 13 & 14 April 1920

81. *WT* 10 May 1920

82. *WT* 27 January 1920, www.

legendarydartmoor.co.uk/manatonchurch

83. *WT* 2 June 1921

84. *WT* 2 & 17 June 1921

85. *WT* 3 May 1921, 24 April 1925

86. *NDJ* 20 May 1926, *D&SN* 20 May 1926

87. *WT* 8 March 1923

88. *TG* 12 June 1925, *NDJ* 12 January 1928, 8 November 1928

89. *MDA* 17 November 1923

90. *TG* 30 October 1925, 30 April 1926.

91. *NDH* 15 January 1920

92. *TG* 15 September 1922

93. *WT* 31 May 1929

94. *WT* 24 October 1919

95. *WT* 1 June 1923, 20 May 1927, 19 April 1929

96. *WT* 11 & 18 February 1919

97. Orme, N., op.cit., p191

98. *D&SN* 6 April 1922

99. *WT* 14 April 1920

100. *WT* 20 October 1922

101. *WT* 3 November 1922

102. *WT* 11 April 1924

103. *D&SN* 28 September 1922

104. *WT* 9 May 1924

105. *WT* 14 May 1926

106. *WT* 22 March 1929

107. Orme, N., op.cit., pp192-194

108. www.oldplymouth.uk

109. *WT* 18 December 1918

110. Devon Censuses 1911, 1921, Kelly's Directories 1914, 1923

111. Cannadine, D., *Victorious Century: The United Kingdom 1800-1906*, p506-512

112. Obituary *NDJ* 19 August 1920

113. Obituary *WT* 18 October 1918

114. *WT* 17 February 1919

115. *NDJ* 26 June 1919

116. *WT* 29 March 1919, Teignmouth Museum file

117. *NDJ* 5 February 1920, 11 March 1920

118. *NDJ* 1 February 1923

119. *WT* 5 March 1920

120. *NDJ* 8 January 1920

121. *Who's Who in Devonshire*, *WT* 12 November 1920

122. *NDJ* 21 February 1924

123. *WT* 13 October 1922

124. *WT* 20 September 1921; Keating,J., *A Child for Keeps: the History of Adoption in England 1918-45*

125. *WT* 24 October 1919, 11 December 1919

126. *WT* 9 & 23 October 1920, 2 November 1921, *D&SN* 6 October 1927

127. *MDA* 1 November 1924, 24 January 1925, 7 March 1925

128. *MDA* 14 April 1923, 26 July 1924, 18 October 1924

129. *TG* 30 November 1928, 1 March 1929, 31 May 1929

130. *WT* 2 July 1919. Female JPs were permitted from 1919

131. *WT* 8 October 1920

132. *WT* 13 July 1921, Parratt, C., *More than Mere Amusement, Working Class Women's Leisure in England 1750-1914*, pp199-202

133. *D&SN* 26 May 1921

134. *NDJ* 19 January 1922

135. *D&SN* 7 September 1922

136. *Who's Who in Devonshire*, *WT* 27 August 1926, 23 May 1930, *D&SN* 24 November 1928

137. *WT* 1/6/23, 25/2/27.

4

THE RECOVERY: TOWNS, TOURISM & TRANSPORT

Towns and tourism

Tourism had faltered during the war, but far from vanished, and quickly picked up again. Resorts hurriedly issued new guide books and ensured Thomas Cook had plentiful stocks. As early as January 1919 Torquay Chamber of Commerce seized upon that fact that travelling to the Continent remained virtually impossible to plan a massive advertising campaign to entice more visitors. New summer entertainments were planned, and the ex-Royal Flying Corps pilots of Cornwall's Navarro Aviation Company received permission to give joy rides around Torbay.[1] At South Molton Show that July visitors were charged a guinea (£1.1s.0d) for a 10 minute ride high above the town in two Avro 504 biplanes. Despite the high price there were long queues.[2] And in September residents and visitors at Torbay, and later Ilfracombe, gazed at the mighty battleship HMS *Queen Elizabeth* with its eight 15" guns moored off the coast as an attraction. Special trains brought in the crowds, the beaches were packed and small boats by the dozen ferried families around the ship.[3] It was much like pre-war summers, except war memorials were still being discussed, not all the men were home yet, and the *Queen Elizabeth* had been Admiral Beatty's flagship at the surrender of the German fleet last November.

100hp Avro 504K aeroplane. (Author's collection).

The Recovery: Towns, Tourism & Transport

The battleship HMS Queen Elizabeth *as she would have appeared before her reconstruction in 1926-27.* (Author's collection).

The Navy never failed to thrill. In July 1920 the full Atlantic Fleet, including the battleships HMS *Valiant*, *Barham* and *Warspite*, as well as *Queen Elizabeth*, anchored in Torbay. For two days a series of rowing races between the crews for the 'Admiral's Cup' added to the general excitement.[4] In 1921 three light cruisers, HMS *Delhi*, *Dragon* and *Dunedin*, visited before joining the fleet for manoeuvres in the Channel. As always on these occasions local crab and lobster fishermen complained about the bar on coastal fishing areas during the exercise.[5] In July 1922 HMS *Warspite* and *Valiant* returned to Torbay and during most summers that decade the warships and coastal towns engaged in receptions, visits, sports and dances – and the occasional rowdiness – while thousands looked on.[6] The *Warspite*, sister to *Queen Elizabeth*, had been constructed not far away around the headland of Start Point in Devonport Dockyard. After a worrying post-war lull the massive dockyard, the largest employer in Devon, went on to build many more warships, including the locally named heavy cruisers HMS *Cornwall* in 1926, HMS *Devonshire* in 1927 and HMS *Exeter* in 1929 that were to face action in the next world war.[7]

Across Devon the superior hotels vied with each other to offer the latest facilities. Even before the war ended hotels in Torquay such as the Grand, Osborne, and Victoria & Albert had electric lighting and lifts, hot and cold running water, garages, tennis courts, croquet lawns and billiard rooms.[8] However when Torquay's huge Palace Hotel opened early in 1921 its advertisements noted not only all these facilities but also a 'ladies' orchestra all the year round' and, best of all, its guaranteed freedom from 'the usual seaside excursionists and trippers.' This was not surprising as double bedrooms cost up to 36/- a *day* and suites up to 5 guineas, and meals were extra. There were rooms for servants and chauffeurs at around 12/6d a day – with board.[9]

The *Times,* however, thought charges in the general run of Devon's hotels were exorbitant. Four guineas (84/-d) a *week* for an 'ordinary' hotel was too high, it asserted, and added that these charge generally failed to include using the bath, having shoes cleaned, and even night time electric light. In addition any meat was 'usually foreign', vegetables tough, and 'for sweets the whole of the coast population is living on stewed prunes'.[10] In 1923 local guidebooks confirm that Ilfracombe's superior Queen's, Runnacleave and Grosvenor Hotels charged between 73/6d and 84/- a week, and similar hotels elsewhere charged much the same.[11] There were, of course, many cheaper ones and thousands of guest houses.

Devon welcomed tourists, but a lingering reminder of the war led many embarrassed traders into court. As price restrictions had not been lifted, in 1919 a long list of bakers, butchers and grocers were heavily fined for charging tourists excessive prices or selling them underweight goods. In many cases tourists themselves had reported the shopkeepers. The items included cocoa, cheese, condensed milk, bread, jam, ham, mutton, veal, sardines, tinned salmon and dried fruit. Some were expensive items – a 1/3d tin of salmon was priced 1/6d, a 2lb jar of jam was priced 2/2½d not the standard 2/1d, and a massive 6lb ham sold for 12/- not the official 9/9d.[12] Nestles Milk made a virtue out of price controls. Late in 1919 its advertisements stated it was illegal to sell tins above 1/3d, and professed pride that despite the vast increase in the cost of milk and sugar a tin was only a ha'penny dearer than at the time of the Armistice.[13]

Over the decade retail grocery prices gradually fell. In one Devon report butter dropped from between 3/8d and 5/- a pound in 1920 to between 2/- and 2/2d in 1922. Beef dropped from 1/4½d to 9d a pound, and pork and mutton from 2/1d to 1/2½d. Chicken stabilised around 1/- a pound, rabbits at 1/- each, and eggs were generally 1/6d a dozen. Fruit remained expensive, though. In 1924 black grapes cost 3/- to 5/- a pound, Cape peaches 1/- each, and dessert pears 8d a pound, although bananas could found for 2d each. Vegetables were much cheaper, with beetroots 1d each, cabbages 2d, cauliflowers 3d, carrots 3d a pound, and potatoes 1/- for 12 pounds.[14] Food still represented a significant proportion of a family's weekly expenditure for the averaged urban artisan earning no more than £3 a week, but most family budgets were a little easier than before the war.

Palace Hotel ballroom. (Mark Ware: Hotel brochure 1924, author's collection).

Stillman's butchers' shop, Exeter. (Mark Ware: WT 20 January 1922: Courtesy of Devon & Exeter Institution Trustees).

Shops were well-stocked, and numerous class-conscious advertisements carefully targeted customers looking for a bargain or those preferring exclusivity. New clothes were expensive with, for example, Barnstaple's celebrated 'Anti-Profiteering Stores' advertising men's cord breeches at £1:9:11½d and hobnail boots at £1:1:11½d. Ladies brogue shoes were 19/11½d and flannelette skirts 4/11½d. In common with many clothing stores, it offered mail order facilities.[15] There were cheaper shops though. In 1925 Costers of Exeter advertised a sale with men's flannel trousers priced from 4/11, raincoats from 12/11d, and sports jackets from 9/11d – representing a 15% reduction on normal prices.[16] And of course swimwear entered the modern age, too, with plentiful advice for women about avoiding green and white 'which seldom look pretty when wet' and the aesthetic advantages of the American style 'which has black or coloured shorts, and a gaily striped top, with which is worn a white belt.' 'Rather thick wool' was the preference of 'front rank swimmers' and not surprising costume prices varied enormously from a few shillings to several pounds.[17]

Leisure items were well-advertised, if expensive. In 1923 Davey & Sons in Exeter sold second hand ladies' and men's bicycles from 50/- although most new ones were nearer £5 and top quality machines with several gears touched £10. Five years after the war the company still proclaimed it stocked 'No German Rubbish'.[18] HMV records cost from 3/- to 8/6d depending on the music and the performers. In 1924 a record with Sir Harry Lauder's comic *I'm the boss of the house* and nostalgic *I like my old home town* cost 6/-, the same as one with two waltz's by Chopin and Tchaikovsky.[19] Wirelesses were making an appearance; the *North Devon Journal* reported 100 licences in Barnstaple in 1927.[20] Smart wooden cased wirelesses cost around £20 but far cheaper kits soon appeared and by the middle of the decade local newspapers had regular columns devoted to 'Hints for Radio Constructors'.[21]

The Victorian commercialisation of Christmas continued apace. For example, among Tavistock advertisements in mid-December 1928, Messrs W. E. Baker & Company thought their electro-plated cutlery, aluminium hot water bottles, and 'Alladin' oil lamps were attractive gifts, while Messrs Burch advertised new lines in HMV records and gramophone players, Mr Ingerson had cabinets of fancy biscuits, chocolates and cakes, Mrs Foster sold Christmas cards, Bibles and prayer books, Messrs Palmer & Son offered prime English beef, pork, poultry, hams and tongue, and Mr East showed off numerous dolls, boxes of handkerchiefs,

A boat trip to Clovelly. (Authors' collection).

manicure sets, powder bowls and brush and comb sets. In addition Messrs Gun had 'everything for the motorist', Mr Tyack everything for the cyclist and sportsman, and Mr Wadge everything for the photographer.[22]

The holiday industry boomed. At Whitsun in May 1920 8,000 people left Exeter's main stations for the sea and moors, 3,000 of whom headed for Exmouth, 1,800 to Dawlish and Dawlish Warren, 1,100 to Teignmouth, 500 to Dartmoor via Ashburton, Okehampton, Moretonhampstead or Tavistock, 450 to Torquay and 150 through the Exe valley towards Tiverton.[23] That August resorts were packed and many who travelled to them without booking accommodation found themselves stranded, and had to search for rooms further inland.[24] A 1920 report on Teignmouth gives the flavour of the post-war summer with rowing matches, swimming contests, paddle-steamer steamer trips, entertainments on the pier, and fairs on the green (the Den) abutting the promenade. A year earlier, a local diarist had noted the crowds were 'principally working class'. They enjoyed cheering the variety shows, keeping the two cinemas busy, sunning and playing on the beach – and, to his disgust, 'kissing'.[25] It did not seem the exclusive resort of a century earlier. And neither did Ilfracombe, where dozens of char-a-bancs ran day trips to Exmoor and other resorts, pleasure steamers ran up and down the coast, the three picture houses showed the latest thrillers, the Gaiety and Alexandra Halls were busy with light concerts, the Victoria Pavilion hosted concert parties and bands, and Runnacleave Hall staged comic plays.[26]

Sundays and Christian festivals were increasingly secularised. In March 1921 Good Friday's church services were reported to be well attended, but nevertheless it was hardly a day of peace said the *Western Times* with crowds attending theatres, picture houses, and football and rugby matches. And, it added, 'piled high up with luggage and smothered in dust, dozens of fine cars passed through Exeter on their way to the seaside and the Moors … motors of every type were throbbing up the hills and along the level all day and well into the night.'[27] As we have seen, many clergy heartily disapproved.

Exeter was a major resort in its own right, and attracted trippers from far afield by rail, motor cars and char-a-bancs. In March 1922 a *Western Times* report on the plight of Exeter's 1200 unemployed was placed next to a far larger article on the city's SHOPPING WEEK opened by the mayor amidst gaily decorated streets, the firing of rockets, a fanfare of trumpets and the release of hundreds of balloons. The mayor emphasised that commerce was vital to prosperity – and employment.[28] In north Devon that Whitsun, where unemployment remained high, Barnstaple's stations dispatched 778 trippers to Ilfracombe and 1050 to Instow. Ilfracombe's major influx, though, was through the paddle-steamers which landed 3600 people that weekend from Bristol, Cardiff and Swansea.[29]

Many towns invested in improvement schemes to attracted free-spending visitors. Their post-war guide books talked enticingly about the tennis courts and bowling greens, generally costing 3d an hour, and the challenges of the new golf courses. Here charges were around 3/- a day.[30] In 1923 public and private enterprise set to work to modernise Newton Abbot by improving its road access, sign posts, street lighting and public gardens, and providing evening entertainments and better sports facilities, especially a golf course.[31] By 1927 the Chamber of Commerce was pleased with the town's future prospects and enhanced 'dignity and prestige', and notably that both the market and railway station had been rebuilt, Alexandra Hall had been renovated, and 224 new houses had been erected.[32]

There were the usual storms that battered Devon's coastline and holidaymakers. In a fearsome thunderstorm in July 1926 the streets of Seaton, Beer, Sidmouth, Pilton and Barnstaple became rivers, camp sites were washed away, power supplies interrupted, small boats smashed, houses struck by lightning, and hailstones 'the size of pennies' hurled out of the sky.[33] However when blue skies returned, holiday makers flocked back to the resorts, and the roads and railways were once again crowded with summer traffic. It was just a few weeks after the General Strike. Indeed local newspapers had been gratified that the rush of cars, motor cycles, and omnibuses meant that resorts had had almost the same numbers of visitors in May 1926 – the month of the General Strike – as in May 1925 despite the cessation of many rail services.[34]

In 1928 eleven south Devon towns cooperated in a major publicity campaign with the Great Western Railway (GWR). Over 400 huge 12' by 10' posters were produced featuring yellows rays of sunshine emanating from a bright red star containing the

Motorists at Dartmeet. (Authors' collection).

names of the towns, and above it was the logo 'South Devon Gems', also in bright red. The GWR placed them in all major cities throughout the country.[35] Mass tourism was the aim, and many resorts were heading steadily down market. One sign was the dilapidated look of the vast over-decorated Ilfracombe Hotel, once the desired venue of wealthy visitors from home and abroad but since the war a steadily decaying monument to a bye-gone era. Those who could afford its luxury were unlikely to return to mingle with the post-war crowds. In 1928 the local council leased part of it as municipal offices, and opened its once exclusive gardens to the general public, but before the decade ended councillors were regretting the Victorian eye-sore could not be purchased and demolished.[36]

Naturally, as in all ages, the post-war frivolity of the young upset their elders. Town councils, churches and welfare charities were concerned that young men and women did not fall prey to unsavoury company, drink, vice and crime. Great efforts were made to attract them to wholesome clubs and activities run by churches and the YMCA. There was modest success: in Torquay YMCA membership topped 230 in 1920.[37] In 1923 Exeter's exclusively male Rotarians condemned 'the lurid placards' advertising cinema films that were 'avidly discussed by factory girls' who then spent 2/- they could not afford on tickets.[38]

Films varied widely. Some had topical war themes such as 'The Man the Army Made' shown in 1919. It portrayed 'the grim side of war' and 'the hero, who had fallen into intemperate habits, rehabilitates himself in the army, performs many deeds of bravery, and at last sees the downfall of the false friend who had tried to lead his wife and himself to ruin.'[39] Innocence and vice, and temptation and redemption, were common subjects, and certainly some descriptions were salacious. In 1919 'A Desert Wooing' told the story of a 'jaded society girl who is placed in the matrimonial market by her impecunious mother to be sold to the highest bidder.'[40] Among the films to see in 1924 were 'Pleasure Mad' which followed the fortunes and misfortunes of a family split up by 'the affections and indulgences which follow the sudden acquisition of wealth'. In 1925 there was 'Mighty Lak' a Rose' telling the story of a poor girl whose sweet nature and violin playing tempt a band of crooks to incorporate her in their plots – only for good to finally conquer evil. Films glorifying the

Ilfracombe Hotel. (Authors' collection).

British Empire were popular too. In 1925 'The Empire Builders' featured Captain Ballard in Rhodesia – 'a real man' whose path to settling the region 'is beset by misguided Boers, resentful natives, and even a well-meaning friend who betrays him.'[41] American Wild West films arrived en masse in the 1920s, and so did the futuristic 'Metropolis – The City of a 100 Years Hence' with its awe-inspiring, even terrifying, advertisements of a future dominated by technology.[42] Interestingly in the light of criticisms of the corrupting influence of popular entertainment, in 1919 the *Torquay Times* praised the Pavilion's pantomime 'Red Riding Hood' for being 'clean' and without innuendo or 'vulgarity passing as wit'.[43]

In June 1919 jazz reached Torquay's Pavilion Cafe and Paignton's Public Hall. The *Torquay Times* happily recorded that 'it caused tremendous excitement, people vying with each other to gain positions of advantage to see the extraordinary movements and grimaces of the drummer.' Perhaps significantly in the light of the gloomy post-war mood the report added 'it attracted some of the best residents of the town', and 'when it commences everyone wants to dance, sing or laugh, and cannot possibly be unhappy.'[44] The newspaper and, it seems, the resorts ignored the widespread condemnation of jazz as a corrupting influence.[45]

Home for Heroes: the problem of housing

This was one of the great post-war issues. It was widely acknowledged in 1918 that much of the housing available for the working classes was hazardous to health, and that a massive building programme was the only way forward to remedy the situation. David Lloyd George, the prime minister, had publicly linked the initiative to the just rewards for ordinary families whose men and women had brought about the hard-won victory. The 'Homes Fit for Heroes' slogan resonated around the nation to help Lloyd George win the 1918 election, and in effect committed the government to fund this alluring ideal. It was estimated that at least 600,000 houses would be needed by 1921, and everyone was aware that expectations were high.[46]

Pre-war Acts of Parliament had permitted local councils to clear slums and replace them with new houses, and a few in Devon had acted positively as exemplified by Plymouth's new streets named after housing committee members, Tiverton's aptly named Council Gardens, and Exeter's Isca Road. Most authorities had merely tinkered with the problem by trying to oblige landlords to improve or replace condemned properties.[47] A few private initiatives had benefited communities. In Victorian times John Heathcoat had built around 150 good quality 'working class' houses near his lace factory in Tiverton.[48] By 1918, though, only public funds could resolve the almost overwhelming nationwide problem.

Lyceum Picture House in Teignmouth.
(Mark Ware: Courtesy of Teignmouth Museum).

The major question was how to build houses of an acceptable standard with modern services for a price which could be repaid within 25 years or so by a combination of rents families could afford, a government grant, and an acceptable rate precept. The Minister of Health, Christopher Addison, came up with an answer in his Housing & Town Planning Act of 1919. Local councils had to identify housing needs and submit plans to meet them. Houses approved by the ministry would receive a grant of up to £260 each, and any justifiable revenue costs above a 1d rate would be subsidised. A year later the scheme was extended to private builders. The Act was generous but the housing standards were high and so were costs of post-war materials and labour, and although nationwide around 176,000 houses were built under the Act the high rents meant most were occupied by better-off families and most slums lay untouched.[49] And by 1921 the recession meant the government largely lost interest in encouraging house building.

Across Devon local councils wrestled with the Act's requirements. There was a general feeling that the new houses should adorn, not despoil, communities, and that women should be on advisory panels to consider house designs and facilities.[50] Most Rural District Councils (RDCs) took care to ensure each village's needs were identified as part of the battle against depopulation.[51] Honiton RDC ended up with 196 new houses on 40 different sites with 146 cottages earmarked for demolition.[52] Conversely Torrington RDC thought 50 houses scattered over its villages were sufficient.[53] Barnstaple RDC argued over whether the working classes needed bathrooms and parlours like 'the parson and other gentlemen'. Eventually, and in common with most councils, it decided all houses should have bathrooms but cheaper ones could do without parlours.[54] In Exeter the city council thought small back and front gardens were best because separate allotments were available for keen gardeners; other councils opted for large back gardens.[55] Searches for suitable sites were often long and hard with the cost of land and provision of services needing to be balanced against the convenience of sites for residents. Readily admitting its hundreds of slums, Torquay Town Council snapped up 28 acres for 150 houses at the back of the tram shed in St Marychurch – perhaps far enough away from the more exclusive parts of the town.[56] Plymouth, meanwhile, stormed ahead with a long-term £4,000,000 scheme for 4500 houses of six different sizes. They became part of a major regeneration and employment scheme, especially as shipbuilding in the naval dockyard slumped after the war. Eight hundred

The Prince of Wales examines plans for Plymouth's North Prospect housing estate with the mayor, 13 June 1919. (Authors' collection).

The River Exe, Exeter's industrial quarter and adjacent housing. (Author's collection).

houses had been built by 1923, many of them covering the old Swilly Estate and renamed North Prospect.[57] Plymouth, in common with Torquay, St Thomas and Exeter, raised funds through issuing 6% Bonds over 5, 7, 10 or 15 years. Keenly promoted, especially by local MPs, they sold well.[58]

Councils' plans were submitted to the ministry only for its inspectors to raise all sorts of questions regarding sites, services, designs, and estimated numbers, costs and rents. Delays proved frustrating, and reports suggest local councils understood few of the rules properly and that different inspectors interpreted the rules differently. There were also suspicions that some councils such as Crediton and Ashburton UDCs were using the delays to drag their heels over building any homes at all.[59] In addition when construction was permitted to start, there were shortages of materials and soaring prices together with endless wage disputes, followed inevitably by council accusations, as at Crediton, that both building companies and workers were holding the country to ransom.[60] Speaking in Exeter Christopher Addison himself asserted 'Trade Union selfishness' was blighting progress and keeping rents high.[61] The delays accentuated the outcries from the Women's Citizenship Association and Dr Adkins, the County Medical Officer of Health, about the rotting, insanitary and rat-infested tenements and cottages continuing to destroy families' health. Critics asserted seven hundred families needed rehousing in Exeter alone.[62]

Despite the general indictment of Exeter's tenements not all of them were ill-maintained. Those in Mermaid Yard off Market Street and in Kendall's Building near Blackboy Road had been built by the city's charitable Improved Industrial Dwellings Company founded in the 1870s and maintained by it ever since. They had two, three or four rooms and water supplies, a toilet, scullery, larder and coal cellar, and rents never topped 1/- a room. Only now, as the 1920s progressed, were they in danger of being superseded by the new but higher priced council houses.[63] However when Dr Charles Lovely moved from Dawlish to Exeter in 1920 the city's West Quarter slums – lived in mainly by the industrial workers of Shilhay abutting the river – so appalled him that he sought the help of like-minded families to create the

The People of Devon 1918–1930

Exeter Workmen's Dwelling Corporation in 1926. Funded by £1 shares, the aim was to rehouse slum families, gradually empty the slum blocks, and ensure their demolition. By the end of the decade the first homes in Looe Street were finished and more were built later on. They were lightly constructed to ensure rents could be kept attractively low as Lovely considered the city council's rents far too high to resolve the slum problem.[64] It took, though, another war and massive reconstruction programmes to come near remedying the housing problem.

Commencing in May 1920 Plymouth and Newton Abbot were probably the first post-war builders of council houses, with Torquay, Paignton, and indeed Exeter, not far behind.[65] The proportions were generous within the costs. A typical house, as at Cullompton, costing 6/- to 7/- a week had 20 yards of garden, 3 bedrooms sized 18'x10'6", 12'x9' and 12'x7'6", a living room 16'x11', a scullery 8'x7', and a coal shed, cupboards, sink, copper, fireplace-cum-boiler, radiators, bath and toilet. Houses costing 10/- a week also had a 10'x10' parlour.[66] By October 1921 1854 houses had been built or were under construction in Devon under the National Housing Scheme with Plymouth leading the way with 630, followed by Exeter with 178 and Paignton with 133.[67] Their very presence accentuated the appalling condition of many older properties, as medical officers of health were quick to point out.[68]

However, progress was soon cut short. In October 1920 Crediton RDC and the Liberal MP George Lambert were in agreement that the heavy burden of national grants and local rates for house building was intolerable during the severe depression. Barnstaple and Kingsbridge RDCs were also dragging their feet despite Ministry pressure to clarify their intentions.[69] Interestingly in that year South Molton RDC found no tenants willing to pay 6/- a week for one of the four new houses in West Buckland. Fearing the misappropriation of

Exeter's varied supply of new housing in the West Quarter between the wars. In the background is a large block of flats built by the Exeter Workmen's Dwelling Company. The light coloured terrace in front of them and the pair on the left were built by the Church Army Housing Ltd. The row of cottages (lower right) facing the steeply sloping Stepcote Hill were erected by the City Council. (Mark Ware: Exeter City Council brochure 1937: Courtesy of City Council).

The Recovery: Towns, Tourism & Transport

Concrete houses in Buddle Lane, Exeter, 1926-28. (Mark Ware: Exeter City Council brochure 1937: Courtesy of City Council).

grants in such circumstances, the Ministry of Health refused any reduction.[70] And by 1922 criticisms were reaching the newspapers about the new houses themselves. Those at Buckfastleigh had constantly dripping taps, ill-fitting floorboards, smoking fireplaces, and toilets right by the front door. 'They are built of rubbish', lamented a councillor after a visit. In 1925 damp was found lifting off the plaster of houses at Moretonhampstead, and those around Axminster also had badly fitted doors, rotting floors and dangerous flues. In 1927 Sir Charles Cave said the Sid Valley houses were blots on the landscape worthy only of being burned down.[71]

In 1921 Addison was removed from the Ministry of Health. His Act was considered over complicated and the depression ensured its demise when cost-conscious councils and government ministers tacitly agreed to cease building. In 1923 a Conservative Housing Act ended controlled rents and offered a flat rate subsidy to builders of £6 a year for 20 years which unsurprisingly benefited private builders and the better-off. The following year the nation's first Labour government had far greater success with an Act that increased the subsidy to £9 a year for 40 years, allowed local councils to add a further £4 a year if necessary and restored controlled rents. Thus encouraged, local councils built half a million houses over the next seven years.[72] In 1925 Newton Abbot Town Council, for example, purchased the Broadlands Estate for 200 houses, Tiverton RDC voted for 104 more houses scattered across 20 villages, and Tavistock RDC for 78 in 11 villages.[73]

For several years the cost and shortage of traditional materials had encouraged experiments with prefabricated concrete panels and steel frames in order to erect houses quickly and rent them cheaply. Tiverton RDC was pleased that its latest houses would be built with concrete blocks and roofed with asbestos slates, thereby allowing rents of 5/-d. They were, it was claimed, cooler in summer and warmer in winter than brick houses.[74] Exeter City Council professed disappointment with its costly progress under Addison's Act but its subsequent choice of concrete blocks enabled 294 houses to be added between July 1926 and May 1928 before brick construction resumed. The city's housing remained expensive, though, with rents

71

varying from 6/-d for one bedroom flats to 9/6d for three bedrooms houses without a parlour and 12/-d for one with a parlour.[75]

A 1926 Act offered grants to rural house owners to renovate properties to rent to rural workers, and a few years later Devon's medical officers of health were gratified at the numerous cottages rendered 'light, dry and airy' by the scheme.[76]

In 1927 Sir Francis Acland reported that Devon's total new 'housing for the working classes' outside Plymouth and Exeter had risen to 5172 of which 2230 were in rural districts. Torquay was singled out with 926, Paignton with 372, and Teignmouth with 219. Many more were 'in the pipeline', but he cautioned,' it was a mistake to regard a great many of the houses built in health resorts as being genuinely houses for the working classes.' He caused consternation among county councillors at his implication that local rates might have been syphoned off as unnecessary subsidies to better-off tenants.[77] A few weeks later Torquay's medical officer of health agreed, saying most of Torquay's subsidised houses were for sale, with only 31 new ones rented in 1926, and hardly touching the slum problem. Modern historians of the decade at large such as Chris Renwick concur.[78]

Sport – the widening appeal

Competitive sports abounded: they were avidly promoted as healthy and character building activities, and often drew large partisan crowds. Local amateur football leagues proliferated after the war, with company teams scattered among them – such as Taw Shipyard, Jenkins' Marble Works, and Willey's Ironworks Cadets.[79] Not everyone appreciated the finer points. In 1920 unruly players and rowdy spectators alarmed north Devon referees to the point that police protection and speedy access to magistrates' courts was seriously considered. Typical incidents that season included several players abandoning the game between Barnstaple Apprentices and Northam when a penalty was considered unfair, and an angry pitch invasion after a goal was declared offside when Bideford played Torrington.[80] Ironically the various competitions and cups, notably the prestigious Hansen Cup given by the Hansen Shipbuilding Company, that aimed to encourage football across north Devon, may well have contributed to partisan support spilling over into unacceptable aggression.[81]

Plymouth Argyle and Exeter City Football Clubs became part of the restored Southern League early in 1919, and in 1920 both accepted an invitation from the Football League to join its new Third Division. Until then the independent Southern League had eschewed contact with the Football League which historically had been the preserve of northern clubs. In 1921 the Division divided into Division Three South and Division Three North, with Exeter and Plymouth residing in the former. Exeter's greatest success was 7th place in 1924-25, but Plymouth was second on six occasions until achieving promotion to Division Two in 1930.[82]

Rugby clubs considered themselves superior to football clubs. In 1923 Devon Rugby Union's secretary praised Newton Abbot for winning the Devon Cup. After noting both the sophistication of the game of rugby and the players' supreme fitness, he could not resist adding that ordinary football's popularity owed much to it being a simple game that could be played whether one was fit or not.[83] In 1928 a civic banquet speech in Barnstaple singled out the rugby club as epitomising the heroic sportsmanship to which other sports should aspire.[84]

Cricket clubs retained their pre-war air of refinement. Nowhere was it more noticeable than in Torquay where the 1920 club dinner resonated with speeches praising elegant team games, such as those prized by major public schools, for instilling the virtues of pluck and determination that won the war.[85] Nevertheless interest was widespread and crossed social boundaries, with, for example, Barnstaple Grammar School playing Shapland & Petters Cabinet Works, and Dartmouth's Royal Naval College playing Jenkins' Marble Works.[86] Perhaps the social mix was exemplified by Tiverton's Heathcoat's Lace Factory whose team included Lieut-Colonel Harry Amory and Captain

Torrington Apprentices Football Team 1923-24. (Beaford Old Archive images: © Beaford Arts).

John (later Sir John) Amory from the factory owner's family.[87]

Lawn tennis was popular too, with district and county competitions characterised by the tell-tale titles of *gentlemen's* and *ladies'* matches. The county championship in 1921 attracted 400 entries.[88]

After the wartime lapse sailing regattas were revitalised in the summer of 1919 with Exmouth's multiple categories extending to sailing and rowing boats and embracing those owned privately, or by clubs or by commercial firms, and crewed by amateurs or professionals, or ladies, being typical for the decade. However, regattas in more renowned sailing centres such as Torquay and Paignton had categories extending to yachts weighing 10 tons or more and drew competitors from far further afield, and reports suggest that the bigger the regatta the less likely it was to cut across the social classes. Reports also revealed that competitors braved most weather conditions but to the chagrin of food and drink stallholders onlookers did not.[89]

Bowling competitions and league tables restarted in 1919 after various club representatives met in Exeter's Rougemont Hotel. Sir Robert Newman was elected chairman of the County Association and everyone agreed that restoring club greens and creating more public greens would provide work for the unemployed as well as attracting members and visitors.[90]

Swimming clubs proliferated, some linked to pools, others to rivers and the sea. In 1920 Exeter Ladies' Swimming Club's annual gala was held near Head Weir on the Exe, Topsham Club's gala was held further down the estuary, and Newton Abbot's Otter Club raced near Stover Canal's Lock.[91]

Music and Arts festivals were popular, bringing together enthusiasts from across the county, and beyond. Just two examples were the Folk Dance Festival at Powderham Castle that attracted 800 participants, and the eclectic Eisteddfod in Sidmouth organised by the Rev. Arthur Lamb and including competitions in choral and solo singing, elocution, recitation, essays, handwriting, piano and violin playing, flower arranging and table decorations.[92]

Ilfracombe's Victoria Pavilion and bowling green, with Ilfracombe Hotel in the distance. (Authors' collection).

Transport by air, sea and land

Aeroplanes and their pilots captured the post-war imagination. Plymouth had had a small naval seaplane base since 1913, and this became RAF Cattewater in 1918. Possibly this experience prompted its Chamber of Commerce to persuade the Ministry of Civil Aviation to undertake trial passenger and parcel flights to and from Birmingham, Manchester and Belfast in 1923 from a potential site for a local airport, probably Chelson Meadow. The much celebrated Alan Cobham was one of the pilots. The trials were considered successful, and in 1925 an airport site was secured north of Plymouth at Roborough. Development and recognition were slow and although a few passenger and transport flights occurred in the late 1920s the official opening was not until 1931.[93]

Amidst massive publicity in August 1929 Sir Alan Cobham (he was knighted in 1926) visited north Devon. Welcomed by local mayors, councillors and members of Chambers of Commerce he took the lucky winners of tickets offered by local newspapers on circuits of the Taw-Torridge estuary in his *Youth of Britain*. Thousands watched and the roads were jammed with vehicles. His visits were to promote air travel generally but primarily to secure business opportunities for his own company. In 1930 he visited Exmouth and Budleigh Salterton, although without his airshow, to promote creating an airfield in their vicinity, and he did the same in Ilfracombe. He offered, for a fee, to select a site and secure government approval, but no progress was made.[94]

Sir Alan Cobham's 'Youth of Britain' (DH61 Giant Moth) at Northam. (Mark Ware : WT 30 August 1929: Courtesy of Devon & Exeter Institution Trustees).

The Recovery: Towns, Tourism & Transport

Sir Alan Cobham. (Mark Ware: WT 30 August 1929: Courtesy of Devon & Exeter Institution Trustees).

In September 1929 the newly established Haldon Aerodrome and School of Flying outside Teignmouth held a spectacular 'Air Rallye'. Thousands attended, and it attracted famous aviators such as Captain Hubert Broad, Flight Lieutenant 'Tommy' Rose and Lieutenant Talbot Baines Bruce – all of them ex-wartime pilots. The high winds and gusts of dust made flying difficult, especially for the pilot of the vertical take-off Autogiro who crashed – but was unharmed. However in the lulls the pilots 'provided thrills galore, as they flew upside down, looped the loop, nose-dived (spirally and otherwise) and made flying at almost any angle look simplicity itself.' The airfield was the brainchild of William Parkhouse, a local engineer and enthusiastic pilot, who became an agent for A.V. Roe and had the gift of attracting influential clients, notably Whitney Straight, the son of Dorothy Elmhirst of Dartington Hall by her first marriage. The site stayed in business commercially until superseded by the new Exeter airport in the late 1930s.[95]

Although it was too early for mass air transport to challenge Devon's holiday resorts, overseas travel by ocean liners and railways was heavily advertised in Devon newspapers to catch wealthy residents and visitors. The Canadian Pacific Railway regularly tempted readers with tickets covering luxurious travel by sea to North America and then across the continent from coast to coast with all hotel accommodation and special visits included. Life aboard a modern liner, even in second class, was portrayed as elegant and carefree with good food, deck games, dances and concerts – just like the first class of pre-war days and far from the cramped sailing ships that had hitherto crossed the Imperial seas.[96]

Aeroplanes and marquees at the Haldon 'Air Rallye' in 1929. (Courtesy of Teignmouth Museum).

Devon's ports had varying fortunes after the war. The bigger ones prospered, the small ones declined. During the decade Plymouth welcomed ocean liners of the Holland-America line and the railways whisked the passengers to and from London. Cunard liners from Southampton, including the 45,000 ton *Acquitania*, also called in before sailing to North America. Warship construction at Devonport dockyard kept many local firms busy supplying timber products, leather goods, upholstery, fire bricks and metalwork. Despite the economic downturns, companies at Dartmouth and along the banks of the Taw-Torridge estuary constructed many small steam driven cargo vessels, tankers, tugs and launches. There was also a vibrant pleasure industry taking tourists by steamers up and down the River Tamar, and along the northern and southern coasts. In other sectors, though, the West Country fishing boat owners had failed to invest in steam driven trawlers or resist the 'invasion' of East Coast vessels into the region, and Exeter suffered by the restricted size of vessels able to use the canal.[97]

Nevertheless the coastal trade remained reasonably buoyant. In 1920 a new opportunity emerged when an oil tanker berthed at Brixham and off-loaded 3,500 gallons of Texas fuel-oil through a special pipe line into the port's new holding tank. Teams of small road tankers then serviced the county's growing number of garages. In 1923 National Benzole established fuel storage tanks at Exeter, and small tankers kept them well supplied. Small colliers serviced the city's large quayside gasworks. Exmouth and Teignmouth in the south and Bideford and Barnstaple in the north were kept busy with ships bringing in supplies of coal, Baltic timber, Dutch bricks, tiles and glass, and Newfoundland fish. Teignmouth was a major exporter of clay from the Teign valley.

The railway network across Devon was almost at its height in 1919. The GWR main line ran east to west from Paddington and Taunton through Exeter and then south of Dartmoor to Plymouth with a second main line branching off at Newton Abbot to Torquay, Paignton and Kingswear. From these main lines branches took goods and passengers from Plymouth to Tavistock and Princetown, from Brent to Kingsbridge, from Totnes to Ashburton, from Newton Abbot to Moretonhampstead, from Churston to Brixham, and from Exeter to Tiverton and Bampton.

Train at Chudleigh station on the winding country line from Exeter to Heathfield and Newton Abbot.
(Author's collection).

The Recovery: Towns, Tourism & Transport

The rival London & South Western Railway's main line ran east to west from Waterloo and Salisbury to Axminster and Exeter and then north of Dartmoor via Crediton, Okehampton and Tavistock to Plymouth It, too, served many other towns with branches from Seaton Junction to Seaton, from Sidmouth Junction to Ottery St Mary, Sidmouth and Budleigh Salterton, from Exeter south to Exmouth and north to Barnstaple, Ilfracombe, Bideford and Torrington, and from near Okehampton to Halwill and Holsworthy.

In summer major junctions such as Exeter and Newton Abbot were hard-pressed to cope with arrivals. As in pre-war days, the vast network meant passengers could travel to numerous places in the county and back in a day. For example, there were cheap day returns from Exeter to stations (now long gone) at Moretonhampstead and Brixham, and guide books abounded with the walks that could enjoyed from rural branch line stations (also long gone) such as Cornwood, Bickleigh and Horrabridge in the far south-west. Amongst the host of offers were summer excursions exploring the Dart valley by a combination of train, river steamer and char-a-banc, cheap Christmas trips to London, and, in 1929, a special train to watch the famous Schneider Trophy air race off Southsea.[98]

One line was added in the decade. In a scene reminiscent of Victorian times, in June 1923 a group of around 20 'navvies' working on a new railway near Hatherleigh became riotous after excessive drinking and ended up assaulting the police constables sent to contain them. The men received sentences of between one and five months hard labour.[99] The new 20-mile line opened with little ceremony in July 1925 and connected Torrington with Halwill which was the junction for lines to Okehampton and north Cornwall. Government and County Council funds as well as private money had financed the remote rural venture in the hopes of stimulating the clay and brick industry around Meeth, revitalising several old quarries, boosting farming centred on Petrockstowe's cattle market, and attracting Ambrosia to open a creamery in the area. By and large all hopes were dashed.[100]

Road vehicles powered by coal or petrol rather than horses had appeared on Devon's roads long before the war. However their proliferation after 1918 contributed much to the county's economy and people's personal convenience while at the same time causing wide-spread consternation at the numerous crashes and injuries, the heavy cost of road improvements, and the creeping destruction of the countryside by tarmac, petrol stations, road signs and litter. Conversely there were constant complaints by drivers about blind corners, hairpin bends, dangerous junctions, potholes, and narrow roads where vehicles could barely pass each other.[101] In 1921 a Londoner's open letter was published asserting what local towns had feared, that the appalling reputation of Devon's roads would have a negative impact on tourism and commerce.[102]

Post-war freight and omnibus companies quickly established highly competitive motorised services throughout the county. Often, to get companies started, they used hurriedly converted surplus army vehicles. In 1919 the Devon General Omnibus Company ran services twice a day between Exeter and Torquay.[103] In 1920 Pennsylvania Garage in Exeter advertised a different freight trip from Exeter on each day of the week, except Sunday. On Thursdays, for example, its lorry wound through villages to Crediton and then up to Winkleigh before returning via Bow and Coleford.[104] Its rival, the Devon Motor Transport Company spread out from its base in Plymouth to run a fleet of lorries and buses between all the major western, southern and mid Devon towns and gradually absorbed several rivals, especially on the lucrative Plymouth to Exeter route.[105] And by 1926 Hardy-Colwill was running more than 20 buses a day between Barnstaple, Bideford and Westward Ho! and a dozen between Barnstaple and Ilfracombe. Competition was already mounting between the railways and bus companies.[106]

Small family cars steadily declined in price during the decade as mass production took hold, and in due course discreetly handled part exchange and hire purchase deals became available.[107] Some Devon garages became manufacturers' agents –

The People of Devon 1918–1930

Devon General Omnibus (solid tyres) with uniformed staff on the Tiverton to Exeter route 1926. (Courtesy of Tiverton Museum).

notably for Ford with its ready supplies and competitive prices. In 1921 a new Ford Tourer cost £195-£202, and the elegant Sedan £310-£375, but they were way beyond most people's pockets when an elementary school teacher's salary was around £160 rising to £300 after 14 years.[108] Not every company survived, but the Okehampton garage that proudly advertised its agency for the Whitehead Car – 'The Triumph of British Mass Production' – was particularly unfortunate when John Whitehead's company folded before any vehicles reached the road.[109] Not quite as ephemeral was the Skootamota frenzy. They were advertised with a youngish woman as driver. Briefly

Radford's Garage at Sampford Peverell (with Tiverton Hospital Week advert to the right). (Courtesy of Tiverton Museum).

manufactured by the ABC Motor Company after the war in partnership with Sopwith, the aeroplane manufacturer, a few Devon garages stocked, and presumably managed to sell, these lightweight 123cc machines. They had a top speed of 15mph.[110]

Advertisement for the Skootamota. (Mark Ware: WT 19 September 1919: Courtesy of Devon & Exeter Institution Trustees).

As early as March 1919 the County Council earmarked nearly £400,000 for road and bridge works, trusting it would secure a 33⅓% government grant. The following year the County Council agreed to take responsibility for all the county's roads as and when local districts agreed. Seven agreed immediately, and negotiations got underway with the Ministry of Transport regarding procedures and grants.[111] Henceforth County Council meetings were full of discussions on balancing heavy spending on road improvement schemes with saving money by restricting heavy traffic, notably traction engines and steam lorries, on awkward and vulnerable roads. Not surprisingly whatever the Council decided was heavily criticised. With regard to tarmac, for example, there were complaints that horses, still a major source of transport, slipped on the surface. By 1924 70 sections of road (other than lanes) had vehicle restrictions in place, but there was also a £1,000,000 main road programme underway.[112] The vast Roadstone Quarries at Bampton with its steam excavator, massive crushers, automatic wagon loaders and good railway connections were kept constantly busy.[113]

In 1920 Exeter's chief constable highlighted the build up of traffic. A survey on Queen Street recorded 34,400 vehicles passing by over six days – some horse drawn, some motor powered.[114] The phenomenal county-wide rise brought injury and death in its wake. Pedestrians found it difficult to judge the speed of vehicles, and children were used to playing happily in village streets. In October 1918 an old man was killed by a car travelling at just 15 miles per hour through Alphington.[115] In August 1919 4-year-old William Dore was playing with friends by the side of the road in Newton Abbot when he darted in front of an approaching car – travelling at just 10 mph – and was fatally injured.[116] Playing in the street also proved fatal to 4-year-old Tom Kersey of Bideford when he tried to emulate older boys by jumping onto the tailgate of a slowly passing lorry but fell in front of a char-a-banc.[117] Cases were fully investigated but courts often found it hard to untangle witnesses' stories and attribute blame. In 1920 11-year-old Victor Newbery was killed when his bicycle hit a pile of stones on an unkempt road near Axminster and he was run over by a passing lorry. The driver was cleared, but only after the court agonised over whether he had had time and space to take avoiding action.[118] Sadly they were far from the only cases of children killed by motor vehicles during the decade.[119]

Char-a-bancs had their share of tragedies. In July 1920, for example, one careered down a hill near Dunsford and crashed into a culvert when the driver lost control. All 30 passengers suffered injuries, and one died. And in May 1928 a char-a-banc hit a car on a narrow bend at Heddon Mill and crashed into a hedge injuring all 14 passengers, one fatally.[120]

In 1919 there were 253 road accidents and 20 deaths across Devon, with the figures soaring to 1,262 and 66 respectively in 1928.[121] There were numerous crashes between speeding motor cycles

Char-a-banc taking Hatherleigh Bible Class on an outing to Torquay, 1923.
(Beaford Old Archive images © Beaford Arts).

and cars, often resulting in injuries requiring hospital treatment. Four were reported in a single edition of the *Western Times* on 8 April 1927. Faulty parts were sometimes to blame. In 1926, for example, a man broke his collar bone in a crash caused by his car's back wheel 'falling to pieces', and a women suffered serious injuries when she lost control of her car, struck a post and was thrown through the windscreen after a shackle spring bolt snapped.[122] And of course women as well as men ended up convicted in court of dangerous driving and thoughtlessly blocking roads when parking.[123]

A county report in 1920 revealed that all Devon's police forces took a hard line on traffic offences, and prosecutions mounted for driving with no lights at night, on the wrong side of the road, and over the legal speed limit of 20 mph. At just one sitting of Paignton's magistrates that August the police presented 11 cases across these three offences.[124] Exeter's chief constable particularly objected to the skirts of 'excited' ladies riding pillion on motorcycles obscuring the rear number plate. It appears the police had some justification,

as in 1920 the Automobile Association claimed Devon had the highest number of complaints against inconsiderate drivers.[125] There seems to have been constant warfare between defiant motorists and the zealous police whom one defence solicitor sneeringly condemned as suffering from 'motoritis' for bringing trifling offences to the court. In this case a car's rear light had occasionally flickered.[126] The 1930 Road Traffic Act finally removed the 20 mph limit for cars after widespread criticism of the police's obsession with speed traps and, bizarrely, an official conclusion that speed limits were unenforceable. Indeed in the 1920s most cars did not have speedometers. The Act did, though, assist the courts by refining the offences of dangerous, reckless and careless driving, and legislated for the introduction of national road signage. Until then some official signs had warned motorists of schools (with a 'torch of knowledge' image) but any other helpful signs had been placed voluntarily by the Royal Automobile Club. Belatedly, in 1930 Devon County Council started to fit traffic lights at dangerous junctions.[127]

The Recovery: Towns, Tourism & Transport

Just as some drivers were accused of reckless joyriding so some char-a-banc passengers upset local communities. At a County Council meeting in 1921 Lord Fortescue supported Ilfracombe UDC's complaint against passengers who delighted in 'singing, shouting, and making a tremendous noise when going through quiet places' and even 'firing apple cores and other missiles' at villagers. A local bye-law making such behaviour an offence was readily approved.[128] In 1922 Parracombe also complained of 'motor cars careering through this little village at all hours of the day and night', and numerous cases of rowdiness outside public houses led Modbury, Ivybridge and Totnes to ban Plymouth char-a-banc trippers arriving in the evening.[129]

In contrast, serious motorists joined one of several 'motorcycle and light car clubs' set up in Devon, and took part in the hill-climbing, cross-country and speed trials they organised. They attracted large crowds and extensive publicity. In 1921, for example, Tiverton's new club attracted 35 entries for its solo, sidecar and light car categories and was well-organised with road marshals, time-keepers and judges. The events were not free from danger, as on occasion riders lost control and machines veered off the track scattering terrified onlookers.[130]

While the motor industry was getting into its stride, horse power was entering its decline. In 1914 *Kelly's Directory for Devon* records 130 traders associated with making, repairing, driving and servicing motor cars, and in 1923 it lists around 750. In 1896 Lady Rosalind Northcote, daughter of the 2nd Earl of Iddesleigh of Pynes, had established the Exeter Cart Horse Parade as part of her life long campaign to promote the care of working animals and instil pride in their ownership. It had lapsed during the war, and although its revival was discussed at subsequent RSPCA meetings, in 1922 the mayor of Exeter's view was accepted that the event 'was a thing of the past' as firms were fast replacing draught horses with motor vehicles.

Part of a Shell advertisement using dashing female motor-cyclists and the thrill of speed.
(Mark Ware: D&S News 17 May 1928: Courtesy of Tiverton Museum).

The People of Devon 1918–1930

Tiverton Motorcycle and Light Car Club hill climb, c1924. (Courtesy of Tiverton Museum).

Forgetting the pleasures of horsemanship, he thought that in a hundred years time 'they would have stuffed horses in the museums.'[131]

REFERENCES

1. *WT* 6 & 8 January 1919

2. *WT* 10 July 1919

3. *WT* 9 & 13 September 1919

4. *WT* 23 July 1920

5. *WT* 7 July 1921

6. *WT* 15 & 18 July 1922, Thomas, S.F., *A History of the Teign Corinthian Yacht Club*, pp25-27

7. Burns, K.V., *Devonport built warships since 1860*, pp74-80

8. *TT* 26 October 1917

9. Torquay Library, Hotel brochure 1924, *TT* 29 October 1920

10. *CC* 16 August 1919

11. Ward Lock & Co., *Guide to Ilfracombe & NW Devon*, c1923

12. *WT* 9, 14 & 30 August 1919, 19 November 1919, 3, 5, 10 & 23 December 1919

13. *D&SN* 27 November 1919

14. *WT* 4 January 1923, 15 February 1924

15. *WT* 15 March 1920

16. *WT* 31 July 1925

17. *WT* 19 July 1919

18. *WT* 11 May 1923

19. *D&S* 10 July 1924

20. *NDJ* 29 December 1927

21. *WT* 6 May 1922, *D&SN* 24 September 1925

22. *TG* 14 December 1928

23. There was the same rush every year, viz. *WT* 25 May 1920, 19 June 1925, 13 June 1930

24. *WT* 3 August 1920

25. *WT* 14 August 1920, Teignmouth Museum, Alfred Best's diary 31 July 1919, 18 August 1919

26. *NDJ* 4 August 1921, 21 May 1925

27. *WT* 26 March 1921

The Recovery: Towns, Tourism & Transport

28. *WT* 31 March 1922

29. *WT* 6 June 1922

30. 1923 Ward Locke & Co., *Guides to Ilfracombe & NW Devon, Plymouth & SW Devon, Teignmouth & SE Devon*, c1923

31. *MDA* 3 February 1923, 14 March 1923, 12 May 1923, 2 June 1923, 6 October 1923

32. *WT* 20 April 1923, 25 March 1927

33. *WT* 23 July 1926

34. *NDH* 27 May 1926, *WT* 6 August 1926

35. *TG* 27 January 1928

36. *NDJ* 24 May 1928, *WT* 4 January 1929. It was not demolished until the 1970s.

37. *WT* 27 March 1920

38. *D&SN* 10 July 1923

39. *DG* 4 January 1919

40. *TT* 14 January 1919

41. The dates are when films were shown in Devon, not the year they were made. *TG* 21 November 1924, 9 January 1925, 11 September 1925

42. *MDA* 15 October 1927

43. *TT* 26 December 1919

44. *TT* 20 June 1919

45. Pugh, M., *We Danced All Night*, pp219-220

46. DeGroot, G., *British Society in the Era of the Great War*, pp197-201

47. Renwick, C., *Bread for All*, pp138-141

48. Brayshay, M., *Southern History*, 13, 82-104

49. Renwick, op.cit., pp142-4

50. *WT* 19 & 27 November 1918, 28 December 1918, 6 January 1919

51. *WT* 27 November 1919, *NDJ* 15 April 1920

52. *WT* 3 May 1920

53. *NDH* 9 January 1919, *WT* 6 January 1919

54. *WT* 15 February 1919

55. *WT* 17 October 1919

56. *WT* 7 March 1919, 18 November 1919

57. *WO* 19 July 1923

58. *TT* 22 October 1920, *WT* 9 January 1920, 1 & 6 April 1920, 10 & 12 July 1920, 19 & 29 October 1920

59. *WT* 28 November 1919, 12 December 1919, 2 January 1920, 4 February 1920, 9 October 1920, 29 July 1921

60. *WT* 3 July 1919, 12 & 15 October 1920, 7 December 1920

61. *WT* 22 February 1921

62. DHC 5631A/M12 Annual Reports of Exeter Medical Officer of Health 1920-1925, *WT* 11 December 1919, 1 February 1921

63. *WT* 6 August 1921

64. Dawlish Museum Dr Lovely collection, www.exeterlocalhistorysociety.co.uk/2018-08-08-dr-lovely

65. *MDA* 15 May 1920, 6 October 1923, *WT* 12 & 21 May 1920, 22 September 1920, 5 November 1920

66. Various designs at *WT* 20 April 1920, 29 October 1920, *NDJ* 10 January 1921, *NDH* 8 July 1920

67. *CC* 29 October 1921

68. *NDJ* 12 July 1923

69. *WT* 15 October 1920

70. *WT* 23 December 1921, 27 October 1922

71. *WT* 26 April 1922, 27 February 1925, 19 June 1925, 1 April 1927

72. *WT* 4 January 1924; Hattersley, R., *Borrowed Time*, pp208-211

73. *MDA* 11 July 1925, 26 February 1927, *D&SN* 23 July 1925, *TG* 18 September 1925

74. *WT* 2 December 1919, *NDJ* 2 April 1925, *D&SN* 19 May 1927

75. Exeter City Council: *Opening of the 2,000th Post War Municipal House 1937*

76. *WT* 26 July 1929, 16 May 1930

77. *WT* 4 March 1927, 8 April 1927

78. *MDA* 14 May 1927, Renwick, C., op.cit., p162

79. *TT* 30 April 1920, *NDH* 26 August 1920, *WT* 22 April 1921, *TG* 24 August 1923

80. *WT* 7 January 1920, 4 February 1920, 16 October 1920, 20 November 1920

81. *WT* 28 April 1920

82. www.grecianarchive.exeter.ac.uk, www.greensonscreen.co.uk/argylehistory, *WT* 8 February 1919, 3 March 1919, 22 April 1921

83. *WT* 1 June 1923

84. *NDJ* 15 November 1928

85. *WT* 31 January 1920

86. *TT* 30 April 1920, *NDJ* 28 June 1928

87. *CC* 27 May 1922

88. *DG* 2 August 1919, *WT* 26 July 1921

89. *DG* 16 August 1919, *WT* 24 July 1919, 20 August 1919, 13 August 1926

90. *WT* 20 February 1919, 4 August 1919

91. *WT* 19 & 20 July 1920, 17 August 1920

92. *WT* 4 May 1923, 27 June 1930

93. www.wikipedia.org/wiki/Plymouth_City_Airport

94. *WT* 30 August 1929, 8 August 1930, 12 September 1930

95. Saunders, K.A., (2006) *Teignmouth's Haldon Aerodrome*, *WT* 27 September 1929

96. *WT* 21 April 1920, 14 May 1926

97. This paragraph and next draws on Duffy, M. and others, *The New Maritime History of Devon, Volume II,* pages 75, 83-84, 229, 238-240, 243-246

98. Maggs, C.G., *Devonshire Railways*, *WT* 23 December 1920, 6 August 1921, 16 August 1929, *MDA* 10 July 1926

99. *WT* 29 June 1923

100. *NDJ* 30 July 1925, www.colonelstephenssociety.co.uk

101. *WT* 9 March 1920, 10 June 1920, 30 July 1920, 26 July 1921

102. *WT* 26 July 1921

103. *DG* 13 September 1919

104. *WT* 3 & 6 February 1920

105. www.oldplymouth.uk, *WT* 17 June 1921, 8 November 1921

106. *NDH* 30 September 1926

107. *D&SN* 6 January 1927

108. Tropp, A., *The School Teachers*, pp274-275, *WT* 2 January 1920, 5 August 1921, 4 November 1921

109. *WT* 5 March 1920

110. *WT* 19 September 1919

111. *WT* 10 March 1919, 9 July 1920, 24 September 1920

112. *NDJ* 7 August 1919, *WT* 13 May 1922, 9 March 1923, 29 February 1924

113. *SMG* 25 February 1922

114. *WT* 16 June 1920

115. *WT* 8 October 1918

116. *WT* 29 August 1919

117. *WT* 12 May 1922

118. *WT* 28 May 1920

119. *WT* 8 & 15 August 1925, *MDA* 14 May 1927

120. *WT* 2 July 1920, *NDJ* 31 May 1928

121. *WT* 1 March 1929

122. *WT* 30 July 1926

123. *WO* 7 October 1920, *WT* 9 May 1924

124. *WT* 14 August 1920

125. *D&SN* 10 June 1920, *NDH* 24 June 1920

126. *WT* 21 February 1920

127. Coaches were limited to 30mph. www.gracesguides.couk/1930_Road_Traffic_Act, *WT* 9 August 1929

128. *WT* 30 September 1921

129. *WT* 5 May 1922, 13 February 1925

130. *WO* 8 September 1921, *NDJ* 28 June 1928

131. *WT* 14 March 19 22

5
RURAL RELATIONSHIPS: THE CHANGING PATTERN OF LIFE

Breaking up the great estates

Not all Devon's countryside was attractive. The guide books eulogised the valleys, woods and moors but carefully avoided the ugly scars caused by hundreds of mines. Most had closed during the long decline of mining since mid-Victorian times but they remained decades away from achieving the status of romantic ruins. Amidst the host of derelict buildings and waste piles, in 1920 a little tin was still extracted at Birch Tor and Vitifer on Dartmoor, a little iron at Brixham, Ilsington and North Molton, no copper but still some arsenic at Wheal Friendship and Wheal Crebor near Tavistock, some barytes in the Teign Valley, and lignite around Bovey Tracey. In contrast the very active clay quarries and processing plants on Lee Moor north-east of Plymouth, in the 'Bovey Basin' around Kingsteignton, Newton Abbot and Stover, and in north Devon around Meeth and Petrockstowe, covered hundreds of acres of countryside.[1]

Over the half century prior to 1914 Devon's farmland had also undergone dramatic changes. Firstly the improvement in late nineteenth century

North Devon Clay Company site, Little Torrington. (Author's collection).

ocean transport brought vast quantities of cheap grain from North America and Russia into the country which threatened the survival of Devon's arable farmers. The deep rural depression from the 1870s onwards only came to an end as the twentieth century dawned with the slow but successful transition to a mixed economy of beef and pork production, dairy produce and market gardening. This was helped by the rapid spread and speed of rail transport to London and the Midlands. Secondly the decision by a growing number of large landowners to sell all or part of their estates began the decline of a rural society dominated by wealthy families whose influence as political figures, landlords, employers, magistrates, and patrons of charities affected many aspects of local life. The reasons were primarily political and financial. The Representation of the People Acts of 1832, 1867 and 1884 had eroded landowners' ability to influence local constituency elections to virtually nothing, and early in the twentieth century a radical Liberal government led by Herbert Asquith and his Chancellor of the Exchequer, David Lloyd George, introduced heavy land taxes and significantly increased the rates of death duty.

All these issues, and the steadily declining income from agricultural rents, made traditional landownership that had heavily subsidised a conspicuously grand lifestyle centred upon the neighbourhood's 'great house' increasingly unappealing on several counts – as a business enterprise, as an adjunct of political power, and as a socially influential way of life. After 1918 more modest households and more discreet lifestyles were generally, although not universally, maintained, and the slaughter of war and the social problems of peace made ostentation seem generally inappropriate, although again not universally, and certainly not in parts of London. Gradually more and more tenants and outsiders purchased the farms, cottages, inns, mills, woods, quarries and hunting and fishing rights as they came onto the market. Some landowners saw business investments giving better returns, some retreated to other estates or their London addresses, and some found themselves in dire straits when their estate income barely covered living costs, mortgages, annuities to elderly relatives, and death duties – which soared from 15% in 1909 to 40% in 1919. However some stayed put and weathered the storms as best they could. Exemplifying the extremes, the Courtenay Earls of Devon kept most of their land along the Exe estuary and elsewhere, while the long-established Strode family in south-west Devon chose to sell virtually every acre by 1920 to invest in mining and railways across the

The Lee Moor clay tramway at Laira, Plymouth. (Author's collection).

world.² The 11th Duke of Bedford had paved the way in 1910-11 when he stunned Tavistock by selling much of the town and surrounding farmland he owned 'in deference,' he asserted, 'to the social and legislative tendencies of the day'. The huge sale over 21 days raised £514,527, and was just part of the Duke's retrenchment across the country.³

Nationally, between 1918 and 1920 somewhere between six and eight million acres of land changed hands – the biggest transfer of ownership since the Tudor dissolution of the monasteries. Such a volatile situation filled rural communities with anxiety. There was a cost attached to the decline of paternalism. Farm ownership gave tenants independence, but the price was usually a heavy mortgage and it cannot be assumed all tenants welcomed the risks of 'freedom'. And the abandonment of the 'great houses' meant the loss of local jobs as indoor and outdoor servants, less business for local traders, and less support for local charities, schools, churches and chapels. However in a speech in 1921 Lord Clinton, probably Devon's largest landowner, explained why he thought agricultural landowners were 'threatened with extinction'. He analysed several estates with rentals averaging £20,300 a year and said that taxes, tithes, rates, mortgages, jointures, maintenance and other costs left owners with about 2/3d in the pound income. He claimed shrewdly investing the money might have brought in nearer 10/- in the pound – an infinitely more attractive proposition.⁴

The selling up that started in Edwardian times accelerated after the war. The immediate post-war agricultural market was buoyant, with tenant farmers assuming wartime prices and government protection would be preserved. As early as Autumn 1918 the Chittlehamholt Manor and Willesleigh House estates in north Devon were sold, and so were the Yarner estate near Bovey Tracey and Rockbeare Court estate outside Exeter. Altogether they totalled 2,367 acres, and included 30 farms.⁵ With auction prices high, the pace increased in 1919 and the age of land accumulation by well-established families was coming to an abrupt end. The heirs of C.W. Hole sold up his 1,996 acre Ebberley estate around

The 21st Baron Clinton. (Mark Ware: Devon DHB: Courtesy of Devon & Exeter Institution Trustees).

Winkleigh in 94 lots for £40,000, and it was an indicator of post-war changes in life styles that no-one wanted the Regency-style Ebberley House itself.⁶ Major Graham, the owner of Pitt House and its estate near Chudleigh, decided to hold onto the house and 30 acres but sell everything else, thereby divorcing the 'big house' from its agricultural tenants.⁷ Similarly in 1921 the wealthy but ageing Lord Cable, who had no male heir, decided to keep Lindridge House near Ideford and its gardens and park but sell off the farms and other properties historically supporting this mansion. A career in Indian commerce had allowed Cable to rent and then buy the whole estate in 1920, and although he spent lavishly on improving Lindridge House and entertaining in it, agriculture and rural Devon in general held little attraction for him.⁸ In 1919 Major Charles Bailey inherited north Devon's Lee Abbey and estate from his uncle but had little interest in either of them, breaking up the 1,868 acres into 14 auction lots before the year was out, and managing to sell the abbey itself in 1924.⁹

Other families, with larger estates, shed just part of their property. Reasons varied. In 1919 the Marquis of Northampton sold 2,047 acres around south-east Devon in 100 lots to help raise, rather urgently, £67,000 to pay a sensational breach of promise

Tawstock Court, near Barnstaple. (Author's collection).

case he lost to the actress Daisy Markham.¹⁰ She settled for a record £50,000. In the same year Sir Arthur Acland of Killerton sold 7,000 acres in 90 lots around South Molton to raise £90,000, largely to pay death duties after he inherited the estate from his brother Charles. In due course Acland reassured his remaining tenants that despite the estate running at an annual deficit of £3,000 there would be no more sales as he believed the traditional Acland landlord-tenant relationship worth preserving.¹¹ Sir William Ferguson-Davie auctioned his Mariansleigh estate of 1,578 acres, including 9 mixed farms, into auction lots. Most of them sold, almost certainly to help rebuild his main property, Creedy House near Sandford, after its destruction by fire in 1915.¹² Some landowners decided to concentrate their holdings to economise administration as well as raise funds. Thus, in 1919 the long-established Walrond family of Bradfield sold 1,800 acres of outlying farmland, and the Earl of Iddesleigh decided to sell off 880 outlying acres at Iddesleigh, ironically the village from which he took his title.¹³

Often, though, virtually everything had to go. In autumn 1919 Sir Philip Bouchier Wrey began the relentless reduction of his family's ancient Tawstock estate in north Devon when 2,763 acres (of the total 10,000) were sold in 50 lots, of which 29 were complete farms. The sale made £83,840. His older brother, the spendthrift Sir Robert who died in 1917, had already moved out of the family mansion, Tawstock Court.¹⁴ A Victorian bankruptcy and lingering financial difficulties led Captain Sir Edward Chichester (of the Raleigh baronetcy) from another centuries-old Devon family, to sell Youlston Park in 54 lots.¹⁵ And at Dartington Arthur Melville Champernowne began to reduce his historic Dartington estate by selling 1,131 acres, but without other sources of income, the diminishing returns from an agricultural estate totalling only about 2,400 acres proved fatal. In 1920 a further three farms made £12,000, and in 1925 the Champernownes were fortunate that the wealthy newcomers Dorothy and Leonard Elmhirst purchased the romantically crumbling Hall and its gardens along with the remainder of the estate – two farms totalling 600 acres and 190 acres of woodland. To the bewilderment of many locals, the Elmhirsts set about creating an unusual rural estate where the carefully managed natural environment would sustain craft communities producing and marketing a variety of high quality farm produce, timber products and textiles.[16]

The sales continued apace. The death of Colonel Follett led to another break-up, that of his family's Culm Davy estate of mixed beef and dairy farms near Uffculme in 1921.[17] Captain Sir George Duckworth decided to end his family's long association with Topsham, and sell all his Wear House Estate including the mansion, two large dairy farms, and various cottages covering 430 areas.[18] The 15th Duke of Somerset's main home was at Maiden Bradley in Wiltshire, and in 1920 he disposed of his Devon estates around Totnes and Sharpham.[19] The banker Sir Charles Cave of Sidbury Manor reduced his estate in south Devon, and his death in 1922 and ensuing death duties forced his heir to sell more land.[20] And the mid-Victorian Watermouth Castle was virtually the only part of the ancient Bassett estate left after several sales of farms – 18 alone in 1920 – by Mrs Penn-Curzon after she inherited it from her father in 1908.[21]

Some farms fetched good prices. For a few years after the war prices averaged an attractive thirty times the annual rental value. In 1921 the Caves of Sidbury Manor secured £3,400 for Manston farmhouse, out-buildings, orchard, and 51 acres of mixed arable and pasture land.[22] When Captain E. J. Holley sold 975 acres of the family estate around Okehampton in 1920 Stockley Farm of 102 acres fetched £3,400 and Fatherford Farm of 154 acres an impressive £6,000.[23] Devon river fishing rights attracted thousands of pounds. In 1921 the '4 miles of excellent salmon, salmon peel and trout fishing' along the River Tavy were enticing highlights when the 5th Earl of Mount Edgcumbe, faced with large death duties and seeking to retrench, was obliged to sell off 23 farms, 78 cottages, extensive woods and numerous market garden holdings.[24] In some places building land was at a premium. The Earl of Devon shrewdly sold his Alphington estate when Exeter was expanding. The 300 acres were divided into 113 small lots, with the cottages mainly purchased by tenants and the land by companies for development. This sale, and a similar one at Newton Abbot, was part of the Powderham estate's recovery, rather than abandonment, which included exploiting cattle grazing and sales of timber, game, deer, and market garden produce, as well as long term investments in stocks and shares.[25]

However, the grander the house the less likely it was to sell, especially when detached from its land. When Sir Frederick Williams auctioned his Upcott estate near Barnstaple in 1921 the farms and fields sold but not the mansion.[26] When Major Style tried to sell the Pickwell Manor estate around Georgeham in the same year he was left with the family's fine mock Jacobean house only built in 1906.[27] In 1922 Arthur Blackburn sold all the farms on his 1,110 acre Stowford estate but he, too, was left with a large unwanted mansion.[28] In 1926 Sir John Pole-Carew of Anthony in Cornwall inherited the baronetcy of Shute and all its property in Devon. He preferred Anthony in Cornwall, and three years later he auctioned Shute House, its deer park, and 4,339 acres comprising 25 dairy and mixed farms and scattered woodlands. Everything sold – except the mansion and deer park.[29] The same happened to Mr and Mrs Harris of Halwill Manor in 1930. As squires they had supported local charities, including the cottage hospital, and he had ridden to hounds, been a JP, and served on the Board of Guardians, They had plans to move to the New Forest, and although tenants and the Forestry Commission purchased the land , the manor house failed to reach its reserve of £2,600.[30]

James Bannatyne, a wealthy Irish flour merchant, had purchased the vast Haldon House on the hills above Exeter from the impoverished Lord Haldon in 1892, and for a brief period it shone as social centre with his wife Emily as hostess. However James died in 1915 and their only son was killed in 1916, and Emily moved away in 1919 leaving the large estate cutting across numerous villages, including Kenn, Dunchideock and Exminster to be put up for sale as an entity. No buyer was found and the estate was broken up piecemeal during the early 1920s but the vast Palladian house remained deserted until much it was demolished. Only the north wing survived.[31] Equally grand, the huge French chateau-style Stevenstone House in north Devon built by the Honourable Mark Rolle between 1868 and 1872 became redundant when all his vast property reverted after his death in 1907 to Lord Clinton who already owned several large houses and thousands of acres. Over the next twenty years, the house was sold on cheaply, large parts of it demolished and the surrounding estate progressively reduced.[32]

After the war the 4th Lord Poltimore failed to auction off his mansion and estate at Poltimore outside Exeter. A few farms were sold to tenants privately, but most lots failed to reach their reserves, and although the recently extended Georgian mansion was realistically advertised as a potential hotel, school or public institution rather than a family home it failed to reach the almost insultingly low reserve of £15,000. Empty of furniture, this remnant of a suddenly by-gone age, was rented by a girls' boarding school in 1923. Although the auctioneer said heavy taxation – death duties after the deaths of the 2nd and 3rd barons in 1908 and 1918 – had caused the sale, Lord Poltimore was also burdened with annuities to aged relatives, heavy mortgage payments and low rental income. He retreated to his preferred Court Hall estate near North Molton, but even here he had sold a thousand acres. Eventually he emigrated to his estate in Rhodesia.[33]

Stoodleigh was yet another extensive estate broken up in the 1920s. Stoodleigh Court and its 18 farms and woods and timber yards, had had several owners in short succession in the twentieth century, but when Frank Shearman's attempt to create a merchant fleet from ex-Royal Naval vessels ended in bankruptcy, everything was parcelled up and sold in 1925 – but no-one wanted the large late Victorian mansion (see picture, page 128). It became Ravenswood School in 1928.[34] Stuckeridge, near Bampton, was yet another mansion – Regency in style – left unsold after tenants purchased the estate's farms in 1926.[35]

In 1921 Harold St Maur, the illegitimate grandson of the 12th Duke of Somerset, was keen to emigrate to Kenya and put up Stover House and its 2,334 acre estate between Newton Abbot and Bovey Tracey for auction in numerous lots, and as usual at this time the farms and woods sold, the former mainly to tenants, the latter to contractors, but not the eighteenth century granite mansion. In 1931 it became (and remains) a private school. In a celebrated court case after the death of the 14th Duke in 1923 without a direct heir St Maur sought vainly for evidence of his parents' marriage to justify a claim to the title.[36]

In an interesting case of family feuds and extravagance proving disastrous, after the war the hitherto extensive Carew estates were whittled down to virtually nothing, and the family's centuries of political and social influence in Devon came to an end. In 1874 Sir Walter Carew left the vast estate to his two daughters, Bessie and Beatrix, but the baronetcy went to his brother's son, Henry. Feeling short-changed, Henry ran up huge debts largely based upon his future inheritance but the two sisters, who never married, were burdened with mortgages and family annuities and, liking hunting and entertaining, also lived way beyond their means. By necessity, the sisters had sold land before the war and continued to do so until their deaths in 1919 and 1921. When everything was finally settled, all Henry possessed was Haccombe House and an estate incapable of supporting it.[37] In 1922 Carew land around Tiverton and Bickleigh was sold although the prices were low, but Tiverton Castle,

Sir Henry Carew, Bt. (Mark Ware: Devon HDB: Courtesy of Devon & Exeter Institution Trustees).

Haccombe. (Mark Ware: Devon HDB: Courtesy of Devon & Exeter Institution Trustees).

a second Carew home, failed to reach its reserve. In 1923 the sale of the family's third estate at Marley comprising 2,650 acres, including 17 farms around Rattery and South Brent, raised £21,000, and in 1924 Marley House, for long a financial millstone, was sold to the Trustees of Syon Abbey for just £5,252.

A few years before the war a twentieth century version of a vast medieval castle began to rise on a massive crag outside Drewsteignton. Called Castle Drogo it was designed by Edwin Lutyens for Julius Drewe whose Home & Colonial Stores had made his fortune.[38] Construction on a limited version of the granite fantasy continued throughout the 1920s but Drewe was almost broken the loss of his eldest son in the war, and such ostentatious buildings and all they represented were fast becoming anachronisms.

Castle Drogo. (Author's collection).

The People of Devon 1918–1930

The survival of patrician influence

The decline of landowners' political influence and the erosion of their traditional authority gained through tenancies, patronage, contracts and the employment of indoor and outdoor staff did not mean that their social prestige faded away as well. And, of course, many landowners retained farms and tenancies even if the prewar heyday of numerous servants to impress numerous guests at numerous social functions was never going to return. Landownership remained the target of heavy taxation, and in an increasingly urbanised nation the protection of agriculture from cheap imports was never going to return, however much political parties continued to express sympathy with farmers during election campaigns.[39] And in a post-war era where unemployment, poor housing and social welfare were key issues, and support for the Labour Party and social equality was growing, any displays of conspicuous consumption in vast over-decorated houses became *passé* even if they still could be afforded. In addition, as the *Western Times* explained in 1919, there was a dreadful problem with servants – in the war they had left to enlist, work in offices and factories, and now 'you can't get a domestic servant for love or money', and those you did find lacked manners.[40] Nevertheless vestiges of the age of deference to families in the 'big house', the pulling power of their names for charitable fund-raising, and their continuing involvement in county affairs, meant that they remained eminently newsworthy.

The 4th Earl Fortescue was an influential and high profile Lord Lieutenant from 1904 until 1928, chairing numerous committees, and Sir Henry Lopes of Maristow chaired the County Council efficiently from 1916 until his death in 1938. And in 1923 *Kelly's Directory* recorded that alongside many farmers, membership of the county council included Earl Fortescue, the Earl of Portsmouth, Earl of Morley, Lord Clinton, Sir Robert Newman MP of Mamhead, Sir John Shelley of Shobrooke, Sir Ian Amory of Knighthayes, Lieut-Colonel Acland-Troyte of Huntsham Court, George Lambert MP of Spreyton, and the Rev. Albany Wrey of Tawstock. The 7th Earl of Portsmouth who died in 1925 had been vice-chairman of the County Council and also chairman of its education, child welfare, licensing, and bridges and main roads committees. Much of the Portsmouth estate in Devon had been sold before the war by his brother, the 6th earl, but the 7th earl's obituary said, he was 'a good friend to the farmer, consistently urging the claims of agriculture.'[41] The landed interest dominated the county council, if not parliament, and the concept of *noblesse oblige*, although fading, was not dead yet.[42]

The Earl of Portsmouth (on the left) smiling at Eggesford Hunt Gymkhana. (Mark Ware: WT 8 August 1930: Courtesy of Devon & Exeter Institution Trustees).

The traditional coming of age celebrations of the heirs of estates were still reported at length. Captain Jack Amory became 21 in May 1915 when he was on active service, and the celebrations at Knightshayes were deferred until July 1919. Gathered with the family on the terraces, Sir Ian's tenants presented his son with an expensive Purdey sporting gun.[43] In August 1919 the tenants of the Fulford estate presented Lieutenant Francis Fulford with an inscribed silver kettle and milk jug, and in

1920 John Molesworth St Aubyn of Tetcott near Holsworthy was given a fashionable dressing case.[44] As tradition required, the oldest tenants presented 'loyal addresses' to which the family graciously replied. At the end of the decade the same format was followed at Sir Robert Throckmorton's coming of age celebrations at Molland (a subsidiary estate to the family's Coughton Court in Warwickshire), and that of 'Squire' Marker, already the owner of the Coombe estate at Gittisham.[45]

The silver weddings of estate owners were also marked by tenants' presentations and loyal addresses – as at Lord and Lady Hambleden's celebrations at Bovey House in 1920 and those of Sir Francis and Lady Acland at Killerton in 1930.[46] The Aclands were a long established Devon family, but the Hambledens were fleeting visitors. Frederick Smith (from 1913 Viscount Hambleden) was the grandson of W. H. Smith, the stationer and bookseller. He had acquired the Bovey estate near Moretonhampstead at the turn of the century, then built the great pseudo-Jacobean manor house in 1907-08, briefly used it as a country holiday home and largely neglected it after the war. He had been, however, in true Edwardian fashion a generous benefactor to the town's church and hospital.[47]

Society weddings received copious coverage too, with full details of flower displays, distinguished guests, key family pedigrees, and brides' and bridesmaids' dresses, such as when Miss Betty Coleridge of Salston Manor, Ottery St Mary married Edward Cave, grandson and eventual heir of Sir Charles Cave in 1922.[48] Villagers turned out to watch and applaud, and often, as at Miss Cicely Fursdon's wedding at Cadbury near the family estate in 1930, local schoolchildren, Scouts and Guides lined the church paths as guards of honour.[49] And on these occasions, too, tenants as well as family and friends customarily gave

Miss Cicely Fursdon's wedding. (Mark Ware: WT 15 August 1930: Courtesy of Devon & Exeter Institution Trustees).

Bovey Manor. (Author's collection).

presents. Large headlines, several photographs and three full newspaper columns were needed to cover the marriage of Miss Eve Cecil, daughter of the Rt Revd Lord William and Lady Florence Cecil, to Commander Richard Shelley RN, second son of Sir John and Lady Shelley of Shobrooke Park in 1929. Many 'county' families attended, with the names Amory, Acland, Acland-Troyte, Buller, Cave, Carew, Coleridge, Drewe, Ferguson-Davie, Fursdon, Kekewich, Newman, Northcote, Portsmouth, Quicke, Sidmouth, Shelley and Trefusis catching the editor's eye. Three other weddings that day received scant attention.[50]

Funerals of members of 'county' families received lengthy publicity. When Lady Susan Fortescue, the current earl's sister, died in 1919 the list of mourners revealed the extensive intermarriage of Fortescues with the aristocratic Bridgeman, Gordon Duff, St Aldwyn and Seymour families.[51] More localised marriages were typified by the 'county families' attending the funeral in 1920 of Lady Gertrude Acland who was the daughter of Sir John Walrond of Bradfield and wife of Sir Thomas Acland, 12th baronet, of Killerton.[52] Countess Fortescue had been a high profile county figure for several decades by the time of her death in 1929. Her funeral was attended not only by mourners from the extended Fortescue family and her husband's many military, hunting and civic associations but also from her own involvement with the Red Cross, Voluntary Aid Detachments, County Nursing Associations, Child Welfare Clinics, Women's Institutes, North Devon Infirmary, North Devon Association for the Help & Protection of Girls, and several north Devon musical and folk dance societies.[53]

When Sir Edward Chaning Wills died in 1921 the Royal Devon & Exeter Hospital lost its president and generous donor, and his 1,300 acre Harcombe estate near Chudleigh lost a keen 'improver' and sportsman.[54] Such figures remained centres of public and financial networks, both commercial and charitable. Sir Frederick de la Pole's funeral in 1926 was attended by representatives from Colyton Grammar School, Devon & Exeter Savings Bank, Axe Vale Harriers, Colyton Parish Council and Feofees, Seaton and Axminster UDCs, the Horticultural Societies of Colyton and Shute & District, Whitton & Lang estate agents, Chard's Mitchell, Toms & Co Brewery, and several other commercial enterprises.[55]

Families in the 'big house' continued to support community projects, including the war memorials that all too frequently commemorated their own sons. It remained fashionable, as before the war, to be leading figures in hospital and medical charities, including maternity clinics, the Cancer Fund, and Exeter's Cripples' Hospital campaign. (see Chapter Six) Several high profile figures, and notably Countess Fortescue, Lady Clinton and Mary Calmady-Hamlyn fresh from their war work, sought to promote the establishment of Women's Institutes (WIs) in Devon villages. It was part of the longstanding concern about rural depopulation stemming from the low wages and arduousness of agricultural life and accentuated by the break-up of large estates.[56] They had elevated aims – practical, moral, and essentially patrician.

Speaking in 1919 Lady Fortescue believed 'the lives of the wives of rural workers especially were dull and grey … They went on with the same daily round, preparing meals, sending children to school, and a great many other tiresome jobs.'[57] Nevertheless she asserted 'women should widen their outlook and bring it more closely to the great questions of the day.' Miss Calmady-Hamlyn said the aim was nothing less than having 'an important share in the great work of reconstruction in England' and by this she meant creating a 'comradeship' of women well educated enough through the WI's educational schemes to influence national affairs 'for the good.'[58] Through instruction and community activities village life could be enjoyed, not merely endured. In 1920 the Federation of Devon Women's Institutes was formed. At its inauguration Lady Clinton itemised the lessons women could attend in cooking, clothes making, the rules of health and child care – the last was important, she said, 'because women after 1,000 years were still experimenting on the bringing up of children'. And, she added, probably sincerely if naively, the WI had 'no distinction of class; every member was of equal importance.' She was duly elected President, with Mary Calmady-Hamlyn as Secretary.[59]

Rural Relationships: The Changing Pattern of Life

Members of High Bickington Women's Institute by a marquee at a local event, c1930.
(Beaford Old Archive images: © Beaford Arts).

By 1922 fifty Devon villages had WI branches, and close working links were established with the county's Village Clubs' Association whose membership included many men. Indeed in 1921 Miss Calmady-Hamlyn was instrumental in setting up the Devon Joint Committee of Women's Institutes and Village Clubs' Associations. After several inaugural speeches highlighting the depressing rural scene, the committee dedicated itself to the spread of community halls and an array of wholesome activities. She became its vice-president, and Lord Fortescue its president. A county survey identified the shortfall in halls, although some were planned as war memorials, and the County Education and Agricultural Committees promised support for rural courses.[60] A fulsome newspaper report in 1922 revealed how the new WI branches were already improving lives by organising trips, tidying up streets, establishing cooperative market stalls, arranging flower shows, and putting on fêtes, plays and dances. Perhaps wryly, it suggested that public houses should be encouraged to reform themselves as communal, not merely male, recreational centres.[61]

In 1925 Lady Clinton was gratified that there were 5,000 WI members in 79 branches across Devon, with numerous courses operating in partnership with the County Council. Interestingly she ended her annual talk that year by asserting the educational programme was more important than the social one, and the overall aim was 'to build up character'.[62] In 1930 Lady Clinton (the president), Mrs Juanita Phillips (the chair) and the Federation's Executive Committee were proud that 102 branches had contributed 5,581 articles to the numerous competitive sections of arts and crafts and produce in the annual exhibition in Exeter.[63] Competition was seen as central to character building in the WI as it was in the nation's schools – as we shall see in Chapter Seven. Lady Clinton was also County Girl Guide Commissioner and her speeches to local companies appear little different to some of those she gave at WI meetings. At one major gathering she itemised 'staunching cuts, cooking economical meals, making garments, feeding young babies' and most of all a heady combination of self-worth stemming from altruistic service and upright living were what the Guides were all about.[64]

The historic County Ball returned after the war. In September 1919 it was held at the Rougemont Hotel soon after the wartime military records staff had left. The newspapers highlighted the presence of Lady Florence Cecil, Lady Peek, Lady May, Lady Hughes, Lady Shelley and Viscountess Sidmouth. Attendees were listed in descending order of their titles and ranks – nobility first, then knights and gentry, and then generals followed by colonels, majors and captains. Probably some of the Ball's grandeur was lost after 1926 when it was held at Poltimore School, Lord Poltimore's old house.[65] Hunt Balls were also resurrected, and attendees also listed in hierarchical order.[66]

A few country house balls survived. Commander and the Honourable Mrs Adams hosted lavish Fancy Dress Balls at Bradfield House in 1923 and 1925 with the Walrond, Clinton and other families attired in costly historical and fictional costumes.[67] Mrs Adams had been the widow of the Honourable Lionel Walrond, killed on active service in 1915. Another Fancy Dress Ball (marking the Haldon Races – see picture on page 47) was hosted in 1929 by Lady Kekewich at Peamore, and no doubt there were others.[68] However although many 1920s Devon MPs came from estate owning families, such as Francis Acland, Lt Colonel Acland-Troyte, Colonel Mildmay, George Lambert, Sir Robert Newman and Cedric Drewe (the son of Julius Drewe, builder of Castle Drogo) Devon's mansions were pale shadows of their former Victorian and Edwardian selves as major political and social centres. Just the partisan fêtes and garden parties kept the tradition alive, as for example when Lady Molesworth St Aubyn hosted a Conservative Garden Party at Halwill in August 1920 and Lady Clinton held a Conservative Primrose League Fête at Bicton in July 1921.[69]

However two local events did possess national significance – but both brought little cheer to Devon's landowners and farmers. In July 1925 Stanley Baldwin, the prime minister, gave a speech at Bradfield House, a staunchly Conservative stronghold, in which he itemised the problems of agriculture – high taxation, death duties, rates, wages, transport costs and foreign competition – but then said government intervention would be limited to encouraging research and good relations between landowners, farmers and labourers.[70] Conversely, in September that year Killerton Park hosted the 'Great Liberal Demonstration' when David Lloyd George, who had gone from being the prime minister (1916-22) to the leader of a mere rump of his old Liberal party, launched an imaginative but doomed programme of land reform. It involved nothing less than the abolition of the present system of land ownership, and its redistribution under state control to ensure maximum output, security of tenure, equitable credit arrangements, and – easily said – good relations with workers.[71]

Village life

Despite all the changes, and the depressing postwar state of agriculture, Devon's rural communities enjoyed a variety of activities, both traditional and new. Some were organised within the village largely for village families such as char-a-banc trips, whist drives, dances, WI meetings, sports days, and school events. Some sought to attract outsiders as well as villagers, such as fêtes, horticultural shows, and football and cricket matches, and some were outside events that enticed villagers to travel further afield, such as county hunts and major Agricultural Shows, Carnivals and Fairs.

In the 1920s villages remained remarkably self-sufficient, despite the greater ease of motorised transport to and from the towns. As *Kelly's Directories* reveal, nearly all villages had a general store, a post office with probably two collections and deliveries a day, a public house or two, an elementary school, an Anglican church and Nonconformist chapel, and residents generally included a seamstress and dressmaker, a cobbler, mason, blacksmith, thatcher and carrier. Most larger villages had a doctor, although in private practice, and access to a trained district nurse was getting easier. Some larger villages had fresh water supplies, although many others still relied on wells and communal pumps. Most houses were still lit by candles or paraffin lamps or, more rarely, gas mantles supplied from small local gas works. Electricity was largely limited to the towns possessing generating companies. Many villages

Rural Relationships: The Changing Pattern of Life

Guy's bakery, delivery van and staff from Exbourne. (Beaford Old Archive images: © Beaford Arts).

Harvest group at Hatherleigh with horses and hay wagon, and baling machine. (Beaford Old Archive images: © Beaford Arts).

had branch railway links with major towns and markets, although trains were often infrequent and slow. Motor cars and omnibuses, along with delivery vans and lorries, were penetrating the countryside and, in common with tractors, replacing horses. This was a gradual process, though, and memoirs of the period readily recall the numerous horses still routinely ridden, and pulling ploughs, rakes, crushers, wagons and carts.[72]

Hunting and shooting remained popular. Self-congratulatory hunt dinners continued to celebrate kills, lament failures, toast the foxes and stags, sing 'John Peel', recall past adventures, thank farmers for tolerating damage, and praise Devon as 'God's own county'.[73] Reports of the meetings of the Hatherleigh Harriers, Eggesford Foxhounds, South Devon Foxhounds, Tiverton Foxhounds and Tetcott Foxhounds showed how hundreds turned out to follow the meetings, although often nothing was killed.[74] The newspapers resounded with the excitement of the chase, especially if it ended with a kill, but not everyone delighted in the sport. In 1926 the League for the Prohibition of Cruel Sports met in Exeter, and then in Lynton, a town surrounded by well-hunted moors, to condemn 'blood sports' as 'the Serpent in God's Garden of Eden'. The League had renowned supporters in Rosalie Chichester of Arlington Court, Issac Foot the politician, and two popular writers with West Country homes, Eden Phillpots and John Galsworthy.[75] In 1930 a Parliamentary Bill to ban stag hunting infuriated many across Devon, especially Earl Fortescue and Lord Poltimore, but it made no progress.[76]

Shooting partridges was popular too. In August 1919 the *Western Times* happily announced, 'The prospects, considering the conditions created by the war, and the increase in vermin, are favourable.'[77] The Culmstock Otter Hounds met around 40 times a year and the lengthy river chases attracted numerous devotees.[78] Badger hunts were common, and the vigorous 'digging out' of setts was reported in minute detail. Early in 1920 three were killed during a single Hatherleigh meet.[79] Hare coursing days were also turned into exciting stories of hot pursuits.[80] And rabbiting with ferrets remained a traditional pastime, especially, it seems, in cold weather when rabbits were slower to bolt.[81]

Village Horticultural and Cottage Garden Shows quickly picked up after the war. According to its report, Broadclyst's Cottage Garden Exhibition in July 1919 was particularly successful because the war had intensified people's interest in vegetable production.[82] There were many others that season, and they proliferated throughout the decade. Over just one weekend in July 1921 the *Western Times* expended much ink on nine almost identical shows, including the joint ones for Kenn, Shillingford & Dunchideock and for High Hampton, Black Torrington, Shebbear & Buckland Filleigh. Several columns were filled with the winners of numerous categories of vegetables, flowers, poultry, cakes and dairy produce. The shows generally had different competitions for farmers, tradesmen and 'cottagers'.[83] And they often involved the village brass bands that prospered across Devon. Hatherleigh was proud most of its bandsmen were ex-servicemen.[84]

District Horse Shows and Agricultural Shows also revived quickly, seemingly little affected by the army's mass purchase of horses and the appalling wartime losses. At South Molton, for example, in 1919 cups and prizes abounded for various categories of brood mares and foals, colts and hunters, hacks and cart horses, and also sheep, pigs, cattle, butter, clotted cream, honey, eggs, cheese, potatoes, onions, peas, beans, carrots and cultivated and wild flowers.[85] For major shows eye-catching advertisements highlighted the prizes on offer. As early as 1921 Tiverton advertised £600 in prizes, along with special parking for motorcars.[86] For Okehampton's Show special excursion trains brought in spectators from Exeter and Plymouth and all the intermediate stations. And the steadily improving village bus routes and timetables were of great help – by 1926, for example, all the villages on the road connecting Barnstaple and South Molton had five buses each way except on Sundays.[87]

Barnstaple Fair remained the county's biggest event; it lasted three days and was essentially divided into two parts – the market for cattle, sheep, pigs and horses, and the fairground and

Rural Relationships: The Changing Pattern of Life

Roundabout with Venetian gondolas at Barnstaple Fair. (Beaford Old Archive images: © Beaford Arts).

sideshows. Launched with great ceremony from the decorated civic chamber, it tended to be accompanied by numerous complaints of the low tone and drunken behaviour of visitors, the fraudsters gulling customers, and regrets that the railway ever reached Barnstaple, especially from Plymouth.[88]

Bampton Fair concentrated on the sale of horses and ponies, and was notorious for the dangers posed by frightened animals being driven through the streets, while Tavistock's 'Goose Fair' had few geese, but plentiful cattle, sheep and horses and, sneered the local newspaper each year, plenty of rouged fortune tellers, itinerant teeth-pullers, 'cheap jack' stallholders, and glib-tongued hawkers of 'quack cures' to fleece gullible country folk.[89]

Carnivals to promote towns and their trade were highlights of the year. Those at Okehampton, Hatherleigh and Holsworthy were major events with several bands, numerous sideshows, plenty to eat and drink, and long processions of noisy and colourful tableaux created by schools, firms, clubs and societies. In 1922 a key attraction at Okehampton was Messrs Day & Sons thirty feet long representation of a torpedo boat destroyer complete with a working searchlight on the bridge.[90] St Peter's Fair at Holsworthy kept up the tradition of selecting its 'Pretty Maid'. In 1928 Miss Gladys Ashby, an 18-year-old Sunday School teacher, won the honour and £2.10s 0d in gold for fulfilling the ancient criteria of being *The prettiest maid: The most noted for quietness and attendance at church: and She maintains peace and goodwill among men.*[91] It does not seem to have been won every year. In 1922 Payhembury Carnival hit the headlines with its revival of the alarming tradition of lighting petrol thrown onto the village pond as an evening finale while the crowd frolicked around.[92] In 1924 Great Torrington revived its May Fair and within a couple of years it proudly announced 'non-stop entertainment from 10am to midnight' with animal displays, bands, sideshows, floral and maypole dancing, athletics match, clay pigeon shooting, football match and a Grand Dance.[93]

Advertisement for Great Torrington May Fair. (Mark Ware: WT 26 April 1929: Courtesy of Devon & Exeter Institution Trustees).

Several district ploughing matches were revived, and were often accompanied by traditional hedging and dairy contests and awards to long-serving farm labourers. Traditionally squires, farmers and clergy had formed the organising committee and provided the cash prizes to help preserve local skills, generate interest in farming, and reward the loyalty of low paid workers. There was always a 'boys' ploughing category.[94] And not surprisingly clergy continued to ensure Harvest Festivals tied key moments of rural life to the Christian faith. Churches and chapels were suitably decorated, special harvest hymns were sung, teas provided for worshippers, and collections made for charities.[95]

Church and chapel outings remained popular. In August 1920, for example, char-a-bancs took Merton's choir and bellringers to Ilfracombe, and the St Giles-in-the-Heath United Methodists to Bude, while trains took Silverton and Moretonhampstead Methodist Sunday Schools to Teignmouth, and Chulmleigh's Anglican Sunday School to Exmouth.[96] In June 1924 two special trains took 850 members of Church of England choirs in north Devon to Wembley's celebrated British Empire Exhibition.[97] At Christmas parishes

Hatherleigh Carnival Procession 1927. (Beaford Old Archive images: © Beaford Arts).

100

Rural Relationships: The Changing Pattern of Life

Harvest Home at King's Nympton Methodist Chapel 1919. (Beaford Old Archive images: © Beaford Arts).

continued to reward loyal Sunday School attendees with parties and presents.[98] Rival denominations were still competing avidly for the hearts and minds of the young, and no doubt some of the young shrewdly chose to patronise the denomination with the better treats.

There were other activities enlivening communities. Many villages fêtes, dances and whist drives supported charities, and St Dunstan's Hostel for blind veterans became a popular cause after the war.[99] Village Sports Days became popular with prizes for adults as well as children in assorted running, jumping and skipping races. Often horse and pony races were included.[100] There were many inter-village football and cricket matches, and associated league tables.[101] Drama clubs put on plays – at Ashreigney the operetta *The Happy Farm* was reported under the telling headlines 'How to Make Rural Life in Devon Brighter.'[102] And at

Ashreigney's operetta The Happy Farm, *January 1921, printed in the* Western Times *under the headlines 'How to Make Rural Life in Devon Brighter'). (Beaford Old Archive images: © Beaford Arts).*

Halberton the local players staged 'The Forty Thieves' in aid of the war memorial hall.[103] Nearly all villages had schools, many all-age ones, and they staged seasonal concerts at Christmas, and sometimes at Easter as well.[104] And alongside the spread of state insurance schemes village Friendly Societies continued to prosper. In May 1929 the 87 members of the Talaton 'Club' marched to church waving their banner to the music of the local band. The bells rang in welcome, and afterwards members went on their annual walk, ate their annual meal at the village inn, and enjoyed their annual sports afternoon.[105]

Farmers and farming

Unfortunately many Devon farms were unhappy places in the 1920s. After the Armistice farmers wanted their sons back quickly, and urged the government to preserve wartime subsidies and impose tariffs on imported food in order to remain competitive. Instead their sons received no special demobilisation consideration, the subsidies went, imported food remained largely tariff free, and all political parties remained far more sensitive to the needs of cities and industry than the complaints of shires and farmers. The only welcome news in Devon was the termination of the draconian wartime directive to expand corn production at the expense of animal husbandry.[106]

There was some talk among government ministers of preserving County War Agricultural Committees under amended names to direct a national agricultural policy aimed at reducing the need for imports. Devon's War Agricultural Committee fully endorsed the idea, but overall it had little support in the general post-war mood of desiring less rather than more state control of local affairs, and the opportunity was lost.[107]

Labour relations were poor. Early in 1919 Devon Farmers' Union (DFU) meetings resounded with complaints that labourers' wages were too high at the legal minimum of 25/- a week.[108] More eruptions occurred when the statutory Wages Board gave labourers a weekly half-day holiday, and said any hours over 48 in winter and 54 in summer were overtime.[109] And in August 1919 the minimum wage rose to 37/6d a week, and in 1920 to 42/- and then 46/-.[110] Even so, skilled country road repairers and lorry drivers were earning several shillings more.[111] Farmers guilty of paying below the minimum wage were heavily fined, and several were named and shamed in Devon newspapers.[112] Rural harmony was not helped by farmers' public complaints that many workers were not worth the money, or agricultural union letters to newspapers citing the deductions mean-spirited farmers made for rent, cider, wood, and even, it was claimed, permission to keep poultry and catch rabbits.[113] In the summer of 1920 more trouble occurred when stories circulated that some workers were refusing to work the longer summer hours.[114] The times were volatile, and tensions were high. Many tenant farmers had become farm owners and were now saddled with heavy mortgage payments and fading political support, and farm workers were becoming more unionised and aware that political parties were vying for their votes.

There were other conflicts too. When the government's price controls on meat and potatoes were lifted in 1919 Devon farmers held back supplies until prices rose. Amidst a storm of protest retailers and shoppers had to pay higher prices, and sales slumped.[115] A far longer lasting row broke out between Devon's dairy farmers and milk retailers over the rising price of milk, with each sector accusing the other of profiteering.[116] A series of convictions against retailers for fat deficient supplies led to mutual recriminations between local farmers and dairies, and both parties were widely suspected of malpractice. A price war evolved between them, and in 1922 the public was threatened with a farmers' milk strike.[117]

The 1922 and 1923 Milk & Dairies (Amendment) Orders created 5 grades of milk based on bottling mechanisms, pasteurisation, the risk of bovine TB and the percentage of bacteria. At a regional conference in 1922 it was not at all certain that West Country farmers and dairies would opt to produce even 'Grade A Milk', which was far less rigorously produced and tested than pure 'Certified Milk' or even the lesser 'Grade A TB Tested Milk', as it would cost 4d a gallon more to produce.[118] As speakers over the next few years noted, the worrying risks of contamination through the lack of dairy hygiene and a reluctance to install costly cooling and pasteurisation machinery lasted right through the inter-war period until legislation forced standards to rise.[119]

In 1921 farmers suffered a severe blow. A year earlier an Agricultural Act reassuringly preserved most of the wartime grain subsidies, but in 1921 it was suddenly rescinded as far too costly – an estimated £30,000,000 a year.[120] The government still rejected import tariffs. Cheap food from wherever it might be sourced, and the avoidance of accusations of favouring agriculture over industry, were important considerations for all political parties.¹²¹ Instead the government sought to boost long term production by encouraging agricultural education and establishing County Conciliation Committees to improve working relationships.

Devon's farmers were outraged at their 'desertion', and DFU meetings resounded with cries of betrayal, but also a dawning realisation that greater efficiency and specialisation were the only alternatives to bankruptcy.¹²² Not surprisingly the DFU subjected the Conciliation Committee to great, and successful, pressure to lower minimum wage levels when deflation occurred in the early 1920s, and, far less successfully, sought government action to provide low interest loans, revise the rating system favourably, lower railway freight charges, and set import tariffs.¹²³ Throughout the decade parliamentary candidates were grilled by DFU branches on all these issues, but the vaguely sympathetic answers never resulted in direct action.¹²⁴ In the Commons in 1928 Lieut Colonel Acland-Troyte, Conservative MP for Tiverton, tried but failed to gain government support for import controls, rate relief and grants.¹²⁵ And Labour Party speakers saying land nationalisation and state investment and controls were the answers did not lead their candidates to remotely threaten the other parties in rural Devon. Farm workers lost out as their parliamentary supporters were too few and the National Union of Agricultural Workers too confrontational to generate wider sympathy.¹²⁶ The nearest any government came to radical reforms was the Conservative 1926 White Paper whose thoughts on modest import tariffs, financial help for farmers' investing in modern machinery and scientific methods, and support for farm workers to become smallholders came to nothing in the face of vocal opposition to any rise in food prices, and any partiality towards farmers and rural problems. The biggest critic, though, was the Treasury.¹²⁷

Although Devon farmers were no longer obliged to produce grain they were faced with the high purchase cost of livestock – prices had tripled between 1914 and 1920 – if they wished to revert to pastoral farming. Many decided to invest in new animals, only for their value to plummet as the devastating 1920-21 slump left them with a deficit economy.¹²⁸ Nevertheless it seemed the only way forward, and across Devon the numbers of beef and dairy cattle, sheep and pigs slowly rose while arable cultivation quickly declined from 356,872 acres in 1918 to 247,071 in 1920.¹²⁹

Not surprisingly, when the initial post-war boom faded some overstretched farmers decided to sell up – as the rising number of advertisements

The Devon County Travelling Poultry School class at Winkleigh. (Mark Ware: WT 5 November 1920: Courtesy of Devon & Exeter Institution Trustees).

revealed. The newspapers also highlighted young people's determination to quit their villages.[130] In June 1923 speakers at Exeter's Rotary Club gave an urban perspective on the Devon countryside, seeing it suffering from low wages, inadequate education, poor returns, insecure tenancies, generally insanitary housing, and devoid of party political interest.[131] Certainly Devon's rural district medical officers of health continued to highlight the houses unfit for habitation, the use of insanitary privies, and the defective dairies.[132]

Despite everything, though, there were some signs of agricultural initiative. In 1926 cider had a resurgence in popularity and Devon's apple orchards received renewed attention and investment.[133] The Devon Butter Producers' Association was essentially a cooperative and through its high standards of manufacture, and accompanying certification, was able to market a top of the range product.[134] Devon's soft fruit and potato growers got together to negotiate cheaper bulk railway rates to Wales and the Midlands.[135] And some farmers, such as Captain Strong at Bow, decided to become producers of eggs and poultry on an industrial scale with vast fenced compounds covering several acres of huts.[136]

Just when the government announced its promotion of agricultural education in 1921 a devastating Board of Agriculture report condemned Devon as England's most backward farming county, stubbornly retaining antiquated methods and scorning new ideas despite subsidies totalling one million pounds in the last twelve months.[137] No doubt angry and dismayed, the County Council revitalised it pre-war programme of short practical courses in rural centres. Among them, the dairy courses included hygienic milking together with cream and butter making, and cheesemaking embraced Cheddar, Wensleydale, Caerphilly and Pont L'Eveque. The travelling poultry school covered breeding, economic feeding, treating ailments, slaughtering, plucking and marketing.[138]

Day courses also proved popular. In just three months – November 1922 to January 1923 – the county agricultural staff gave 130 lectures in 54 centres on aspects of horticulture, poultry keeping, dairying and farriery with an average attendance of thirty. The sessions rose rose to 186 with 6,446 attendees for the period October to December 1926.[139] Demonstration classes in bottling and preserving fruit, and in aspects of dairying and horticulture, were held at local agricultural shows.[140] The DFU realised many farmers were hopeless at keeping accurate accounts, and probably ended up paying too much tax, and in 1922 secured the County Council's provision of book-keeping courses.[141] The County Council also organised advisory visits to farms, lectures in schools, and district discussion groups led by forward thinking farmers.[142]

From 1919 the County Council purchased several dozen large farms at auctions to be broken up to provide demobilised officers with smallholdings.[143] One unfortunate consequence was county council bidding forcing up auction prices and evoking complaints from tenants seeking to buy their farms.[144] Applicants for the new smallholdings had first to complete an intensive year-long training courses at a converted farm at Holcombe.[145] A significant minority failed the course, but there were successes, capped in 1922 by one ex-serviceman winning 'best smallholding' at the Bath & West Show and 'best calf' at the South Molton Show.[146]

In 1919 Devon had the new Seal-Hayne Agricultural College in its midst at Newton Abbot, but, said the Board of Agriculture's report in 1921, it was remarkable that no Devon students attended it.[147] In 1903 the wealthy Charles Seale-Hayne from Dartmouth had left his fortune to create a college specifically to bring Devon farming up to date. Things were a bit better in 1922 with Devon providing 25 of the 90 students. However critics were soon mocking the County Council's provision of an annual grant of £3,000 merely to show farmers how to do their job. In retaliation Seale-Hayne's bursar railed against Devon's farmers foolishly scorning modern scientific methods and refusing to allow their sons to attend courses, and hitting a particularly sensitive issue he derided the bookish curriculum in elementary schools which pushed boys away from rural occupations.[148] Two years later the County Agricultural Committee came to the conclusion that rurally sited farm institutes taking school leavers at 14 were preferable to Seale-Hayne's courses which were only offered to 16 year olds.[149] As a start the County Council opened up all its own agricultural courses to 14-year-old school leavers.[150] As far as Devon was concerned the college's use was confined mainly to its research into the eradication of plant and animal diseases, and the soil components best suited to particular crops, and the willingness of staff to visit farms on request with advice.[151]

REFERENCES

1. Burt, R. *Mining in Cornwall & Devon: Mines & Men*, pp35-48; Edwards, R.A., *Devon's Non-Metal Mines*, pp106-152

2. Perrin, R., *Agriculture in Depression, 1870-1940*, pp7-36, Rothery, M. (2007) 'The wealth of the English landed gentry 1870-1935' in *Agricultural History Review* 55,II, pp251-268

3. *TG* 23 June 1911; Parker, D., *Edwardian Devon*, pp85-86

4. *WT* 5 November 1921, Austin, A., *The History of the Clinton Barony 1299-1999*, pp214-223

5. *SMG* 23 November 1918, *WT* 4 October 1918, 14 & 17 December 1918

6. *NDJ* 16 January 1919 J.S.C. Davis, Devon VAD Director became its tenant

7. *WT* 12 December 1919

8. *WT* 13 January 1921, 1 April 1927

9. *WT* 30 August 1919; www.landedfamilies.blogspot.com/Bailey of Lee Abbey

10. www.stagebeauty.net/Daisy Markham, *WT* 24 October 1919

11. *WT* 4 July 1919, *D&SN* 20 October 1921

12. *NDJ* 27 March 1919

13. *WT* 8 August 1919

14. *WT* 16 October 1919, Lauder, R., *Devon Families*, p156

15. *NDJ* 11 March 1920, www.historicengland.org.uk/listing/Youlston Park

16. Emery, A., *Dartington Hall*, pp88-91, Young, M., *The Elmhirsts of Dartington*, *WT* 19 July 1919, 16 October 1920

17. *WT* 27 September 1921

18. *WT* 3 December 1920

19. *WT* 29 May 1920

20. *WT* 22 June 1920, Lauder, R., *Devon Families*, p34

21. The castle itself was tenanted. *NDJ* 19/8/20. The similarly long-standing north Devon Elwes and Stucley families also parted with hundreds of acres in 1920 – *WT* 12 March 1920, 23 July 1920

22. *WT* 2 September 1921

23. *WT* 17 & 27 September 1920

24. *TG* 24 March 1921, *WT* 17 September 1920

25. *WT* 26 April 1922, Jackson, A.J.H., (1996) 'Managing Decline: The Economy of the Powderham Estate in Devon 1870-1939', *Rep. Trans. Devon. Ass.*128, pp197-215

26. Upcott House house was let to Maxwell Thornton, MP for Tavistock 1922-24, *NDJ* 7 July 1921, *WT* 9 August 1921

27. *NDH* 18 August 1921

28. *WT* 18 July 19/22

29. Sale sheet, Colyton Heritage Centre, *WT* 18 October 1929

30. *WT* 21 March 1930, 9 May 1930

31. *WT* 13 March 1920, 24 April 1922, Lauder, R., *Vanished Houses of South Devon*, pp6-21

32. *WT* 5 September 1930, Lauder, R., *Vanished Houses of North Devon*, pp48-66

33. Hemming, J., *A Devon House*, pp21-60, *D&SN* 23 October 1919, *WT* 2, 24 & 27 September 1921, *CC* 21 July 1923

34. *D&SN* 3 June 1926, DHC PWDRO 1096/280 Stoodleigh Court estate

35. *WT* 28 May 1926.

36. *MDA* 5 November 1921, www.wikipedia.org/wiki/Harold_St-Maur.

37. *WT* 29 February 1922, 16 March 1923, Carew, Sir Rivers, *Footprints in the Sand*, pp165 et seq. Haccombe was sold in 1940

38. Cherry, B., & Pevsner, N., *The Buildings of England, Devon*, pp245-247

39. *TG* 29 November 1918, *WT* 3 November 1922, *D&SN* 6 December 1923, *NDJ* 7 July 1927

40. *WT* 10 February 1919

41. *TG* 11 September 1925

42. Phillips, G., 'The Social Impact' in Constantine, S. and others, *The First World War in British History*, pp119-122

43. *D&SN* 31 July 1919
44. *WT* 8 August 1919, 14 September 1920
45. *WT* 21 June 1929, 19 July 1929
46. *MDA* 24 January 1920, *WT* 1 & 5 September 1930
47. *WT* 19 September 1919 By 1930 Bovey House had become a GWR hotel.
48. *WT* 20 July 1922
49. *WT* 15 August 1930
50. *WT* 19 April 1929
51. *WT* 13 February 1919
52. *WT* 13 August 1920 She had been prominent in the Exeter Anti-Suffrage League.
53. *NDJ* 18 July 1929
54. *WT* 18 October 1921
55. *WT* 19 February 1926
56. *NDH* 4 December 1924
57. A point confirmed by Gail Braybon in 'Women & The War' in Constantine, S., op.cit., p167, *WT* 8 November 1919
58. *WT* 8 November 1919
59. *WT* 12 June 1920
60. *WT* 26 & 27 November 1920, 22 March 1921, *CC* 20 August 1921
61. *WO* 16 November 1922
62. *WT* 23 January 1925
63. *WT* 9 May 1930
64. *NDH* 24 June 1920
65. *WT* 18 September 1919, 30 September 1921, 9 January 1925, 27 August 1926
66. Viz East Devon Hunt Ball in Rougemont Hotel, *WT* 7 April 1921
67. *WT* 12 January 1923, 9 January 1925
68. *WT* 6 September 1929
69. *WT* 6 August 1920, 29 July 1921
70. *WT* 3 July 1925
71. *D&SN* 17 September 1925
72. *Kelly's Directory* 1919, 1923, Devon Federation of WIs, *Devon Within Living Memory*, pp10-19, 38-48, 58-67, 142-149
73. Viz Axe Vale *WT* 10 December 1920
74. *WT* 7 January 1920, 28 January 1921, *D&SN* 9 January 1922
75. *NDH* 2 September 1926, *WT* 26 February 1926, 16 August 1929
76. *WT* 4 April 1930
77. *WT* 29 August 1919
78. *CC* 16 August 1919, *WT* 4 January 1923
79. *WT* 7 January 1920, 24 March 1922, 2 January 1925
80. *WT* 15 & 23 January 1920, 28 January 1921
81. *WT* 1 January 1926
82. *WT* 31 July 1919
83. *WT* 28 & 29 July 1921, 17 July 1925
84. *WT* 12 August 1921
85. *WO* 10 July 1919, *WT* 15 July 1920, 2 September 1921
86 *D&SN* 7 July 1921
87. *WT* 2 September 1921, 3 September 1926
88. *WT* 15 September 1921
89. *CC* 29 October 1921, *TT* 16 October 1919, 11 October 1929
90. *WT* 5 December 1919, 10 November 1922, 15 November 1929
91. *D&SN* 12 July 1928
92. *WT* 10 November 1922, 8 November 1929
93. *WT* 2 May 1924, 30 April 1926, 26 April 1929
94. Viz Dalwood, Bovey Tracey *WT* 23 October 1920, 16 October 1925, 26 September 1930
95. Viz Withleigh, Penton and Burlescombe *D&SN* 27 September 1928
96. *WT* 6 & 13 August 1920
97. *MDA* 21 June 1924
98. Viz Hartland, Kilkhampton, *WT* 7 January 1920, 28 December 1921
99. *WT* 6 & 31 January 1919, 7 February 1919, 7 March 1919, 7 July 1922
100. Viz Gulworthy *TT* 2 January 1925, Cornwood *WT* 3 June 1926, Hemyock *D&SN* 5 June 1930
101. *D&SN* 15 January 1920, *NDH* 1 January 1920, *WT* 16 March 1923, 7 March 1930
102. *WT* 28 January 1921
103. *D&SN* 23 December 1926
104. Viz Exton, Inwardleigh *WT* 2 January 1922, 2 January 1925

105. *WT* 24 May 29, also Kentisbeare Club *D&SN* 5 June 1930

106. *WT* 29 November 1918, 25 January 1919 *D&SN* 2 January 1919, 6 February 1919

107. Whetham, E. H., *The Agrarian History of England & Wales* Vol.VIII, pp118-123, *D&SN* 23 October 1919, *WT* 4 & 17 January 1919, 14 November 1919

108. *WT* 1 & 7 February 1919

109. *WT* 27 February 1919, 30 January 1920

110. *WT* 15 August 1919, 16 April 1920, 20 August 1920, 28 January 1921

111. *WT* 4 July 1919

112. *WT* 20 August 1919, 26 November 1926

113. Whetham, E.H., op. cit., pp124-132, *WT* 15 February 1920, 16 April 1920, 10 May 1920, 12 June 1920

114. *WT* 30 August 1920

115. *WT* 16 April 1920

116. Whetham, E.H., op. cit., pp144-148, *WT* 19 December 1919, 28 April 1920

117. *D&SN* 31 March 1921, *SMG* 7 June 1919, *WT* 14 April 1920, 14 March 1922, 8 April 1922

118. *MDA* 3 February 1923

119. *D&SN* 6 January 1927, *TG* 27 January 1928

120. Whetham, E.H., op. cit., pp139-141, *WT* 12 August 1921

121. *WT* 12 August 1921

122. *WT* 27 September 1921, 17 December 1921, *WO* 23 August 1923

123. *WT* 4 & 10 January 1922, 29 December 1922

124. *WT* 18 July 1922, 25 January 1924, *NDJ* 10 January 1924

125. *D&SN* 8 March 1928

126. *NDJ* 26 May 1927, Penning-Rowsell, E. C. (1997) 'Who 'Betrayed Whom? Power & Politics in the1920/21 Agricultural Crisis' in *Agricultural History Review* 45, II, pp176-194

127. Sheail, J. (2010) 'The White Paper, Agricultural Policy, of 1926: its contest and significance' in *Agricultural History Review* 58, II, pp236-254

128. Whetham, E.H., op. cit., 124-127, 137-139

129. *SMG* 18 June 1921; *Kelly's Directories* 1919,1923

130. *WO* 9 March 1922, *WT* 20 April 1923

131. *WT* 29 July 1923

132. *TG* 8 June 1923, 9 April 1925, *WT* 29 June 1923, 17 July 1925

133. *WT* 23 December 1926

134. *WT* 23 December 1926, 23 August 1929

135. *WT* 23 May 1930

136. *WT* 20 June 1930

137. *WT* 18 November 1921

138. *WT* 13 August 1920, 13 October 1920, 5 November 1920

139. *DHC DCC* Agricultural Education Sub-Committee 15 March 1923, Agricultural Committee 17 March 1927)

140. *TG* 20 March 1925

141. *WT* 31 March 1922, 5 May 1922

142. *WT* 19 January 1923, DHC DCC Agricultural Committee 17 March 1927

143. *DHC DCC* General Purposes Committee 25 May 1919, 11 December 1919, 17 June 1920, *WT* 9 December 1919

144. *WT* 19 November 1919

145. *DHC DCC* Smallholdings Sub-Committee 29 September 1921

146. *WT* 21 July 1922

147. *WT* 18 November 1921

148. *WT* 28 June 1921,13 & 27 October 1922

149. *WT* 25 April 1924, 17 April 1925

150. DHC DCC Agricultural Committee 18/3/26

151. *WT* 16 May 1924

6
HEALTH & WELFARE: WORKING TOWARDS A SYSTEM

The 1918–19 influenza pandemic

On its onward march around the world the influenza pandemic struck Devon in October 1918 adding yet another horror to countless families who had already endured four years of war. Believed erroneously to have originated in Spain, the disease probably spread from east to west across Europe with its advance hastened by the bad conditions in devastated cities, overcrowded military camps and hospitals, and the never-ending movement of troops, casualties and refugees. The army medical department thought it originated in the Ypres Salient and was carried by Allied troopships and hospital ships to Great Britain and the Americas. Some modern historians suspect a virus transmuting from poultry in the vast Allied training and transit camp at Etaples was to blame.[1]

On 9 October the alarming number of children struck down in Exeter led the Education Committee to close all schools for a fortnight, and a week later staff sickness led to unprecedented reductions in the tram service. On 18 October the *Western Times* pictured young Dorothy Prouse who had been a tram conductor in Exeter throughout the war but died from influenza that week. By then it had killed several people in Tiverton and Appledore, and by 22 October it was rife in South Molton and Paignton. On 24 October all schools in Newton Abbot Rural District were closed, including Bishopsteignton, Chudleigh Knighton and Moretonhamstead. On 25 October the *Western Times* publicised the plight of five children whose desperately sick mother had thrown herself out a window. By the end of the month the pandemic had spread across Bideford Rural District and killed people in remote villages such as Chagford and Chittlehampton. By the end of November the newspaper was recording the mounting death toll in Dartmouth, Totnes, Newton

Dorothy Prouse, a victim of influenza. (Mark Ware: WT 18 October 1918: Courtesy of Devon & Exeter Institution Trustees).

Advertisement for Zip and its claim to cure influenza. (Mark Ware: WT 7 February 1919: Courtesy of Devon & Exeter Institution Trustees).

Abbot, Exeter St Thomas and Plymouth. The catalogue of misery went on into the new year when a second wave of influenza arrived, and cases only began to decline in the Spring. Mysteriously the pandemic disappeared almost as quickly as it arrived.[2] Perhaps enough people had developed antibodies. A milder form of the virus appeared in 1922 but it still laid many people low and killed several children across Exeter.[3]

As the *Western Times* noted, hospitals, doctors and nurses were constantly busy, especially when patients' influenza led to pneumonia with the probability of a terrible choking death.[4] Barnstaple RDC's Medical Officer reported whole families becoming ill, with 17 deaths from influenza and 17 from pneumonia in the latter part of 1918.[5] There was little he or any other doctor could do to help victims other than recommend salt water mouth washes, rest, warmth and drinks. Medical advice to the healthy extended to keeping off the streets and cancelling indoor meetings and events.[6] Local chemists advertised dubious remedies and preventives such as Stories' Influenza Mixture costing 1/3d a bottle that asserted 'The First Dose Relieves – One Bottle Cures. Angiers' Emulsion claimed to stimulate bodily resistance to the disease, and Condy's Fluid was a strong disinfectant sniffed up the nose and exhaled through the mouth.[7] The 1918-1919 outbreaks alone killed an estimated 228,000 people across Great Britain, and although contemporary medical researchers believed transmission lay in minute organisms in victim's sputum, the virus itself was not isolated until 1933.[8]

Hospitals: voluntarism and the battle to survive and expand

If people desired medical treatment for influenza, or indeed anything else, they had several choices depending on their locality and wealth. They might be able to afford to pay a qualified doctor they visited or who visited them, or the full charges levied by a hospital – in which case they would occupy a carefully secluded private bed. They might posses medical insurance through private companies, friendly societies, company schemes or the 1911 National Insurance Act that entitled them, and under some policies their families, to treatment. For those without these resources any treatment in a voluntary maintained hospital or a dispensary would depend upon the earmarked charitable funds held by those institutions, or upon the annual 'subscribers' to hospitals possessing 'tickets' they could to give to people they thought deserving of free treatment.[9]

Finally there were the Victorian workhouses. In Devon, as elsewhere, the spate of highly critical *British Medical Association* reports in the 1890s on the abysmal state of workhouse sick wards and their staff had led to the construction of new self-contained purpose-built infirmaries. The Boards of Guardians in Bideford, Exeter, Newton Abbot, Okehampton, Plymouth, Tiverton and Totnes were among those shamed by public condemnation of their sanitation, bedding, lighting, heating, ventilation, food and record keeping into making radical improvements. These infirmaries accepted patients, mainly elderly and mentally ill paupers and single women due to give birth, free of charge once they had been verified by the local Board of Guardians. Often such patients had come before the magistrates who 'recommended' them to the Guardians for admission. Across the nation in the 1920s the workhouse infirmaries provided 80,000 beds, the municipal hospitals in major towns 74,000 and other entirely voluntary hospitals 56,000.[10]

Hospitals underwent a sea change in the decades straddling the war regarding both the breadth of treatment they offered and the public's positive perception of their success rate. In 1899 Dean Clarke's Hospital in Exeter was visited by the Duke and Duchess of York and it was renamed the Royal Devon & Exeter Hospital (RD&E). Much else was changing there too, notably the quality and quantity of nurses, and the the construction of a new operating theatre, additional wards, more nurses' homes, and an 'accident room' for emergencies. However, here as everywhere else across Devon, modern hospital developments depended upon traditional and worryingly uncertain sources of funding. These included interest from existing endowments, new legacies,

The Royal Devon & Exeter Hospital in Southernhay. (Mark Ware: Courtesy of Devon & Exeter Institution Trustees).

annual donations, never-ending fund raising events, dipping into reserves, and patients' fees.[11] In 1919 Sir Edward Chaning Wills, the RD&E's Chairman of Governors, pinpointed the issue in his remark at the annual meeting that a unblemished reputation for a successful balance between efficiency and economy was vital if people were to continue supporting the hospital.[12] Fortunately for this hospital, and most others, the age-old habit of humanitarian philanthropy remained strong after 1918 despite, or perhaps because of, the massive demands made upon medical care in the war. And the post-war government's concern for the health of mothers and their babies – welcomed as the new generation of defenders of the Empire – all helped maintain the charitable momentum as well as raising the issue of permanent, rather than just wartime, state intervention. Indeed, for a long time after 1918 the War Office and Ministry of Pensions paid hospitals, including some in Devon, to treat ex-servicemen, notably those with shell-shock, TB or venereal diseases. Nevertheless, two questions – who the hospitals should accept for treatment, and who should pay for it – bedevilled the era.

Although voluntary cottage hospitals were small, in a county of small towns spread widely apart they served a vital purpose, but many of them lived perilous financial lives as the cost of staff, services and equipment soared. They could fail, as happened in Chulmleigh in 1922.[13] In 1920 Dartmouth's hospital closed, and only reopened after great efforts to secure the £1,000 a year costs through increasing fees and annual subscriptions, and successfully offering all local trade union members reduced subscription rates of 2d a week.[14] And it took the threat of closure for Dawlish to save its cottage hospital through fundraising galas, fêtes and dances and persuading 400 new subscribers to pay 2d a week.[15] Around the same date Ashburton and Buckfastleigh Cottage Hospital also neared closure until patients' fees were increased and local villages organised fund raising events. In 1923 this hospital treated 70 in-patients, 55 operations were carried out, and a fortuitous rise in donations kept patients' fees down to between 7/6d and 12/6d a week.[16]

Ottery St Mary's cottage hospital, in common with most others, survived on subscriptions, legacies, church collections and donations far more than on

Health & Welfare: Working Towards a System

'A Midsummer Night's Dream' at Bovey Tracey Fête in aid of the cottage hospital and voluntary Nursing Association.
(Mark Ware: WT 16 July 1920: Courtesy of Devon & Exeter Institution Trustees).

fees. It was also fortunate to have the active support of the patrician Coleridge family and the distinguished scholar and diplomat, Sir Ernest Satow, who lived there in retirement.[17] Some other hospitals were equally fortunate. Although Lord and Lady Hambleden were rarely at Bovey Manor after the war they continued to support Moretonhampstead's cottage hospital, as did Colonel Mildmay, the local MP, whose wife had been a dynamic VAD regional director during the war.[18] In Axminster money from a few large legacies supplemented by public donations and subscriptions allowed the cottage hospital to be rebuilt just before the war, but the 1920s witnessed a struggle to fund a X-ray machine, improve sanitation, and employ more nurses.[19] Few cottage hospitals had adequate endowments to subsidise the expanding world of modern medicine and rising popular demand. In this respect Exeter Eye Infirmary was fortunate that it could subsidise poor patients through a complicated system whereby a governors' sub-committee decided how much a patient could pay and then made up the difference after agreement with the surgeon and administrator.[20]

Okehampton & District War Memorial Hospital. (Mark Ware: WT 5 July 1929: Courtesy of Devon & Exeter Institution Trustees).

Not all districts possessed hospitals in 1918. Various pre-war pressure groups in Okehampton had failed to generate enough interest, and people were left with the choice of the workhouse infirmary or lengthy and costly trips to hospitals in Exeter or Plymouth. However when peace returned a proposal by a returning army chaplain, several local doctors and other influential residents that fifteen neighbouring parishes should collaborate on raising funds for a war memorial hospital received widespread support. Running costs would be met by local charities together with a scale of charges ranging from nothing for the deserving poor to sizeable fees for a private room. After successful fund raising a foundation stone was laid in 1925, but only at the second attempt. The first had been abandoned after aggrieved ex-servicemen

noted the stone made no mention that it was a war memorial. The 8 public and 2 private beds in Okehampton 'Memorial' Hospital received their first patients in late 1926. It had cost £7,000, and 154 patients were admitted in its first year.[21]

Although costs and demand were rising, many hospitals held fast to the voluntary principle and disliked the involvement of local authorities or government departments in their affairs. The Victorian objection to the state's encroachment upon individual and community decision making remained strong. In a typical example of autonomy, in 1921 Earl Fortescue, whose family had long supported Barnstaple's North Devon Infirmary, praised the voluntary funding of its new electric lift by the hospital's Ladies Association as the means of keeping state involvement at bay. To laughter and applause he asserted, 'one did not want to see hospitals becoming a State Institution like sewage works or the police station.'[22] In 1922 the North Devon Infirmary was in financial crisis, but the district rallied to ensure its survival. Under the leadership of the mayor of Barnstaple several influential figures across the district agreed to organise particular events. They included plays, concerts, dances, whist drives, sports days, a 'confetti carnival', street collections, a boxing tournament, and 'a mile of pennies'. Within the year £1,235 was raised.[23] Fortified by this success, an endless series of events across north Devon kept the infirmary solvent, in good repair and well-equipped. Another thousand pounds was raised in 1925, and a massive £10,000 was the target achieved in 1926, its centenary year.[24]

After the war Tavistock Hospital set about renovating its neglected building, and began a never-ending period of internal and external modernisation that relied heavily on voluntary support. Among several events in 1921 the award winning Gunnislake Choir donated performances and a high profile 'Hospital Sunday' church service and collection was boosted by a procession including Tavistock's Girl Guides, Boy Scouts, Comrades of the Great War, Salvation Army, Cooperative Society and Trades & Labour Council. In 1926 the procession at Tavistock Hospital

The prize winning Nursing Association float at Sandford Carnival, 1925.
(Beaford Old Archive images: © Beaford Arts).

North Devon Infirmary, Barnstaple. (Author's collection).

Carnival had 17 competitive classes totalling 200 gaily decorated motor cars, motor cycles and sidecars, lorries and vans, horses and riders, farm carts and wagons, and prams. The day raised £1,085.[25]

Teignmouth raised £17,000 for a new hospital with support from Lady Cable and a mix of donations, subscriptions, grants and funds raising events. In 1925 the old Sion House hospital was replaced by a new one in Mill Lane with two 10 bed wards and 4 private rooms. It was soon serving over 100 in-patients and 700 out-patients a year. Here, too, local 'Hospital Sundays' were important, with the one in nearby Bishopsteignton in 1920 drawing in local schools and clubs, and their bands, in the procession to and from the parish church.[26]

Things were easier in wealthier Torbay. In 1919 the Governors of Torbay Hospital decided its cramped Victorian building, and its excessively noisy site after the increase in motorised traffic, required massive improvements or, ideally, replacement. Amidst endless wrangling about the estimated £100,000 cost of a new hospital and the potential humiliation of failing to raise it, the Governors and Town Council were relieved when a wealthy resident, Mrs Ella Rowcroft, donated £8,000 to purchase a large site. In 1925, with just a further £16,000 raised locally, Mrs Rowcroft donated the full £100,000. Her only stipulation was the town boosted the hospital's Endowment Fund. She gave a further £6,500 so that the hospital chapel could be staffed by a Church of England chaplain 'free from the teachings of the Anglo-Catholic Church and the Roman Catholic Church.' Not surprisingly her offer was accepted, and she laid the foundation stone in June 1926. (see picture on page 45). In an imaginative gesture, the architect, builders and other donors paid for 21 tiled panels featuring nursery rhymes to adorn the new children's ward. The town's Endowment Fund reached a healthy £40,000 by the time the hospital opened in September 1928. Mrs Rowcroft dedicated the hospital to her parents. Her brother was Sir Edward Chaning Wills, and their father was Sir Edward Payson Wills (1834-1910), a director of the Imperial Tobacco Company.[27]

The 'Bowring' Children's Ward in the Royal Devon & Exeter Hospital, 1928. (Mark Ware: RD&E Hospital Annual Report 1929: Courtesy of Devon & Exeter Institution Trustees).

In January 1920 the Royal Devon & Exeter Hospital launched a campaign for £33,000 to build and equip a Victory Wing adding 100 beds to the 200 currently available. As a ward would be temporarily reserved for discharged soldiers the Ministry of Pensions gave £2,000 to add to the £2,000 donated by Sir Edward Chaning Wills and £10,000 from the British Red Cross Society. Nevertheless the remaining money was a tall order on top of the hospital's running costs of £20,000 a year. Costs were not helped by the average stay of each patient being 30 days – a not unusual time in this era when bedrest rather than 'getting up and about' was the norm. The Governors came close to thinking they had overstretched themselves as the Victory Wing costs progressively exceeded the estimates, and drug prices were rising, and staff salaries needed improving. Some emergency fund raising ideas were sought, and these included asking twenty key supporters to raise £100 each. Several hundred pounds were raised by a massive day long carnival in St Thomas in Exeter in November 1920 embracing various public sports, a minstrel show, numerous 'Old English Fair' sideshows, and an evening carnival procession of tableaus on lorries and carts. It was repeated the following year.[28] Amidst all the fund raising, including a vast bazaar in Exeter full of items donated by county dignitaries, the Victory Wing was opened in June 1922. A justified obsession with hygiene meant all internal corners were curved and traditional brass fittings abandoned.[29]

Many RD&E annual reports have survived, and they reveal the extent of community efforts on the hospital's behalf. Here, as elsewhere, in-patient numbers were constantly rising – to 3,471 in 1928. Ominously, the total included 335 road accident cases. Nevertheless voluntary support that year through money and goods easily matched the £12,818 paid in fees by patients and insurance companies, and did so every year. Legacies raised £4,800, donations £3,750, the Alexandra Rose Day £500, St Thomas Carnival £340, Hospital Sunday £50, firms' collections £219, collecting boxes in hotels, shops, public houses and around the hospital £203, subscribers' purchase of 'recommend tickets' 845gns, several hundred church and chapel collections £1,450, and 'entertainments' such as fêtes, carnivals, whist drives and dances £1,912. In addition each annual report listed many hundreds of gifts of eggs, meat, seasonal fruit and vegetables, tea, sweets, sheets and pillows, toys and games, books and magazines. The hospital also kept alive the pre-war tradition of local egg collecting on its behalf, and at Easter 1920, for example, it set a target of 12,000 for immediate use or preserving. Well-wishers in schools, churches and firms across the county set to work, and the huge egg collections lasted throughout the decade. In 1928 well over 20,000 were collected.[30]

As medical knowledge advanced, hospitals were keen, even vied, to keep up to date. For centuries TB had debilitated and killed countless people, especially young men and women in the supposed prime of their lives. Although Robert Koch had identified the tubercle bacillus in 1882, and the BCG vaccine was being perfected in the 1920s, the main treatment was the patient's isolation in a sanatorium under a regime of rest, good food, clean air and chest exercises. In post-war Devon great efforts were made by the combined forces of medical practitioners, local authorities and insurance companies to isolate sufferers, using the force of law if necessary, in the sanatoriums at Smyrna in Torquay, Didworthy on Dartmoor near South Brent, Ivybank in Exeter, Hawkmoor outside Bovey Trace, Bolham outside Tiverton, and Hawley House in Barnstaple. The latter two used converted army huts fitted with extra windows and wide open verandahs.[31] As Devon found out, many men returning from active service were sufferers – at least 397 according to a county report early in 1920.[32] The sanatoriums, just like the government funded war hospitals, counted on local events to provide 'extras' such as books, games, and gramophones and records. Voluntary efforts, including those by patients and their families, meant a new children's ward and schoolroom could be added to Hawkmoor in 1927.[33] And all the time district medical officers' reports and speeches constantly pointed to the dirty homes, unboiled milk, piles of refuse and the habit of spitting as the lairs of the deadly TB bacillus in waiting.[34]

Hospital Sunday procession leaves Exeter Cathedral after the special service. (Mark Ware: WT 18 October 1929: Courtesy of Devon & Exeter Institution Trustees).

The verandah at Bolham TB Hospital.
(Mark Ware: WT 8 July 1921: Courtesy of Devon & Exeter Institution Trustees).

Cancer was the other great horror, with Dr Adkins, the County Medical Officer, reporting a rising death rate from it.[35] In 1920 Newton Abbot Hospital acknowledged its good fortune when several large donations enabled it to instal an X-ray machine and begin radium treatment.[36] By 1924 the hospital saw itself as a pioneer in cancer treatment and used a combination of scare tactics – 'In its ravages it attacks all ages and classes' – and reassurance that radium treatment has 'gratifying results' to raise £15,000 for further supplies of radium and treatment rooms along with new sanitation systems. All this had been achieved by 1927 when the Prince of Wales opened the extensions.[37] In 1925 Exeter's Civic Hall hosted an elaborately staged three day County Fair in October 1925 with thousands of pounds as its target to instal radium treatment in other hospitals, notably the RD&E. As with many such events the advertisements highlighted the important figures who would be attending – in this case Earl Fortescue, Lady Seymour, Lady Clinton, Sir Robert Newman MP and most of the county's mayors.[38]

The demands on hospitals were relentless with the wider recognition that they could actually treat, or at least relieve, more and more ailments successfully. The experiences of thousands of servicemen had largely confirmed it.[39] In 1928 the RD&E discharged 3,062 of its 3471 in-patients 'Cured & Relieved'. Of the remainder 185 died, 202 were long term patients and 22 discharged themselves.[40] In addition an increasing number of people with little money became able to secure admission for treatment through subscribers' 'recommends', by possessing state or friendly society

Hospital collection during the 1920 Tiverton Carnival. (Mark Ware: WT 15 October 1920: Courtesy of Devon & Exeter Institution Trustees).

insurance certificates, or in the last resort gaining permission from Poor Law Guardians who sometimes paid for their patients to have operations in better equipped hospitals. This growth, and conversely the provision of relatively costly private beds, meant that hospitals increasingly catered for people of all social classes, although no doubt with varying degrees of respect and comfort. In Tiverton, for example, the hospital in Bampton Street developed gradually from being a day dispensary in the late nineteenth century to provide wards for in-patients, fit surgical appliances, operate on accident cases, and conduct X-ray treatment. In 1928 it had 26 'free' and 5 private beds, and was proud that recent donations had paid for electric lighting and a wireless system complete with patients' headphones. Now it hoped that the new contributory scheme whereby single people paid 2d a week, and families 4d, would ensure financial stability. Typically, the scheme provided 'free' care up to 2/-d a day together with X-rays, massage and electrical treatment, and the services of an ambulance. However the hospital still needed Tiverton's streets to be packed for the annual 'Hospital Week' carnival with its many sideshows and musical events.[41]

Mothers and babies: the recognition of need

For many decades the appalling rate of infant mortality across the nation had been widely known but largely seen as an inevitable part of the human condition. In addition, many middle class commentators were too ready to assume poor families were careless families, and to associate impoverished surroundings with dirt and contagion because mothers were feckless and ignorant rather than striving against impossible odds. In 1914 some Devon districts, but far from all, had trained midwives, and some parishes had lying-in charities or blanket clubs, but other than destitute women, usually single, who gave birth in workhouse infirmaries or charitable hostels, babies were born at home amidst all the risks the homes might present. It took the First World War to engender a belated admiration of working class families for their sacrifices and powers of endurance, and also a fearful recognition that the defence of the nation and its Empire required future generations to be as numerous and as fit as possible.[42] A seminal event was a Scott's Emulsion advertisement in September 1916 stating that the number of infants dying each year was equivalent to four army corps. In confirmation the NSPCC (National Society for the Prevention of Cruelty to Children) calculated that 109,725 British men had been killed in the first 13 months of the war but during that time 140,370 babies had died.[43]

The resulting pressure from newspapers, medical officers, and influential families such as the Astors, led to the creation of several wartime day nurseries and maternity clinics in Plymouth and Exeter, and then in Barnstaple and other towns. They were served and supplied by volunteers but also received local authority advice and support. However the day nurseries failed to survive the war. Although Devon's Women's Citizenship Association fought for their survival to fill the two year gap between the maternity clinics and full time schooling their hopes were frustrated by the post-war depression.[44] The clinics, however, prospered throughout the 1920s complementing the wider efforts of local authorities to improve public health by eradicating soil closets, polluted water courses and unhygienic milking parlours and dairies.[45]

Gradually the voluntary groups, health visitors, school nurses and medical officers created networks of support and publicity that led mothers to trust the clinics, and not feel demeaned by them. In January 1919, for example welcoming tea parties were held at the St Sidwell and Heavitree Maternity and Child Welfare Clinics in Exeter. In December Father Christmas gave 130 children tea, chocolates and extra clothing at Exeter's Magdalen Street Clinic.[46] In 1920-21 the donations that supported Exeter's clinics diminished in the depression but the determined use of Flag Days by dozens of supporters kept them solvent. They served over 500 families. A report the following year recorded the significant pockets of poverty in central Exeter, notably the West Quarter's crowded tenements, where mothers benefited from the council's free milk, the Lying In Charity, and well-wishers gifts of grocery tickets and linen.[47] Exeter's Nursing Association, historically funded by voluntary contributions but supplemented in recent years by public grants, was closely linked to the city's new maternity home and training school for midwives. A high moral tone prevailed. In 1922 a Lying In Charity speaker said the maternity home gave mothers the determination 'to try to lead cleaner, healthier and better lives.' And in 1923 a Nursing Association speaker claimed there was 'no more noble work than the alleviation of suffering in homes where the inmates, through circumstances over which they had no control, could not possibly provide proper nursing or other arrangements.'[48]

The Maternity & Child Welfare Act of 1918 obliged local authorities to survey local facilities and remedy inadequacies, and Devon County Council found it had many gaps in both midwife and clinic provision. There were just 14 maternity and child welfare clinics, and 107 parishes were without access to a trained midwife.[49] Networks were taking shape though. In January 1919 Torquay's Clinic Committee agreed to liaise closely with the School Medical Officer to ensure children were fit to start school.[50] A few years later Barnstaple's Medical Officer praised the close links between its Maternity and School clinics; it helped that they were in the same building.[51] However, 'national efficiency' – the maintenance of a healthy race to ensure British supremacy – was everything, and sometimes genuine sympathy for the mothers seemed in short supply. In January 1919 a new clinic opened in Totnes. During the ceremony the County Superintendent, Miss Booker, revealed her lingering Victorian perspectives in a speech that lamented the 12% of babies who grew up weak and undersized to 'be a burden on some one', and 'the heaps of homes' with grossly inadequate mothers.[52] Motherhood was now tantamount to national service. At the opening of Torquay's third clinic in March 1919 Dr Dunlop, the borough medical officer, stated 'when they considered the great number of lives lost in the terrible war, it was the duty of every parent to endeavour to bring up their children in an absolutely healthy condition.'[53] A few months later a speaker from the Children's Era Movement urged clinics to embrace the moral as well as hygienic training of children – as they, being British, are the future leaders of the world.'[54] Whatever the motives, the overall policy was successful. In November 1921 Sir Napier Burnett, a distinguished obstetrician, gave a speech in Exeter that highlighted the achievement of clinics in 'imparting knowledge to mothers' and reducing the national death rate of children under the age of one from 140 to 80 per thousand between 1913 and 1920.[55] Tiverton's medical officer concurred. The borough's clinic provided maternity classes and cheap clothing, tooth brushes, milk, Ovaltine and Virol He believed that the 16 babies who died in 1920 did so from imperfect prenatal development, infantile convulsions, pneumonia or septic meningitis, but not maternal 'mismanagement and neglect.'[56]

Galas and fêtes raising funds for hospitals often incorporated Baby Shows and 'Bonny Baby' Competitions. Local doctors were usually among the judges, and took it as a tribute to the new generation of trained midwives, health visitors, and clinic staff that so many proud mothers and healthy babies were on display.[57] In July 1920 Sidmouth's clinics received fulsome praise when 27 of the 90 babies at a Baby Show received full or very high marks 'and the rest (with few exceptions) were highly creditable specimens.'[58] Often proud mothers would see their names recorded in the local newspaper.

However Dr Adkins, the County Medical Officer, was less sure of universal success. In September 1922 he lamented the deaths of 30 mothers and 500 babies 'sacrificed every year in this County to what should be preventable causes.' Not surprisingly local newspapers made much of this apparent slur on local efforts. A *Western Times* headline questioned 'What's Wrong With Devon?' but irate county aldermen and councillors preferred to ask what was wrong with their chief medical officer. Earl Fortescue was Chairman of the Maternity & Child Welfare Committee, and with his wife had done much during the war to promote grants to the Nursing Association and maternity clinics. He said Adkins had given 'a very false impression.' He pointed out that Devon's infant death rate of 62 per thousand births was way below the national average of 83, and 'it was simply absurd to imagine they could have 7,658 confinements without a certain number of casualties.'[59] Nevertheless a flurry of public letters claimed infantile TB sprang from district councils failing to condemn filthy cow sheds and milking

Mothers and babies at Meshaw Hospital Fête Baby Show, 1926. (Beaford Old Archive images: © Beaford Arts).

parlours, and blamed the deaths of mothers and babies on the appalling housing conditions about which too little had been done. Adkins remained unabashed, and speaking at Honiton's new clinic a month later, he strongly implied that Devon's councils could do much better.[60]

Whether deliberately or not, Adkins raised the profile of public health and (as we saw in Chapter Three) local newspapers gave extensive coverage in October 1922 to the Women's Local Government Society's national conference in Exeter. It was a seminal county event and seized by campaigners. Here Dr Adkins and Dr Stirk, his city counterpart, were guest speakers detailing the roles of good housing and pure milk in promoting family health. There were many women speakers from Devon – notably Juanita Phillips on the state's responsibility to mothers, Alice Vlieland on educating public opinion on the purity of milk and combating TB, Clara Andrew on child adoption, Edith Splatt on the dangers inherent in fostering, Mrs Roberts on the problems of boarding out pauper children with local families, and Mrs Kitson and Mrs Shave on 'rescuing' unmarried mothers. After covering the controversy and the conference the *Western Times* carried the provocative headline: 'CALL TO THE WOMEN OF DEVON: Their Help Never More Necessary Than Now'.[61] In March 1927 Dr Adkins opened the county's 26th maternity and child welfare clinic in South Molton. It, too, was supported by both voluntary and public funds, and the mayor acknowledged the central work of local women, including the mayoress, health visitor and district nurse, in securing its foundation.[62]

Those on the edge

Attitudes towards single women expecting babies often remained punitive but there was a slowly growing sense that although they could never shake off the humiliation of their situation society must support some degree of rehabilitation and not degrade them further. The 1920s saw a greater degree of cooperation than hitherto between the police, magistrates, church missioners and volunteer 'rescue workers' to give vulnerable women shelter, care and advice. In Exeter, for example, St Olave's Home, founded by the Church of England in the previous century, took in pregnant women while St Elizabeth's Home, grant-aided by the post war Ministry of Health cared for women with venereal diseases. The police and magistrates were reluctant to use prisons or workhouses in such cases, and as Miss Sharpe, a missioner, claimed of St Olave's, 'None are too good and none too bad to be taken in', and Bishop Cecil added rather vaguely, 'I think the guiltiness lies very largely on the whole of Society.'[63] Reports revealed both homes were in great demand, and parishes were urged to devote collections to them. During 1921 58 women stayed at St Olave's and 63 at St Elizabeth's.[64] In a significant display of patrician charity in 1921 a group of prominent women in Exeter raised funds by organising a costume doll competition and follow-up exhibition. It was hosted by Lady Davy of Southernhay House whose husband, Sir Henry Davy was a distinguished physician and Chairman of the Diocesan Association for the Care of Friendless Girls.[65]

There were at least a dozen other charitable 'homes of mercy' across the county.[66] For example, churches and chapels together with magistrates and the police cooperated with the North Devon Association for the Help and Protection of Girls vigorously led by Countess Fortescue and two local JPs – Mrs Brannam and Miss Adams. Its shelter was kept busy, as were its rescue staff. At Ilfracombe watch was kept for young girls arriving alone by ship. The Association's meetings often had visiting speakers, and a common theme was the danger posed to young women by the far greater freedom they possessed during the war, and now after it, then ever they did before it. Not surprisingly they found it easy to blame the modern world with its 'flimsy fashions', salacious films and racy novels that 'were turning girls' heads' and ensuring the 'want of romance was the cause of many tragedies.'[67]

The *Devon & Somerset News* offered advice, but unfortunately sometimes contradictory, in its new *Whispers for Women* column. In March 1921 it strongly advised mothers not to let their daughters stay in hotels by themselves, or go to dances, restaurants or the theatre with a man they had not vetted first. It ended ominously, saying 'A maiden can so easily lose the fresh bloom of her femininity, which is, after all, the chief charm of a woman.' Conversely, a few months later the column avidly defended the modern young woman's desire for freedom as just and right.[68]

In June 1925 the County Education Committee suffered an alarm when a report by Dr Corkery, a district school medical officer, supported the persistent early twentieth century worries about 'national degeneration' by claiming Devon's rural children were degenerating into lowly C3 specimens of physical and mental health. When questioned by a special sub-committee he stood firm on his assertions that inter-marriage, the migration of fit and healthy families out of villages, and the drift into them of urban 'weaklings' and 'misfits', were major contributory factors. Committee members were divided in their opinions, but a substantial number agreed with Corkery. They were not alone as across the nation eugenists were at the height of their influence arguing that only selective breeding could save the nation from degeneration. By implication, Corkery's report suggested many Devon villagers should be discouraged from having children. After a confused, and clearly embarrassing debate, Corkery's report was formally accepted, but never re-examined.[69]

The Barnardo's girls from Exeter who were 'received' at Buckingham Palace. (Mark Ware: WT 13 April 1923: Courtesy of Devon & Exeter Institution Trustees).

There were other, and more readily acceptable, ways of dealing with children who were burdens on communities. In April 1923 four uniformed girls from the Barnardo's Home in Exeter had the honour of being 'received' at Buckingham Palace prior to their emigration to Canada.[70] They came from the orphanage at 13–14 Clifton Street that housed 50 girls aged between six and fifteen, and they followed thousands of orphans who had been sent over many decades by various charities to uncertain and sometimes perilous futures with foster parents and employers in Canada and Australia. The voyages seemed a sound way to ease the problem of the poor while stocking the colonies, providing labour and offering a chance of advancement. The shocking reports of cruelty and mismanagement had led to some improvement in placements and monitoring procedures before the war, but, as much later twentieth century revelations unearthed, there remained many opportunities for abuse.[71]

In 1924 the assiduous Dr Adkins came up with a cost-effective treatment plan for crippled children. He found Devon had 400 cases within the school age range and 200 below it. Most were suffering from TB, rickets and paralysis, and he believed 80% of cases were curable if treated early. He cited Shropshire's example where children had short stays in hospital for the compilation of treatment plans which were then carried out by specialist orthopaedic 'travelling nurses' at home or in welfare clinics. The County Council concurred, and offered to pay administrative costs and patients' fees.[72] Once again the voluntary principle came into play, with Lady Clinton and Dame Georgiana Buller addressing public meetings and having little difficulty in engaging influential supporters, such as Major General Sir Robert Jones, a key orthopaedic surgeon. By the end of 1925 a site had been donated in Exeter and £5,000 raised, primarily through the promoters' aristocratic and civic contacts, including Sir James Owen, the newspaper proprietor and ex-mayor of Exeter who ensured maximum publicity.[73] Throughout 1926 many Devon mayors hosted balls, schools sponsored 'cots', churches and chapels earmarked collections, and communities organised yet more fêtes, dances, and whist drives.[74] In November a lavish County Bazaar in Exeter raised £1,000. It was opened by the Duchess of Somerset and attended by the Amorys, Caves, Clintons, Ferguson-Davies, Owens and Peeks. Sir George Newman, Chief Medical Officer to the Board of Education and Ministry of Health, gave a speech of support. However, he came close to saying cripples were not 'citizens'. A crippled life, he asserted, was a wasted life as it was not productive, and 'unless they saved these children when they were young and mended them, we were going to pay for them all through their lives.'[75] By January 1927 £15,000 of the £18,000 target had been raised.[76]

The new orthopaedic 'hospital school' was opened on Gras Lawn by the Duchess of York on 16 November 1927 and named after her daughter Princess Elizabeth. It had voluntary status, but was recognised by the Ministry of Health and Board of Education, supported financially by the Local Authorities, and worked closely with the orthopaedic clinics established in local towns that were visited regularly by specialist staff from Exeter. VAD staff were employed as assistants, and transport was provided by ambulances and private volunteers. Dame Georgiana Buller who had been instrumental in the campaign became chairman of its trust.[77] It was busy from the outset, not only in formulating treatment plans, training more staff and supplying orthopaedic appliances, but also in training patients in vocational skills, and – a key aim – finding paid employment for at least some of them.[78]

Other wealthy philanthropists were still to be found. In the middle of the decade Mr Robert Living provided a children's convalescence home in a mansion facing the sea amidst spacious gardens between Lynmouth and Lynton. With honorary visiting doctors, well-respected local families administering it, and a corps of paid nurses and domestic staff, the home catered for 24 children at a time and was an instant and lasting success.[79]

Workhouses and their infirmaries: the end in sight

The *British Medical Journal*'s exposure of workhouse infirmary shortcomings in the 1890s meant that by 1914 most Devon Boards of Guardians had built new well-equipped hospitals adjacent to their workhouses, but carefully separated from them. All Boards had to find adequately skilled doctors and trained nurses. In the early twentieth century various benefits provided by traditional Friendly Societies were increasingly complemented by government pension, unemployment, health insurance and sickness benefit schemes, and this meant workhouses became mainly the preserve of the elderly infirm, people with severe mental health issues, some unmarried mothers, and the evening intake of vagrants. Alongside them were a few families caught by the depression and obliged to enter workhouses temporarily, and sometimes magistrates had little choice but to commit deserted mothers and neglected children to the care of Boards of Guardians.[80] Most other claimants on the Guardians' purse stayed outside the workhouse and received 'out-relief' payments after due investigation of their circumstances. Soon after the war the unpalatable word 'Workhouse' was replaced by the slightly less off-putting 'Institution'. For the sake of clarity, however, they are referred to as 'workhouses' throughout this chapter.

However Guardians viewed single able-bodied male applicants with great suspicion, thinking that their lack of unemployment benefits, or if their entitlement to them was exhausted, meant they were habitually unwilling to work. Exeter's Guardians put such men to work within the workhouse or in its adjacent brickyard and they were paid in cash or kind, usually grocery tickets, but well below the city's average weekly wage of 32/-.[81] Sometimes suspicions were justified, and sometimes not. In September 1922 three dozen angry members of Newton Abbot Unemployed Association invaded a Board of Guardians meeting and after a verbally bruising encounter the local relief rates were raised. However, at 10/- a week for an adult and between 4/- and 6/- for each child they remained well below average wages. A few months later the Guardians clawed back payments from the claimants they found benefiting from other schemes.[82]

Alongside the harsher aspects of workhouse life, the Victorian custom of well-wishers ensuring inmates had a hearty Christmas dinner and tea, and presents of tobacco, beer and sweets, continued across Devon well into the 1920s.[83] Christmas Day 1922 was the first time men, women and children had eaten together in Tiverton Workhouse. Hitherto families had been kept apart, even on the rare festive occasions.[84] For some, there was a summer trip, usually to the seaside. In June 1926 the 150 inmates at Barnstaple enjoyed a trip to Combe Martin and a strawberry tea.[85] However the cautionary note sounded by the Poor Law Inspector visiting Guardians in Bideford and Newton

Map showing Exeter Workhouse and the early twentieth century detached infirmary. The workhouse has gone but the infirmary remains in use as a hospital.
(1906 Ordnance Survey map).

Abbot in 1923 still held firm that life in workhouses must not be too comfortable, even for children, as inmates would want to return 'and have everything done for them.'[86]

Few children resided in workhouses in the 1920s. Some were 'boarded out' with approved families, but the practice caused endless problems for everyone concerned – for vulnerable and difficult children, for the reputations of families coping with them, and for Guardians faced with investigating unpalatable issues in the full glare of publicity. As late as 1923 Dr Ley, a vigilant Newton Abbot guardian, thought many boarded out children became no more than 'poor little slaves' of the adults with whom they lived.[87] Other children lived in 'Scattered Homes' where a dozen or so children lived with care staff under the overall authority of Guardians, but they too were exposed to adverse publicity when – as in Barnstaple in 1921 – children ran away and staff were suspected of cruelty.[88] Interestingly, in 1923 37 pauper children in Tiverton were moved from an old house in Shillingford to completely renovated premises in Uffculme, where at school, said one visitor, their cleanliness compared well with the dirty village children.[89]

Vagrants were the bane of Guardians' lives. Where possible they were housed in 'casual wards' away from other inmates. Conditions remained relatively harsh, and sympathy was thin on the ground, but as the decade wore on even some Guardians raised questions about the inadequate heating and sanitation, leaking roofs, lack of hot water, filthy bedding, and overcrowding.[90] Differentiating between the 'professional tramp' and genuine migrants seeking work, such as on the new Torrington to Halwill railway, was often difficult. Embarrassingly for Guardians, as we have seen, some vagrants turned out to be ex-servicemen while others pretended to be by wearing purloined medals and trying to convince workhouse staff they were disabled. A few had children with them. Between 1919 and 1922 daily admissions trebled, and Guardians everywhere fretted about the cost of bread and cheese for vagrants, and their reluctance to undertake the customary breaking of stones (for road repairs) or chopping of logs in return for their board and meals.[91] In 1926 the exasperated Devon Vagrancy Committee believed thousands of vagrants were 'crawling over the county and getting food.'[92] In 1927 Tiverton's Guardians, nearly overwhelmed with around 55 vagrants a night,

The Mayoress of Barnstaple visits children in a 'Scattered Home' at Christmas. (Mark Ware: WT 20 January 1922; Courtesy of Devon & Exeter Institution Trustees).

thought most of them should be sent to domestic 'labour colonies'. Possibly the pioneering pre-war colonies of the Salvation Army – rather than memories of the notorious convict colonies – had given them the idea. To some extent Tiverton got its way as in 1930 an empty mansion at Blackborough was opened as a residential training centre for young vagrants.[93]

Boards of Guardians were also guardians of district rates, and were forever balancing their views on appropriate expenditure on poor relief – which was not always mean-spirited – with local public opinion which could easily accuse them of extravagance. It was the Guardians' susceptibility to the swirling currents of rate-payers' views and erupting scandals that contributed to bringing the whole system into disrepute and ripe for abolition at the end of the decade.[94] In January 1920 Exeter's MP, Sir Robert Newman, publicly denounced district Boards of Guardians as too small for the establishment of an equitable system across the county, and workhouses as too large and inflexible for housing elderly people.[95] In common with many reformers he agreed with Christopher Addison, the Minister of Health, that county councils should take over all aspects of what was being called Public Assistance. Not surprisingly most Boards disagreed with him. Newton Abbot's chairman asserted that locally elected people knew what was best for the local people who fell on hard times. He claimed county councillors were already overworked, and distant officials could never act as 'lovingly, carefully, and tenderly as Guardians.' His colleagues wholeheartedly agreed.[96] The tide of opinion, however, was against such a view. A ex-inmate's convincing pen picture of life in Tiverton's workhouse published in 1926 praised the institution's staff and cleanliness but recorded the frequent 'anxiety', 'melancholia' and 'irritability' brought on by the relentless monotony, and all-pervading sense of incarceration and helplessness.[97] In 1925, and again in 1929, Bishop Cecil of Exeter had no compunction about declaring the Poor Law to be 'harsh', its officialdom 'profligate', its uneven interpretation of regulations 'unfair', its end products 'hardened outcasts', and its abhorrent Victorian stigma beyond redemption.[98]

Tiverton workhouse. (Courtesy of Tiverton Museum).

Speaking in Newton Abbot in 1926 a Poor Law Inspector conceded the bishop's final point. Perhaps he felt free to do so as the previous year the government had outlined its proposals to transfer responsibility for public assistance and health care to county councils.[99]

The change of responsibilities had began as early as 1921 when Crediton's Board of Guardians agreed that part of its underused workhouse could become a county council mental hospital, and soon afterwards workhouse wards at Newton Abbot and Barnstaple were similarly reserved.[100] In 1921 Honiton's Guardians voted to open up its well-equipped infirmary and maternity ward to paying patients, primarily those in insurance schemes.[101] Honiton's medical officer initially sought the use of the lying-in ward and its staff partly because the town's Nursing Association persistently refused to attend the confinement of single mothers. In a celebrated case the Association only backed down when threatened with the loss of all grants by the Minister of Health.[102]

Board of Guardians across Devon held their last, and highly emotional and self-congratulatory, meetings in 1930, although some members were soon elected to the new larger public assistance committees.[103] The County Medical Officer's team had already surveyed all the workhouses to identify new uses for them, notably as public hospitals, mental health institutions, and homes for the elderly. They would be under county council control. However there was much to do. The report was alarming.[104] It criticised the inadequate categorisation of 'mental defectives' across the county, and found many 'ordinary' inmates, especially elderly ones, suffering from severe mental illnesses and without any form of remedial treatment. Many workhouses were in a poor state of repair, and the report itemised the high windows no-one could see out of, the dangerously worn flagstone floors, the rough unplastered walls, the inadequate number of toilets and baths, the obsolete laundries, the absence of central heating, and the prison-like outside walls.

However ten workhouses possessed entirely separate infirmaries, and these were deemed suitable for speedy renovation and use as general or specialised hospitals. The report recommended that infirmaries in Axminster, Crediton, Honiton, Okehampton, Plympton, South Molton, Tavistock, Torrington and Totnes could become specialist institutions for various grades of mental defectives, and some had further space for the physically infirm elderly. Barnstaple, Newton Abbot and Tiverton infirmaries were deemed fit for the elderly, and probably also maternity cases. Bideford and St Thomas were earmarked as maternity and general hospitals, and Holsworthy could become a home for either children or old people. Kingsbridge was in such a poor state that no recommendation was made. In all cases some adjacent buildings would be converted for accommodation for medical staff, but it was thought that much of the fabric of the workhouses should be removed. The report decided that eleven of the twelve children's homes – six of them in Newton Abbot – were good enough to continue in operation. Only Barnstaple's home was condemned as having 'the atmosphere of an Institution.' The workhouses infirmaries in Exeter and Plymouth became city hospitals in 1930, although both had significantly widened their patient intake several years earlier. While all these changes were taking the buildings took on new identities as part of a county wide reorganisation of medical and welfare facilities – but to many families they still looked like workhouses, and no doubt felt like them inside.

REFERENCES

1. *TT* 18 April 1919, www.nationalgeographic.com/history/Spanish_Flu

2. *WT* 9, 18, 19, 21, 22, 24 & 25 October 1918, 1, 12, 13 & 22 November 1918, 6 December 1918, 7 & 23 March 1919, *NDH* 13 March 1919

3. *WT* 26 January 1922, 24 February 1922, 2 March 1922

4. *WT* 9 October 1918

5. *NDH* 7 August 1919

6. *WT* 2 November 1918; *CC* 26 October 1918

7. *WT* 7 February 1919, 9 February 1922, 19 January 1923

8. *TG* 28 March 19819, Pugh, M., *We Danced All Night*, pp5-6

9. *WT* 29 January 1920

10. Parker. D., *Edwardian Devon*, pp146-173, Pugh, M., op.cit., p55

11. Caldwell, J., (1972) 'The History of Dean Clarke's Hospital' in *Rep.Trans.Devon.Ass.*104 1972 pp175-192

12. *WT* 28 February 1919

13. Bolt, B., *The Hospitals & Asylums of Devon*, p10

14. *WT* 30 November 1920

15. *DG* 2 & 16 August 1919, *WT* 30 May 1921, 18 November 1921

16. *WT* 28 January 1921, *MDA* 16 February 1924

17. *WT* 31 January 1919

18. *WT* 19 September 1919

19. Sutton, C.M. (1986) *Axminster Hospital 1866-1986*

20. *WT* 2 November 1918

21. *WT* 4 May 1923, 3 July 1925, 25 June 1926, 5 July 1929

22. *WT* 10 August 1921

23. *NDJ* 19 January 1922, 23 March 1922, 13 April 1922, 10 August 1922

24. *WT* 13 April 1923, 27 August 1926, *NDJ* 30 July 1925, 3 September 1925

25. *TG* 28 February 1919, 24 March 1921, 6 May 1921, 9 September 1921, 17 September 1926

26. Teignmouth Museum hospital file, *WT* 2 July 1920

27. Payne, F.J. *The History of Torbay Hospital 1844-1980*

28. *WT* 29 January 1920, 21 February 1920, 30 July 1920, 29 October 1920, 4 November 1920, 18 October 1921

29. *WT* 20 June 1922

30. DHC 1260F/O/HA/33-59 RD&E Annual Statements, *WT* 20 April 1920, 9 May 1924, 24 February 1925, 14 April 1927

31. DHC DCC Public Health & Housing Committee 16/6/21; *CC* 13 March 1920, *MDA* 17 March 1923, *WT* 5 December 1919, 15 October 1920, 24 March 1921

32. *WT* 5 March 1920

33. *D&SN* 6 October 1927

34. *WO* 13 May 1920

35. *WT* 17 July 1925

36. *WT* 31 January 1920

37. *MDA* 26 July 1924, 5 December 1925, 11 June 1927

38. *WT* 9 & 16 October 1925

39. Pugh, M., op. cit., pp41-51

40. DHC 1260F/O/HA/59 RD&E Annual Statement 1929, p31

41. *D&SN* 15 October 1925, 3 May 1928

42. Degroot, G., op. cit., pp214-223, Renwick, C., op. cit., pp97-125

43. *WEH* 5 September 1916; Parker, D., *The People of Devon in the First World War*, pp160-161

44. *WT* 18 January 1919

45. *TG* 8 June 1923, 9 April 1925, *WT* 4 April 1924

46. *WT* 13 January 1919, 29 January 1920

47. *WT* 8 October 1921, 6 May 1922

48. *WT* 9 May 1922, 4 May 1923

49. DHC DCC Child Welfare Committee 13 March 1919

50. *WT* 8 January 1919

51. *NDJ* 12 July 1923

52. *WT* 29 January 1919

53. *TT* 23 March 1919

54. *WT* 1 December 1920

55. *WT* 5 November 1921

56. *WO* 12 May 1921

57. Viz Ottery WI Fête – *WT* 19 June 1921, Bovey Tracey Carnival – *WT* 18 November 1921

58. *WT* 30 July 1920

59. *WT* 29 September 1922

60. *WT* 6 October 1922

61. *WT* 13 October 1922

62. *WT* 4 March 1927

63. *WT* 21 April 1921

64. *WT* 21 February 1920, 27 April 1922

65. *WT* 27 May 1921

66. www.childrenshomes.org.uk/list/Devon.shtml

67. *NDH* 24 July 1924, *NDJ* 25 July 1925, 18 February 1926, 7 October 1926,

68. *D&SN* 18 March 1921, 6 April 1922

69. Overy, R., *The Morbid Age*, pp93-135, *WT* 6 February 1925

70. *WT* 13 April 1923

71. See canadianbritishhomechildren.weebly.com

72. *WT* 20 June 1924, 6 & 27 November 1925

73. *D&SN* 10 December 1925, *WT* 11 December 1925

74. *WT* 1 April 1926, 19 November 1926, 14 January 1927

75. *WT* 19 November 1926

76. *WT* 21 January 1927

77. *WT* 4 March 1927

78. *WT* 25 July 1930

79. *NDJ* 12 June 1924, 2 April 1925, 26 July 1928

80. *WT* 20 April 1920, 21 January 1921

81. *WT* 26 April 1922, 27 May 1922

82. *WT* 22 September 1922, 23 February 1923

83. *NDJ* 10 January 1924, 5 & 19 January 1928, *WT* 28 December 1921

84. *D&SN* 28 December 1922

85. *WT* 25 June 1926

86. *MDA* 20 January 1923, WT 4 May 1923

87. *MDA* 27 January 1923

88. *NDJ* 14 July 1921, 8 September 1921

89. *D&SN* 4 October 1923, 4 September 1924; *WO* 27 September 1923

90. *TG* 23 November 1923; *NDJ* 7 & 21 February 1924, *WT* 18 January 1929

91. *WT* 3 July 1920, 16 & 29 August 1921, 15 June 1923, 15 February 1924

92. *WT* 18 June 1926

93. *D&SN* 20 January 1927, 5 June 1930

94. *NDJ* 27 February 1919, 11 March 1920, *WT* 23 December 1919, 5 March 1920

95. *WT* 20 January 1920

96. *WT* 10 March 1921, see St Thomas *WT* 14 May 1926; Tiverton *D&SN* 10 June 1926

97. *D&SN* 7 January 1916

98. *WT* 24 April 1925, 12 June 1925, 22 February 1929

99. *MDA* 20 March 1926, *WT* 11 December 1925

100. DHC Crediton PLU/36 Guardians' Minute Book (GMB) 27/3/20, Tiverton PLU/1 GMB various entries 1921; *WT* 29 March 1921

101. DHC PLU Honiton PLU/5 GMB 15/4/21; *WT* 15 July 1920, 5 September 1921

102. *WT* 15 November 1921

103. *WT* 14, 21 & 28 March 1930, 2 May 1930

104. Devon & Exeter Institution, *DCC Report of the County Medical Officer on the General Condition, Accommodation & Future Use of Institutions handed over to the County Council in pursuant of the Local Government Act 1929*

7

CHILDREN & SCHOOLS: STRENGTHENING THE DIVIDE

The 1918 Education Act: opportunities and omissions

In 1914 educational opportunities mirrored the class divisions within British society. Indeed the Victorians and Edwardians deemed it axiomatic that gradations of wealth should be reflected in the type of education necessary for one's role and position in society – as, say, an aristocratic landowner, or a middle class professional, or a working class artisan. Fundamentally families paid for the schooling they wanted or could afford, and poorer families who could not afford to do so were provided with the type of schooling the State thought fit for them.

Families who could pay the most had access to the handful of exclusive private institutions confusingly called 'public schools' such as Eton, Rugby and Winchester but 'below' these were a host of private day or residential schools of varying cost, quality and reputation from which to choose. As long as parents paid the fees, and their children had a modicum of ability, these schools provided older pupils, notably boys, with courses preparing them for 'white collar' jobs, and entry to military and naval academies, the Civil Service, and universities. Among local examples there were St Hilda's and

Stoodleigh Court. (Author's collection).

Advertisement for the privately owned Hoe Grammar School, Plymouth. George Dymond became a Plymouth Alderman, and Frank was his son.

(Mark Ware: Kelly's Directory 1923: Courtesy of Devon & Exeter Institution Trustees).

Mount Radford in Exeter that for a time rivalled the city's Maynard's Girls' School and Exeter School for Boys in fees, courses and reputation. In north Devon West Buckland School sought to restore its fortunes by ignoring the agricultural bias over-optimistically planned by its Victorian founders – the local rector and the Fortescues of Castle Hill. In the south-east Ravenswood Preparatory School was opened in Paignton by an ex-army officer in 1921 and became successful enough to move into the aristocratic, but empty, Stoodleigh Court near Tiverton seven years later. Among the county's many ancient foundations All Hallows School in Honiton prepared the sons of middle class families for the professions and entry to major public schools.[1]

The vast majority of children attended 'elementary' schools. Some were termed 'provided' as the state wholly funded them via taxation and rates and they were maintained by County Councils and County Boroughs. Others were termed 'non-provided' as they were maintained by the Anglican parishes or Nonconformist and Roman Catholic congregations who originally founded them, although for decades they had been fortified by state grants. It was known as the 'Dual System', and the all-important difference was 'non-provided' schools could provide religious instruction according to the tenets of a particular church whereas 'provided' schools had to avoid any doctrinal bias. The schools varied in size from small pseudo-Gothic village schools nestling by the parish church with a couple of dozen children to huge two or three storied town blocks containing several hundred pupils. Elementary schools usually accepted pupils around the ages of 4 or 5 until 14, but in most counties, including Devon, local regulations allowed children to leave school at the ages of 12 or 13 if they had achieved the not-very-high average standard of work of a child of 14. As school logbooks dismally recorded, many parents needing their children's wages took full advantage of this. In rural areas many families simply ignored the attendance regulations for several days at a time at harvest time. And as many logbooks also noted, many school buildings were in a lamentable state of repair – with inadequate lamps and fires, damp floors and walls, insanitary middens for toilets, no running water, and dirt yards as playgrounds.[2]

Ever since an Education Act in 1902 County Councils and County Boroughs (such as Exeter and Plymouth) had been permitted to spend up to a 2d rate on what was termed secondary education. This was a predominantly academic education, including Classics, up to the age of 16 or 18 such as offered in those fee-paying schools generally known as grammar schools. Some of then were centuries old, and from 1902 Devon, Exeter and Plymouth chose to grant aid a dozen or so grammar schools, and Devon County Council planned as couple of new ones. All of them were small with less than 100 pupils, and attending them gave pupils, and their families, a significant measure of social prestige and unlocked doors to 'white-collar' careers. In 1907 the Board of Education said that 25% of pupils admitted to grant aided secondary schools should not pay fees. Anyone could take the scholarship examination. Children already at fee-paying schools were at a significant advantage at this examination, but a trickle of able children from elementary schools were successful in accessing council scholarships or the bursaries offered by the grammar schools themselves. However access to the tiny secondary school sector remained way beyond the reach of the vast majority of working class families. In recognition of this a few towns such as Ilfracombe, Okehampton, Plymouth and Devonport, had small 'higher elementary schools' that catered for able children unable to access secondary schools due to distance, cost or just missing scholarship standards.[3]

During the war a major Education Act battled its way through both Houses of Parliament to receive the Royal Assent on 8 August 1918. The main reason for its success lay in the determination of the new Prime Minister, David Lloyd George, back in December 1916 to stiffen national resolve in the darkest days of the war by offering ordinary families a glimmer of hope that their never-ending sacrifices would be rewarded once victory was achieved. He persuaded Herbert Fisher, the respected Vice-Chancellor of Sheffield University, to become President of the Board of Education by assuring him of the necessary political and financial support.[4]

Fisher trod positively but warily. Eschewing a ferocious wartime battle with the churches he left the Dual System untouched. And to avoid confrontation with local authorities he left the awkward administrative arrangements imposed by the 1902 Act unreformed. Devon County Council and its Education Committee possessed responsibility for 'the superintendence' of elementary education everywhere except in Barnstaple, Tiverton and Torquay. These boroughs were responsible for their own elementary schools – but not the secondary ones. The County Council was also responsible for grant aided secondary schools everywhere except in Exeter and Plymouth. These retained authority over both their elementary and secondary provision. When dealing with education all these councils were termed Local Education Authorities (LEAs).

Many reform groups had urged Fisher to make secondary education more accessible, even free and universal (as it became in 1944), but the 1918 Act was limited to removing the 2d limit on secondary education support. Instead Fisher deliberately fostered the elementary sector. His Act preferred to build on the Board's pre-war encouragement of courses enhancing the essentially utilitarian skills working class children were thought to need as future artisans, labourers, servants and parents. Fisher undoubtedly deepened and broadened the elementary school curriculum but at the expense of widening the gap between it and the academic bias prevailing in secondary grammar schools. Thus the Act banned any child from being exempted from schooling before the age of 14. LEAs were encouraged by grants, and by Board pressure, to introduce 'advanced instruction' for older boys in handicraft and gardening, and for girls in cookery, laundry work and needlecraft, although in a few *avant garde* schools girls took gardening and handicraft lessons. Further grants were available to provide playing fields and access to swimming pools. In lieu of formally expanding the prestigious secondary sector Fisher obliged all LEAs to introduce compulsory part-time 'continuation schools and classes' for elementary schoolchildren aged 14 to 16. Their syllabuses would be partly academic and partly vocationally biased towards each locality's job opportunities.[5] Naturally there were diverse views on what was necessary. In March 1919 the *Torquay Times* welcomed the Ministry of Reconstruction's Women's Advisory Commitee urging all LEAs to provide good quality grant-aided courses to encourage and train more girls to enter domestic service. The strong link between working class education and social training was exemplified in 1925 when Budleigh Salterton's Evening Continuation Classes were praised because they inculcated better quality speech and engendered 'a higher faculty of judgment' that stopped the working classes 'being swayed by the agitation of the moment.'[6]

Another key clause broadened the scope of the School Health Service. Created rather reluctantly in 1907 as a belated response to the alarming

The forbidding exterior of the Western Counties Institution at Starcross. (Author's collection).

percentage of 'defects' found in recruits for the Boer War of 1899-1901, it had limited itself to obliging LEAs to appoint medical staff to identify 'defects' in children and inform parents who then had to seek remedies. However the School Health Service's pre-war statistics of the shocking percentage of children unable to see, hear or breathe properly, with skin complaints, or alive with lice, contributed significantly to the post-war campaign to avoid 'national degeneration'.[7] The 1918 Act firmed up the treatment process by obliging LEAs to ensure parents acted on the advice they received or, if that proved financially impossible, providing free or subsidised treatment in clinics and hospitals.

Children characterised by the brutal definition of 'mentally defective' had become the responsibility of LEAs under a 1913 Act. However the categorisation procedures were primitive, and finding and training special staff proved difficult. In Devon the large Western Counties Institution at Starcross, founded fifty years earlier, sought to train 'mentally defective' but educable boys and girls in good habits and behaviour and in practical skills such as gardening, basic handicraft, cooking, laundry work and needlework. If the institution's reports are accurate the training was undoubtedly successful but the high standard of the children's work they describe, and reveal in illustrations, casts grave doubt on the accuracy of the initial assessments. One suspects their initial admission had stemmed as much from disruptive behavioural issues as intrinsic learning difficulties.

Nevertheless the greatest problems arose when the children left Starcross at the age of 16. A few found and kept menial jobs, some disappeared back home, but as the principal lamented in 1920 many ended up in lunatic asylums or the workhouse.[8] Most children with lesser learning difficulties, and any associate behavioural problems, remained in ordinary schools whose staffing levels rarely gave them time for special lessons. In 1927 there were just three special classes for 'dull and backward' pupils across the vast county – one each in Plymouth, Bideford and Tavistock. Perhaps Tiverton education committee's confession of ignorance that year about the needs of such children, and its decision to leave matters to headteachers to sort out as best they could, represented the general feeling.[9]

Devon's response

Fisher's Act met with varying responses. These included enthusiastic support from teachers and the Press, cautious approval from the financially embarrassed Church of England, sullen resentment from die-hard employers fearing the loss of cheap young workers, and outcry from all those who perennially opposed the costly intervention of the state in people's lives. Devon's branches of the Cooperative Society and Workers' Educational Association urged the massive extension of vocationally oriented 'advanced instruction' in elementary and continuation schools, complete with grants for clothes, travel and books.[10] Conversely in February 1919, a diatribe against government controls and waste by the Rev. H. Rosson Hudson, a Wesleyan minister at Barnstaple concluded with the argument 'that underlying all the causes of unrest was the increased education of the people, which led them to look for new ideals' – and to him this meant militant Socialism.[11]

The 1918 Act permitted LEAs to fund nurseries for children 2 to 5 years old. Their advocates usually adopted class-based social training arguments about nurseries offsetting the inability of poorer parents, through lack of time, interest or knowledge, to train young children in vital developmental activities such as washing and dressing, acquiring manners and good speech, and playing together cooperatively.[12] The lobby was doomed to disappointment across Devon, as nearly everywhere else. As we have seen, Devon possessed a growing number of maternity and child welfare clinics, and the nearest the County Education Committee came to filling the gap between these and mainstream schooling was in 1923 when it refused to exclude children between four and five years of age from 'normal' schools, even during the depression. Pragmatically committee members agreed schools would 'tame' these infants ready for 'normal instruction' and stop them 'running wild' on the streets and succumbing to evil influences.[12]

At the other end of the age range the future of impressionable elementary school leavers had worried many teachers, politicians and social reformers long before the end of the war. Indeed across Devon there were many wartime reports of wild juvenile offenders ending up being fined, birched or dispatched to reformatories.[13] The Board of Education hoped the strict new leaving age and continuation classes would help, but it urged the spread of Juvenile Employment or Advisory Centres. An early Juvenile Advisory Centre for Tiverton and its surrounding villages was established in December 1917 with Sir Ian Amory and Miss Lazenby on its committee. It operated a programme of visits to schools, regular discussions with employers, teachers and children, and made determined efforts to find employment for those leaving schools without confirmed posts. The Centre kept in touch with school leavers until the age of 18 to encourage further education, resolve any difficulties and advise on career opportunities.[14]

Tiverton and Exeter were probably the first Devon LEAs to restructure their bye-laws, in May 1920, to restrict the out-of-school employment of children between 12 and 14 years of age to light work and to just an hour before school and in the evening. Work was barred in potentially morally damaging places such as commercial kitchens, billiard halls and public houses, and no girl under 16 or boy under 15 could engaged in street trading. And when engaged in street trading they could not actively tout for business or 'use any bell, gong, or noisy instrument.'[15]

Towns across Devon were much relieved at the thought of the higher government grants. Barnstaple, Newton Abbot, Tiverton and Torquay along with Plymouth and Exeter already possessed institutions offering advanced classes in several vocational subjects.[16] In September 1919, for example, Tiverton's Technical, Science & Art School advertised a new range of courses for those considering careers in the building trade, commerce and mechanics. The Art courses covered drawing, painting, design, geometry, and stone and wood carving; Science included metal and wood work, and chemistry and domestic economy; Trades centred on painting, decorating, lettering and carpentry; and Commerce embraced shorthand, typewriting, book keeping, English, arithmetic and business practice.[17] Barnstaple's programme included a particular emphasis on the skills needed in the local ship-building and joinery works.[18]

Plymouth and Devonport were particularly favoured; both had successful Technical Schools, Schools of Art, and Schools of Domestic Economy & Trade Dress Making, and Plymouth had a specialist School of Navigation. In a significant decision Plymouth had chosen to build a Technical School rather than a statue or clock tower to celebrate Queen Victoria's Jubilee in 1887. It opened in 1892 complete with suites of lecture rooms, specialist laboratories, and art, craft and engineering workshops. Well before 1914 its daytime programme ranged from foundation courses for elementary school leavers up to London University external degrees, and its evening classes targeted local workers seeking further skills and qualifications.[19]

In 1919 Barnstaple LEA took two decisive steps. It decided to turn two all-age elementary schools into senior elementary schools offering 'advanced' classes for older pupils, and to work closely with the County Council in offering secondary school scholarships and maintenance grants to more local children of the required ability. In addition it modified its hitherto inflexible rule that women teachers had to resign when they married after a committee member suggested there could be cases, especially after the war, where a husband was totally incapacitated and his wife needed to work to avoid reliance on state assistance.[20]

In a significant move Devon LEA also approached towns to discuss whether one elementary school could become a 'senior' school for children over the age of 10 or 11 with neighbouring ones becoming 'junior' schools up to those ages. It was thought, not unreasonably, that children clustered together at a senior school would benefit from the cost-effective concentration of specialist staff and facilities. In urban Tavistock the suggestion that the Council School became a junior school and the Church of England School became the senior one was not seriously challenged – although it took from 1923 to 1928 to take effect. A similar agreement was reached between the LEA and Church of England in Totnes, although here the church school became the junior school. In other places, as exemplified by Ogwell in 1923 where its senior pupils would have to go to Newton Abbot, resistance stiffened at the long distances to be travelled and the likely closure of the much diminished village school. Ogwell only succumbed

Devonport Technical School. (Author's collection).

to 'junior' status in 1929.[21] In marked contrast the villagers of Shirwell voted *en masse* to tell the LEA that attendance at an urban school was infinitely preferable to children enduring the primitive sanitary facilities and sub-standard teaching at their local school where no-one ever won a scholarship. However the school stayed all age until 1944.[22]

In 1919 Exeter LEA thought the city's existing range of elementary and secondary schools, together with the advanced courses at the Royal Albert Memorial College, was about right. That August John Stocker, chairman of the city's education committee, expressed pride that in September 43 scholarship holders from the city would enter Hele's Boys School and 'about the same number' would go to the Modern School for Girls. (These were second tier secondary schools below Maynards Girls' School and Exeter Boys' High School.) It sounded fine, but in 1921, the city was publicly revealed to be an abysmal 78th out of 82 in the English County Borough league table of secondary school places per head of the child population.[23]

In Plymouth the dynamic Secretary of Education, Chandler Cook, tried something radically different. He embarked upon a visionary reorganisation policy aimed at creating a web of junior and senior elementary schools, raising the leaving age to fifteen, providing extensive professional, technical and commercial course in the final year, and boldly freeing secondary schools from fees. Amazingly in the brief post-war euphoria he secured the full backing of the Education Committee, and support of most parents and employers, but the half-fulfilled scheme was wrecked by the government's reduction in educational expenditure in 1922. Fees had to be restored and final reorganisation delayed until after the next world war.[24]

The health clauses in the 1918 Act were acted upon across the county. The compact urban LEAs – Barnstaple, Exeter, Tiverton, Torquay and Plymouth – created comprehensive inspection, treatment and follow-up services by mid-decade. In 1925 Dr Dunlop, Torquay's School Medical Officer, painted a generally gratifying picture of post-war improvements. All children were medically inspected three times during their school career, and there was close contact with Health Visitors and Child Welfare Clinics regarding children due to start school. Few children were dirty, and Dunlop believed the 'surprise cleanliness parades' of hands and nails,

Lettie Sanders, aged 13, never missed a day's schooling at Thornbury and King's Nympton during her nine years of education (1912-20) – a remarkable avoidance of all the illnesses blighting children's lives. (Mark Ware: WT 30 April 1920: Courtesy of Devon & Exeter Institution Trustees).

and feet and boots, conducted by teachers were invaluable. He listed the common ailments he ensured were treated – defective teeth, sight, hearing and breathing – and the less common ringworm, scabies and running sores. He was an advocate of removing tonsils and adenoids, and said their loss contributed much to children's health. There were, though, things beyond his control, primarily the intermittent and widely feared epidemics of measles, mumps and scarlet fever. All three had 'gradually traversed the whole town' in 1924-25. He worried, too, that there were no 'special difficulty classes' for 'misfits' which he defined as the 'dull and backward' children who deserved better consideration than wasting their time, and taxpayers' money, in ordinary classes.[25]

Devon LEA began extending its School Health Service in February 1919. The number of assistant medical officers doubled to six, contracts were signed with more dentists and oculists, and plans were pushed forward for expanding the open-air school at Hawkmoor for children with tuberculosis.[26] However, Dr Adkins had to tread carefully as his status as a salaried expert fulfilling the costly expectations of government policy did not always fit easily with the gentrified and generally cost conscious aldermen and councillors he seemed so often to be telling what to do. Adkins held his ground, though, and repeatedly explained the need for greater health education of parents and children, and better sanitation and ventilation in schools. In 1923 he submitted a detailed indictment of the deteriorating condition of many schools, especially 'non-provided' ones where parishes were increasingly hard pressed to raise funds for repairs and improvements.[27] There had been earlier warnings. In July 1921, for example, one assistant medical officer bluntly wrote that 'many of the school playgrounds were really disease traps' containing 'rough rubble and dust, and often one could not see the children playing in them for the clouds of dust that were raised.'[28] However the immediate, and almost certainly unintended, effect of Adkins' diatribe was to channel members' thoughts towards closing some of the smaller schools.[29]

The 1919–21 depression and the battle for progress

The post-war depression soured all hopes of reform, except in the national priority of child health. In March 1920 Devon's council chamber resonated with complaints of unacceptably high education rates and the government's 'orgies of extravagance'. The allegedly hard-pressed pockets of ratepayers took priority over the interests of children, and two years later the vocal economy lobby was still asserting Devon's elementary schools represented poor value for money. Devon Education Committee minutes reveal the paltry number of schools receiving attention to broken desks, defective windows, leaking roofs, outside toilets, damp walls, suspect water pumps and blocked flues, and it can be safely assumed that any renovations had been long delayed by the war. In the ultimate gesture of economy in 1922 some on the Education Committee suggested older elementary school children could replace caretakers.[30] Even secondary schools came in for criticism. In September 1922 Devon LEA raised their fees from 10 guineas a year. The decision was accompanied by the highly revealing comment that if the rise meant some fee-paying pupils had to leave early so much the better as secondary schools were notoriously overcrowded with sub-standard pupils who had bought their way in.[31] In that year, too, Devon County Teachers' Association (DCTA) used its annual conference to highlight the plight of many village schools where a single teacher sought to cope with 30 or 40 children aged between 4 and 14, often in cramped and depressing conditions.[32]

Village schools were directly in the firing line. Overall the numbers in Devon's elementary schools were in steep decline – from 54,712 in 1914 to 41,544 in 1923 – and rural emigration was much to blame.[33] However over the decades village schools had become important parts of the community, and most had the support of local clergy and families in the 'big house' who graced events, donated prizes, paid for Christmas parties and summer trips, and often employed school leavers.[34] However from 1919 onwards many villages were appalled to learn their schools might close, and endured months of anxiety and protest. In 1919 Bishopsteignton Luton and Rockbeare Marsh Green schools closed, and two years later so did Bicton, Loxhore, Swymbridge Travellers' Rest and Powderham. However so great was the protest at Powderham that the Earl of Devon reopened the school privately.[35] And arguments of the depressing loss of village amenities and significant inconvenience to poor families failed to save other tiny schools during the decade, including Bishops Nympton Newtown, Coffinswell, Cornwood Lutton, Dean Prior, Holbeton Mothecombe, Marwood Endowed, Monkton, Rattery, and Sampford Spiney.[36] Each one saved around £200 a year in costs, while more and more children trudged to distant schools.

In 1922 the infamous 'Geddes Axe' fell after the government accepted a policy of massive cutbacks recommended by an emergency committee chaired by the Conservative businessman Sir Eric Geddes.[37] In April 1922 the DCTA angrily charged the Geddes committee with having 'a bankrupt faith in human development', and in Tavistock an emotionally charged public meeting agreed that the cutbacks 'must inevitably degrade education below the inadequate standards prevailing before the war.'[38] The protestors had reason to be concerned as the long awaited 'continuation schools' were put on temporary, and then permanent, hold. For their critics it was a surprising but welcome triumph of the age-old criticisms of the waste and folly of over-educating the working classes. In Devon one new part-time continuation school biased towards Engineering had started in Newton Abbot, and another at Tiverton was linked vocationally and financially to Heathcoat's Lace Factory. A third biased towards Commerce in Torquay had got no further than planning.[39]

A well-publicised incident in Bideford was indicative of the acrimony. In 1920 Devon LEA converted the old Gunstone School in Bideford into a domestic subjects and handicraft centre for local schools. In 1922, when Devon was in the grip of depression, local county councillors scornfully asked how it could 'justify its existence', and the centre triumphantly obliged by altering its syllabus to show how girls could produce 'better and cheaper meals than their mothers'. It received widespread praise for producing tasty cottage pie,

Village school at Broadhempston. The building is on the left in the vaguely Gothic style of many late Victorian elementary schools. (Author's collection).

cabbage and currant pudding for 6d a head, liver and bacon, potatoes and fruit pie for 6d, and lentil soup and jam roly-poly for 3½d.[40]

By early 1923 relations between Devon LEA and its teachers had slumped to an all-time low with the DCTA threatening strikes over salaries and in return being accused of Socialism and Bolshevism by irate councillors. In January the DCTA voted to refuse to accept any voluntary pay cuts requested by the government. In February the County Council's special Public Economy Committee recommended a salary reduction of 10% for headteachers and 5% for assistant teachers. The increasingly militant DCTA refused to budge, but in June the warring parties agreed a compromise of a 3¼% reduction on the current scales, but only until 1925 when a higher scale would be introduced.[41] Neither side wanted an all-out strike, and although the modest cut saved the face of the LEA it barely masked the teachers' victory.

With the depression biting deep, the small independent Schools of Technology, Art & Science in Barnstaple, Bideford, Newton Abbot, Paignton, Tiverton and Torquay acknowledged they were in dire financial straits. Student numbers were falling, costs were rising, fees could not be raised for fear that numbers would fall even further, and the County Council's grants, although welcome, were too small to bail them out. After debating every possible avenue, Devon LEA believed the Schools were worth saving, primarily as training grounds for keen working class people likely to benefit local trade and industry. In a major step, it voted to accept full responsibility for their maintenance and development. This meant the Schools would receive higher government grants, and in effect they would serve much like alternative 'continuation schools'.[42] Applications soon recovered, with Newton Abbot having 800 students spread over dozens of award-bearing courses in 1923-24.[43] The typing, shorthand, book-keeping and commercial arithmetic courses attracted many female students. As the *Tavistock Gazette* asserted in January 1923, 'Formerly any smattering of education was considered good enough for girls, but that has been changed now that they have to compete for employment in the professional and business world.'[44]

Later troubles and advances

Reports by Dr Adkins in the early 1920s showed that the cases of skin complaints, rotting teeth, and poor vision and hearing were steadily falling, but Sir George Newman, the Board of Education's Chief Medical Officer, shocked Devon when his 1924 annual report stated that the physical condition of Devon's rural children was actually worse than before the war.[45] Significantly the Council Council made no public response. And in 1927 it had some difficulty in refuting the disgust expressed by Dr Christopher Addison, the ex-Minister of Health, that Devon LEA still allowed schools to be without fresh water supplies. At the LEA meeting debating a response members were well aware the charge was true, and their only defence was an assertion that schools without taps or wells were adequately served by nearby village pumps or with water stored daily in tanks. The following year Adkins was gratified to record that no less than 68 schools had had sanitary repairs and improvements.[46]

However complaints about school conditions were never-ending. In 1926 it was the erratic water supplies for schools such as Fogintor and Wiggaton, and the utter condemnation of Langtree School where water had to be drawn from a local well, lamps had to be lit all day for the children to see to work, the road had to be used as the playground, and, most offensive of all, the adjacent churchyard drained towards the constantly damp back wall of the school.[47] Earlier Boasley Cross Council School near Sourton had sprung into unwelcome prominence as a result of its lengthy closure as the suspected source of TB followed by a local protest that the children 'were running wild'. In the end the walls were stripped, re-plastered and whitewashed, and all pens and books destroyed and replaced, and everything else disinfected. However everyone remained suspicious of the building, and the school was rebuilt in 1927.[48]

Early in 1924 a strike by parents in Morwelham revealed other issues affecting rural children's health. Families refused to send their children, many as young as five years old, three miles to Gulsworthy School where there were no facilities to heat their midday pasties and no transport home over hilly Devon lanes. Parents said they were unable to dry drenched clothing in time for school the following morning. Under great public pressure Devon LEA grudgingly agreed to provide horse drawn traps in winter, but not in summer. Although schools were not legally responsible for children during the midday break, the LEA also provided a stove in the play shed for the children themselves to warm their food.[49]

In January 1925, amidst criticism of the poor state of many old church schools, the Exeter Diocesan Conference accepted the need to raise £20,000 to help parishes improve them.[50] The more active parishes set to work at once. Among the events that year, the vicar of Fremington's garden was given over to fête with a fancy dress parade, country dancing and teas to help repair the school roof.[51] In Newton Abbot the managers and staff of Wolborough School organised a two-day fair that drew upon the full support of the parish, including Lady Churston who was better known as the celebrated singer and actress Denise Orme.[52] By April 1926 the diocesan fund had reached the halfway stage, with Lady Florence Cecil prominent in the campaign to promote church schools as the only guarantors of a Christian education in a country that, she claimed, was rife with unrest, secularism and materialism.[53] The aristocratic Cecils easily secured the support of the Earl of Devon, Lord Clinton, Viscount Sidmouth, Major General Sir Edward May, Sir Charles Cave and Sir John Kennaway and their families for the Anglican campaign. A high point was the well-patronised fête at the Bishop's Palace opened by HRH Princess Beatrice in June 1927.[54]

Rural communities continued to think they were misunderstood. In January 1923 Basil Peto, MP for Barnstaple, told an audience of north Devon farmers what they wanted to hear – that in his opinion rural elementary schools were moving dangerously away from preparing children for rural occupations. And in 1928 the chairman of the North Devon Teachers' Association came close to agreeing with him when he argued that a sound knowledge of the natural environment and the occupations associated with it would show 'the good service schools can do to agriculture.'[55]

The same argument occurred later in the decade when the County Education Committee embarked on the major task of creating senior elementary schools everywhere. Late in 1926 the Board of Education's Consultative Committee published a major report recommending that all children should pass from primary schools to secondary schools at the age of 11, and that there should be two types of equally funded secondary schools – 'Grammar' with an academic bias and 'Modern' with a practical one. In 1928 the government got round to publishing *The New Prospect in Education* that gave lip-service to the recommendations but in practice rejected them. All existing secondary schools were to be known as 'Grammar Schools', and were to be modestly expanded, but the 'Modern School' disappeared from view as an equal partner to be replaced by the creation of senior elementary schools taking children at the age of 11 from several surrounding schools that would become 'junior' in status. It was a cheap option – both financially and educationally. Secondary education would remain relatively exclusive, and subject to fees or scholarships, and most older children would remain in a revitalised but essentially elementary sector funded by the inferior elementary grant formula.[56]

Devon LEA planned for 80 senior schools and up to 500 'feeder' junior ones by the end of the decade. The new schools would cost £500,000 although the government grant covered 50%, and school transport would rise to around £30,000 a year. The council chamber resounded to complaints of hefty rate rises, a dictatorial government, and utter waste of money. Many education committee members from rural areas rejected the alleged educational benefits of grouping older pupils together far from home. All manner of ills were forecast including the dilution of staff in village schools, the failure of senior schools to pay attention to rural education, the poor attendance of children faced with long journeys, and the greater migration of families to towns.[57] The consultations between LEA officials, school managers, church organisations and teachers' associations were endless, and delaying tactics were common, especially by parishes whose church schools stood to lose their older pupils. However the DCTA welcomed the new groupings, and in March 1930 its president spoke warmly of the advanced courses in domestic subjects, gardening and manual training that were already in operation.[58] Such utilitarian working class thoughts by an influential elementary school headteacher must have been some compensation for critical county councillors. Torquay, Barnstaple and Tiverton LEAs also began reorganising their elementary schools during the decade, although the process was not finished until well into the 1930s. In a typical example, Tiverton's senior schools not only served Tiverton itself but also drew children from the surrounding villages of Loxbeare, Calverleigh, Butterleigh, Stoodleigh and Templeton.[59]

Teaching and learning: the age of competition

Meritocracy reigned supreme. There were competitions in nearly everything – in all aspects of sport, and also handicraft and needlework, and singing, country dancing and art. They were held to stimulate effort, encourage perseverance, and train pupils to be modest in victory and stoic in defeat. Many schools, and indeed several towns, held exhibitions of children's handicraft and needlework and the prizes on offer gave them a strong competitive dimension. Each year Tavistock Church of England Girls' School held a public exhibition of needlework, handwork, Nature

Classroom at Torwood Church of England School, Torquay, c1925.
A world map highlights the British Empire, photographs portray key national figures, including Admiral Jellicoe, the framed scroll probably lists 'Old Boys' killed in the war, and the wall tiles level with the children's heads say: 'abhor that which is evil; cleave to that which is good. Be kindly affectioned to one another with brotherly love (St Paul's Epistle to the Romans 12:9-10) Typically the classroom has a high window, a wooden floor, gas lights and what appears to be a protected coal or coke fire. Hopefully children's work adorns the walls.

(Beaford Old Archive images: © Beaford Arts)

Study, housewifery and cookery in the Town Hall. The displays of embroidery, bouquets, basketwork, dresses, drawings, and desserts were judged by local dignitaries who were no doubt gratified at the quality of training given to the town's future wives, mothers – and domestic servants.[60] In Exeter, Ladysmith Road Boys' and Girls' Schools were proud of the practical training the children received. In 1919 a public exhibition featured the boy's fretwork designs, animal drawings, and models of mills, aeroplanes, moving figures, and electrically lit boats and houses, and the girls' flower paintings, friezes, dresses, knitted clothes and embroidery.[61] Schools also vied for prizes in choral singing. In 1927 the headteacher at Beer proudly underlined his entry in the school logbook when his boys' and girls' choirs won first class certificates in the Rural Schools' section of the County Music Festival.[62]

By the late 1920s Devon was covered with district football leagues for elementary schools. Better roads and transport made matches easier to organise, and it became fashionable for landowners to give or lend fields to local schools. In 1926 Earl Fortescue formally established Devon's branch of the National Playing Fields Association and the Earl of Portsmouth got the movement off to a start with the gift of three acres to Morchard Bishop.[63] Winning the Devon Schoolboys' Shield was the pinnacle of achievement for an elementary school. In the early 1920s it was dominated by the rivalry between Ladysmith School in Exeter and Heathcoat School in Tiverton. Some indication of the unacceptably partisan fervour this evoked was the unsuccessful attempt by the organisers in 1923 to keep secret the ground selected for the final between these two teams. When the news leaked out that the venue was Exminster 'a mad stampede' occurred.[64]

The most striking competitions, though, were the secondary school scholarships dangled before able elementary school boys and girls. Although proud of sporting and musical successes, many elementary schools considered scholarship passes to be their greatest achievements.[65] Ironically the best thing for an elementary school's reputation was for able children to leave it for a more prestigious establishment. Indeed there was a tendency for Devon Education Committee members to crudely equate an elementary school's

A proud moment. Bickington (all-age) Church of England School Football Team with teachers, school managers and District Challenge Shield, 1921-22 season. (Beaford Old Archive images: © Beaford Arts).

Children & Schools: Strengthening the Divide

Pupils of Holy Trinity School, Barnstaple, in Empire Day costumes, May 1921. Britannia stands supreme with her possessions encircled protectively by the army and navy. (Beaford Old Archive images: © Beaford Arts)

overall worth by the number of scholarships it gained. In 1922 no-one disagreed with one member who sneered that some schools were not capable of preparing pupils for the examination.[66] In 1924 the *Western Times* said the two rare scholarships won by Ashwater boys to Okehampton Grammar School were a 'great credit' to the headmaster's diligent training.[67] And when Beer won 2 places at Colyton Grammar School in 1922 and 3 in 1926 they were considerable achievements for a school of 90 pupils.[68] However not every family's finances, or indeed attitudes, allowed scholarship winners to take up the place. When, in the summer of 1918, the headmaster of a Teignmouth elementary school recorded that his scholarship winners to Hele's School in Exeter had risen from 4 to 6 after two families elsewhere had turned down the awards he was drawing unhappy attention to this fact.[69]

One lingering aspect of the war continued to hold schools in its grip throughout the 1920s. Although there were few public celebrations of Empire Day, local clergy, school managers and civic leaders ensured its awesome watchwords of 'Responsibility, Sympathy, Duty and Self-Sacrifice' were drummed into the nation's children. The Earl of Meath had successfully advocated a day of celebration of British Imperialism in the wake of the grimly unedifying 1899-1902 Boer War, and Queen Victoria's birthday, 24 May, duly became Empire Day. During the First World War the day was imbued with deep religious significance and children listened to sermons, sung hymns, said prayers, saluted the Union Jack, and sometimes dressed up as historic British heroes, or Britannia and her Allies, prior to a half-day holiday. This intensity persisted after the war, with children frequently being told that God would remove the Empire from Britain's charge if they failed to 'live the watchwords'.

With Bolshevism threatening Europe's fragile reconstruction, and a fractured society at home, Empire Day remained important in generating an aggressive patriotism, and preserving essentially conservative attitudes towards the future that included, by implication, British superiority over its subject races. At Ladysmith Road School in Exeter in 1921 the songs were the popular 'There's only one England' and 'Flag of our country', and the address highlighted the collapse of ancient empires, and recently the Austro-Hungarian, German and Russian ones, 'because of something inherently rotten within.'[70] In Bideford it became an annual custom for children and teachers to place wreaths on the war memorial, and then processed with the Town Band, Mayor and Corporation to a park where the mayor's chaplain conducted a service.[71] In 1928 the vicar of Lynmouth told children that the great sailors Sir Walter Raleigh and Sir Francis Drake were primarily God's servants bringing Christianity to 'remote and heathen countries.'[72] However on Empire Day 1924 Bishop Cecil of Exeter had a different message. Visiting Barnstaple, he bemoaned the diminishing birth rate in Devon. 'If he had his way, when the girls' schools came to salute the flag he would put a cradle beside the flag and make every girl salute the cradle, for the greatness of England depended on the cradle.' Teachers, he said, should instil in girls the importance of motherhood.[73]

Not everyone liked Empire Day. The post-war League of Nations was receiving enthusiastic support, and speakers across Devon were highlighting its essential role as a peacemaker. They urged schools to ensure History and Geography syllabuses encouraged international understanding and respect rather than perpetuating Imperial aggression and a sense of British racial superiority.[74] Some thought Empire Day should be linked to courses in Citizenship leading children to contribute positively and ethically to local and national affairs, and to challenge all those eaten up 'with corrupt and lowly ends.'[75] And there were others who thought the Empire was an abomination. In 1920 there had been fears in Devon about the spread of Proletarian Sunday Schools promulgating Marxist ideology. In 1922 the *Western Times* and Church Army organised a petition against suspected plans to establish one in Exeter, and all communities were urged to be watchful. And in 1926, as the General Strike loomed, Chudleigh's Parochial Church Council had been among those formally petitioning the government to ensure teachers in council schools were not promoting Communism.[76]

Very occasionally things could go horribly wrong in schools. In 1924 Barnstaple's Roman Catholic School received a particularly abysmal HMI's (His Majesty Inspector's) report, and in desperation after a lengthy period of dissatisfaction its managers secured the LEA's permission to dismiss all the teachers.[77] This was a rare disaster, and although HMI were often critical of some aspects of school life many elementary schools received encouraging praise for both maintaining academic standards and trying out more modern methods of teaching. HMI often commented favourably, as at Exton in 1922, on pupils fresh air activities such as gardening, nature rambles, visiting historic sites, swimming and team games.[78] HMI also liked schools where pupils were given problems to solve through group discussions and experimentation, and where subjects such as gardening and handicraft had clear links with other subjects such as English, Mathematics, Art and Science.[79]

Infant teaching was encouraged along moderately liberal lines. In 1920 HMI praised Tavistock Council School's infant department for its 'happy tone' and social training. 'Hand-work is well thought out, and singing, stories and games play a very important part in refining manners and training the children in healthy activity.'[80] At St Mary Magdalene Infants School in Barnstaple HMI was particularly gratified that children from poorer homes had been trained in 'clear and pleasing' speech.[81]

Many county as well as church schools received good or excellent grades for the quality of their religious instruction. Unusually in Devon the Diocesan RI Inspectors examined both types of schools. Among many examples, in 1927 inspectors had high praise for both the hymn singing and Bible knowledge of pupils at the Heathcoat, Bolham, Cove, Withleigh, Chevithorne and Elmore Schools in and around Tiverton.[82] In these difficult post-war times for the churches, one suspects the inspectors were only too pleased to find things to praise.

The secondary grammar schools: diverging paths

In the 1920s Devon's grant aided secondary schools were a mixed group of ancient foundations, largely restructured and revitalised in the later nineteenth century, and new schools founded by LEAs just before or after the war. Revised statutes and public money had reinvigorated the ancient grammar schools in Ashburton, Barnstaple, Bideford, Braunton, Colyton, Crediton, Kingsbridge, Ottery St Mary, Tavistock, Tiverton and Totnes. Similar Victorian reforms of ancient foundations had provided Exeter with the ambitious Maynard's Girls' School and High School for Boys and the cheaper and socially inferior Hele's Boys' School and Episcopal Girls' Modern School. The Boys' High School retained the hugely enticing gift of 18 scholarships to Oxford and Cambridge Universities. Edgehill Girls' College at Bideford and Shebbear Boys' College were Victorian Bible Christian foundations. They were well-equipped and their nonsectarian atmosphere made them popular. After prolonged negotiations they, too, secured LEA grants in 1920 and helped fill gaps in the county's provision.[83] There were, though, extremes of fortune. Although Barnstaple had had its old town chapel site replaced by a purpose-built secondary school in 1910, for most of the 1920s Kingsbridge School made do with an old convent when fire destroyed its buildings in 1914, and Totnes waited impatiently until 1928 for a new girls' school to complement King Edward VI's Boys' School.[84]

Outside Exeter and Plymouth, the county's secondary schools were small, rarely topping 200 pupils during the decade. Pre-war plans by Devon LEA for new secondary schools in Newton Abbot and Torquay reached fruition in 1915, and soon after the war Ilfracombe and Okehampton's 'higher elementary' schools were relabelled mixed secondary schools but at least they possessed science laboratories, domestic science rooms, handicraft workshops, gardens, music rooms, and asphalt, not gravel, playgrounds.[85] Several other new secondary schools started life in far less auspicious circumstances. In 1920 the old Winterbourne House in Teignmouth, together with its grounds and motley collection of outbuildings became a new county secondary school drawing its 150 pupils from as far away as Exminster and Chudleigh as well as Teignmouth and Shaldon. The school had no gymnasium or library, just one basic laboratory, and no level

The new Totnes County School for Girls. (Author's collection).

playing field. In 1921 an army hut gave it 3 more classrooms and a second in 1923 provided an assembly hall.⁸⁶ New secondary schools in Exmouth, Dartmouth, and Plympton similarly started their lives in unwanted old houses together with an army hut or two.⁸⁷ In 1923 a new site was earmarked to replace Colyton Grammar School's medieval schoolroom, but the building only opened in 1930.⁸⁸

Issues of social class constantly swirled the admissions criteria for fee payers and scholarship winners. During a conference in Exeter in 1920 on 'The Link between Elementary and Secondary Education' one elementary school headmaster insisted the scholarship examination was manifestly unfair as children of poor parents were handicapped by large elementary school classes, fewer books and crowded homes while richer parents paid for coaching, provided comfortable homes and could always fall back on fees. The headmaster of Exeter High School cynically agreed, adding that no secondary headmaster would want to accept a boy from an 'unsatisfactory' home.⁸⁹ At least by then Devon LEA had standardised the examination to embrace Arithmetic, English Composition and Dictation, and General Knowledge, including History, Geography and Nature Study, that were all included in elementary school syllabuses.⁹⁰

During the 1920-21 depression several Devon secondary schools were short of fee-paying pupils, and they offered to increase their intake of publicly funded bright elementary school children. There was an acknowledgement, probably grudgingly given, that some scholarship winners were adding greater lustre to secondary school reputations than many less able fee-payers. However it was the same depression, and no doubt the fears of revealing that many more poorer children were capable of secondary schooling, that led Devon LEA to reject the offer.⁹¹

The Rivals' staged by Tiverton Boys' Middle (Secondary) School. The title 'Middle' was contemporary usage signifying the school served the middle classes and came somewhere midway between major public schools and local elementary schools. (Courtesy of Tiverton Museum).

Children & Schools: Strengthening the Divide

Classroom at Tiverton Girls' Middle (Secondary) School. The sender of the postcard said the teacher, Miss Smith BA, taught Science and Mathematics and 'Elle est bonne'. (Author's collection).

Two years later, in 1923, there were still only 4,273 pupils in Devon's secondary schools, and no more than 30% of these were scholarship pupils or lucky holders of bursaries.[92] In 1925 just 21 boys and 25 girls from across the whole of north Devon won scholarships to Barnstaple Grammar School. Eight of the boys and four of the girls came from the large Ashleigh Road School in Barnstaple. Arguments raged in council chambers and newspapers over whether all north Devon's elementary schools were doing their best, and whether more scholarships should be created.[93] Grudgingly over the decade LEAs increased the number of scholarship places in tacit recognition that the number of pupils meriting them far exceeded the number of places available.[94]

Once at secondary school – whether at 11 as scholarship holders or much younger as fee-payers – pupils embarked upon predominantly academic studies with plenty of homework and regular tests. This was interspersed with physical training and team games leading ultimately to a variety of external examinations at 15, 16 and 17. 'Show' events for parents included winter plays and summer sports day, and Speech Days resounded with the successes of football, cricket, swimming and hockey teams against schools of similar status. Remarkably, several girls' secondary schools in Devon had cricket teams.[95] The academic curriculum embraced English Language and Literature, Latin, French, Mathematics, Science, History, Geography, Art and Religious Instruction. The golden prizes, such as the Oxford and Cambridge Locals and Senior Locals, London Matriculation and Civil Service Examinations, prepared pupils for 'white collar' and professional careers and university entry. A number of girls won Royal Drawing Society and London Institute of Fine Needlework prizes. However although Speech Days made much of such successes the pupils actually achieving them were few in comparison to the numbers on roll.[96] In 1924 the *Mid Devon Advertiser* lamented how early leaving blighted children's careers and thereby the reputation of Teignmouth's secondary school. In 1925 the headmaster of Okehampton Grammar School said much the same. He blamed parents' short-sighted desire for their children to secure what he derided as low level jobs for his school's few successes in public examinations.[97] Perhaps he had forgotten it was a perilous time for gaining employment of any sort.

Differentiation by appearance – superior school uniforms for boys and girls. (Mark Ware: WT 16 April 1920 & 8 April 1927: Courtesy of Devon & Exeter Institution Trustees).

Single, successful and generally self-sufficient, secondary school headmistresses were keen to promote academic success as the key to satisfying careers and independent lives. Typically, at Speech Day in December 1918 Miss Jenkin at Barnstaple welcomed both the Education Act and Franchise Act, adding 'Most of the girls might now anticipate that it would one day be their duty to take a part in the government of the country, and they would now take a much more intelligent interest in political life.'[98] In 1919 Miss Belcher at Crediton asserted her aim was 'to lay a foundation that will fit the woman of the future to take up almost any profession or public work.'[99] In 1920 the mayor of Exeter was less progressive, telling the girls of Maynard School that if women made happy homes they were doing their very best 'to promote the health and happiness of the country we all loved.'[100] However, in 1928 the girls of Barnstaple Secondary School heard Sir Robert Newman, Exeter's MP, say that their opportunities now embraced membership of the House of Commons where, he said, physical strength was no advantage and language flowed freely, 'in which the ladies were not deficient.' He thought there might be a female prime minister one day.[101]

Aspirations of greatness led some schools openly to scorn local links. In 1921 Exeter City Council took control of Exeter School for Boys but in 1929 the school reverted to direct grant status because, the new ambitious headmaster explained, 'a dependent existence was prejudicial to the spirit of an English public school.'[102] It sought fees, recognition and status far beyond the city and county boundaries. During this decade Blundell's School in Tiverton also continued its march towards 'public school' exclusivity. Although still accepting public money, in 1921 its headmaster sarcastically described a recent HMI inspection as 'an irritating process' from which 'we learnt little that was really useful.' Here was another Devon school, founded originally for able but poor local children, whose Speech Days and ambitions increasingly concentrated on the wealthy few.[103]

Both Exeter and Plymouth hoped their technical and art colleges would become University Colleges offering London University degrees. Exeter won the race in the 1920s, but not without difficulty. Although the ambitious City Council designated the Royal Albert Memorial College in Gandy Street its University College in 1908 it did so in contravention of accepted usage as it failed three times – in 1901, 1906 and 1910 – to gain the appropriate grants. The investigating teams found its finances too precarious and its advanced students too few. The College set about remedying the situation by creating an influential College Committee dedicated to campaigning for a spread-out South Western University College incorporating several existing technical and art colleges. However in 1919 Herbert Fisher at the Board of Education rejected another plea for University College status and higher grants on the same grounds as before.[104] At this time the college had around 450 students funded variously by fees and grants from the City and County Councils and Board of Education. About half were undertaking teacher training and half studying various Art and Science courses up to degree level.[105]

The campaign for recognition by the University Grants Commission went on, and in a stroke of luck in 1922 Streatham Hall and 11 acres of land were purchased by W.H.Reed, a wealthy supporter of the College project, and immediately donated as a new campus to replace the rooms and boarding houses scattered awkwardly across the city. In 1922, too, the College became incorporated, and aggressively set a fund-raising target of £100,000 for further buildings, facilities and staff.[106] In 1926 a *Times* article greatly admired the College

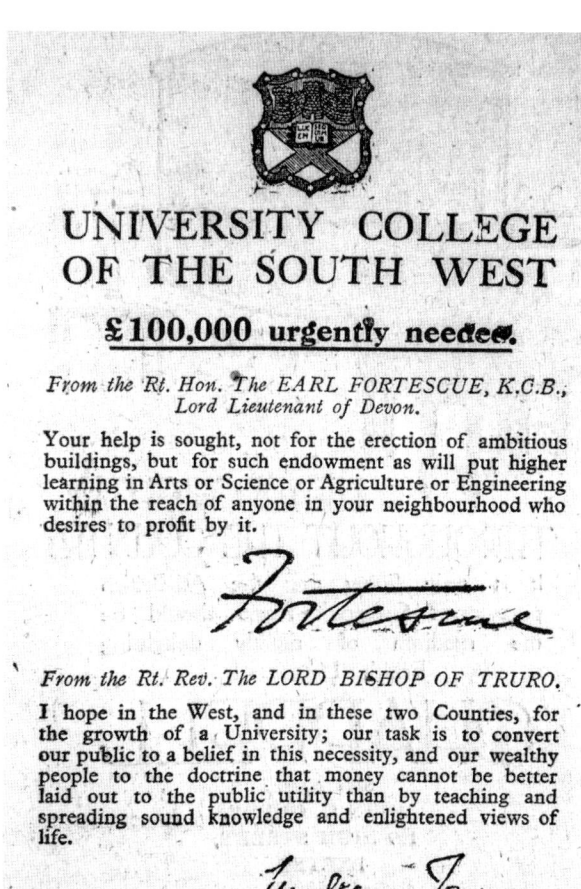

University College of the South West promotional advertisement. (Mark Ware: WT 9 October 1925: Courtesy of Devon & Exeter Institution Trustees).

'Group of Pretty Grammar School Girls in Barnstaple'. A photograph taken during the House Sports and probably not the headline desired by the headmistress. (Mark Ware: WT 13 August 1920: Courtesy of Devon & Exeter Institution Trustees).

Committee's energetic programmes for developing the Streatham Campus and a range of degree level courses in close association with Plymouth's Technical Colleges, Seale-Hayne Agricultural College and Camborne School of Mines. As a reasonably sure sign of government approbation, in 1927 the University Grants Commission awarded £5,000 towards a boarding hall.[107]

REFERENCES

1. *WT* 6 May 1921; Edmunds, J., *A History of West Buckland School,* Holladay, R., *Ravenswood School: Some memories of its first 27 years 1921-48,* Bovett, R., *Historical Notes on Devon Schools,* pp416-417

2. Parker, D., *The People of Devon in the First World War,* pp167-169, *WT* 11 & 28 February 1919

3. Lowndes, G.A.N., *The Silent Social Revolution,* pp78-105, Bovett, R., op. cit., pp417, 421-422, www.oldplymouth.uk/education

4. Andrews, L., *The Education Act, 1918,* pp16-19

5. Ibid., pp35-51

6. *TT* 14 March 1919, *WT* 9 October 1925

7. Lowndes, G.A.N,., op.cit, pp169-179

8. *WT* 1/6/20; Radford, J.P. & Tipper, A., *Starcross: Out of the Mainstream*

9. *D&SN* 3 March 1927

10. *WT* 16 & 23 February 1920, 23 March 1920, 21 December 1920, *D&SN* 25 March 1920

11. *WT* 11 February 1919

12. *NDJ* 24 April 1919, 10 June 1920, *WT* 6 April 1923

13. Parker, D., *The People of Devon in the First World War,* pp190-192

14. *WT* 21 & 24 January 1919

15. *D&SN* 27 May 1920, *WT* 7 June 1920

16. *WT* 15 May 1920

17. *D&SN* 18 September 1919

18. *NDJ* 16 September 1920

19. www.oldplymouth.uk/Plymouth/Technical_College, Kelly's Directory 1923

20. *NDJ* 6 February 1919, 8 January 1920, 10 June 1920, *WT* 15 October 1920

21. *WT* 23 March 1920, 23 February 1923, 9 & 16 March 1923; *MDA* 3 March 1923, Bovett, op. cit., pp296-298, 235, 339-341

22. *NDJ* 19 March 1925, Bovett, op.cit., p273

23. *WT* 6 August 1919, 16 February 1921

24. Walling, R.A.J., *The Story of Plymouth,* pp261-266

25. Torquay LEA: School Medical Officer's Annual Report for 1925

26. *WT* 28 February 1919

27. *WT* 2 February 1923

28. *WT* 22 July 1921

29. *WT* 8 February 1924

30. Viz. DHC DEC 11 December 1919, DCC Finance Committee 15 June 1922, *WT* 12 March 1920, 1 July 1921, 5 & 17 May 1922, *WO* 3 June 1920

31. *WT* 7 January 1921, 8 September 1922

32. *MDA* 1 July 1922

33. *WT* 11 January 1924

34. Viz. *WT* Exton 2 January 1922, East Down 17 March 1922, North Lew 2 January 1925, Postbridge 23 December 1925

35. Bovett, op.cit., pp6-7, 25-26, 29-30, 199, 253-254, 257, 293, 306-307

36. *WT* 1 July 1921, 23 February 1923, 11 January 1924; Bovett, op.cit.. pp28, 73-74, 80, 90, 167, 206-207, 217, 255, 264-265; DHC DEC 15 March 1923

37. *WT* 13 December 1921

38. *WT* 18 April 1922, *TG* 3 March 1922

39. DHC DEC 11 December 1919, 16 December 1920

40. Bovett op.cit., pp26-27, *WT* 5 April 1920, *NDJ* 15 June 1922

41. *WT* 5 January 1923, 6 April 1923, 15 June 1923

42. *WT* 9 December 1921, *WO* 14 April 1921

43. *MDA* 17 January 1925

44. *TG* 26 January 1923

45. *WT* 2 May 1924, 6 & 20 November 1925

46. *WT* 4 March 1927, 8 April 1927, 24 May 1929

47. *D&SN* 29 May 1924, *WT* 8 October 1926, 29 April 1927 A new Langree school was built in 1930 – Bovett,op. cit., p194

48. *WT* 4 May 1923, 14 January 1927

49. *TG* 22 & 29 February 1924. Morwelham had lost its school around 1907 when local mining had collapsed

50. *WT* 23 January 1926

51. *NDJ* 18 June 1925

52. *MDA* 26 September 1925

53. *WT* 5 February 1926, 16 April 1926

54. *WT* 3 June 1927

55. *WT* 26 January 1923, *NDJ* 23 February 1928

56. Simon, B., *The Politics of Educational Reform 1920-1940,* pp116-144

57. *WT* 13 December 1929, 3 March 1930, *NDJ* 7 November 1929, 5 April 1929, 31 May 1929

58. *WT* 7/3/30

59. *D&SN* 27 September 1928, 24 January 1929, 14 March 1929, 11 April 1929

60. *TG* 25 July 1924

61. *WT* 19 December 1919

62. *NDJ* 29 December 1927, DHC 2269C/EFL2 Beer School logbook, 7 March 1927

63. *NDJ* 30 April 1926

64. *SMG* 12 May 1923

65. Viz. Exeter Practising School *WT* 23 December 1919, Highweek, Newton Abbot *MDA* 29 December 1923, 2 January 1926

66. *WT* 8 September 1922

67. *WT* 30 May 1924

68. DHC 2269C/EFL2 Beer School logbook 29 May 1922, 19 May 1926

69. Teignmouth Exeter Road Boys' School logbook 2, 4 & 17 July 1918

70. *WT* 30 May 1921

71. *WT* 30 May 1924

72. *NDJ* 24 May 1928

73. *TG* 26 May 1922, *WT* 18 May 1923, 16 May 1924

74. *WT* 2 August 1921, *NDJ* 13 April 1927

75. *WT* 22 August 1921

76. *WT* 11 November 1920, 3 & 6 May 1922, 23 April 1926

77. *NDJ* 15 May 1924

78. *WT* 2 January 1922

79. Viz. Teignmouth, Exeter Road Boys' School logbook 14 December 1926, 25 May 1927, Barnstaple, Ashleigh Road Senior Boys' School *WT* 19 March 1925

80. *TG* 17 September 1920

81. *NDJ* 10 May 1923

82. *D&SN* 28 April 1927

83. *WT* 11 October 1918, Bovett, op. cit., pp390-438

84. Bovett, op. cit., pp391-393, 4018-420, 434-436

85. *WT* 20 January 1921

86. *WT* 29 November 1918, 7 February 1919, Stephenson, J. A., *Teignmouth Grammar School: The First Fifty Years,* DHC DEC 11 December 1919, 11 March 1920

87. *WT* 4 December 1919, 2 June 1922, Bovett, op.cit., p394

88. *WT* 4 May 1923, 3 October 1930

89. *WT* 16 February 1920

90. *WT* 7 February 1919

91. *WT* 22 July 1921, 7 October 1921

92. *WT* 11 January 1924

93. *NDJ* 18 June 1925, *TG* 23 December 1925, *WT* 14 May 1926, 2 July 1926

94. *NDJ* 11 June 1925

95. *NDJ* 17 December 1925, *WT* 16 October 1919, 23 December 1921

96. *WT* 19 December 1918, 11 December 1920, 23 December 1921, *NDJ* 17 December 1925, 20 December 1928

97. *MDA* 4 October 1924, *WT* 27 November 1925

98. *WT* 19 December 1918

99. *CC* 6 December 1919

100. *WT* 11 December 1920

101. *NDJ* 20 December 1928

102. Bradbeer, D.M., *Joyful Schooldays,* pp74-75

103. *WO* 28 July 1921

104. *WT* 3 February 1919, Hetherington, Sir Hector, *The University College at Exeter 1920-1925*

105. *WT* 31 October 1919, 9 December 1919

106. *WT* 16 October 1925, 9 July 1926

107. *WT* 15 October 1926, 11 March 1927

BIBLIOGRAPHY

Newspapers

Crediton Chronicle (CC)

Dawlish Gazette (DG)

Devon & Somerset News (D&SN)

Edinburgh Gazette

London Gazette

Mid Devon Advertiser (MDA)

North Devon Herald (NDH)

North Devon Journal (NDJ)

Paignton Observer (PO)

South Molton Gazette (SMG)

Tavistock Gazette (TG)

Torquay Times (TT)

Western Evening Herald. (WEH)

Western Observer (WO)

Western Times (WT)

Books

Acland, A., *A Devon Family: The Story of the Aclands* (Phillimore, 1981)

Aggett, W.J.P., *The Bloody Eleventh: History of the Devonshire Regiment, Vol. 2 1815-1914 & Vol. 3 1914-1969.* (Devonshire & Dorset Regiment, 1988)

Andrews, L., *The Education Act, 1918* (Routledge & Kegan Paul, 1976)

Anon., *Guide books to Ilfracombe & NW Devon, Plymouth & SW Devon,* and *Teignmouth & SE Devon* (Ward Locke & Co., c1923)

Anon., *Who's Who in Devonshire* (Wilson & Phillips, Hereford, 1934)

Atkinson, C.T., *The Devonshire Regiment 1914-1918* (Eland Bros., Exeter, 1926)

Austin, A., *The History of the Clinton Barony 1299-1999* (Lord Clinton privately, 1999)

Bolt, B., *The Hospitals and Asylums of Devon and Their Records* (Devon Family History Society, 2000)

Bovett, R., *Historical Notes on Devon Schools* (Devon County Council, 1989)

Bradbeer, D.M., *Joyful Schooldays: A Digest of the History of the Exeter Grammar Schools* (Sydney Lee, Exeter, 1973)

Burns, K.V., *Devonport built warships since 1860* (Maritime Books, Liskeard, 1981)

Burt, R., *Mining in Cornwall & Devon: Mines & Men* (University of Exeter, 2014)

Cannadine, D., *The Decline & Fall of the British Aristocracy* (Macmillan, 1992)

Cannadine, D., *Victorious Century: The United Kingdom 1800-1906* (Penguin, 2018)

Carew, R., *Footprints in the Sand: The Story of the Carews of Devon 1086-1945* (DuBois, 2018)

Cherry, B., & Pevsner, N., *The Buildings of England: Devon* (Penguin, 1991 ed)

Constantine, S., Kirby, M.W. & Rose, M.B. (eds.) *The First World War in British History* (Edward Arnold, 1995)

DeGroot, G.J., *British Society in the Era of the Great War* (Longman, 1996)

Devon Federation of WIs, *Devon Within Living Memory,* (DFWI and Countryside Books, Newbury, 1993)

Duffy, M., and others (Eds), *The New Maritime History of Devon, Volume II* (Conway/University of Exeter, 1994)

Edmunds, J., *A History of West Buckland School* (Aycliffe Press, Barnstaple, 1983)

Edwards, R.A., *Devon's Non-Metal Mines* (Halsgrove, 2011)

Ellis, A.C., *Historical Survey of Torquay* (author + Torquay Directory, 1930)

Emery, A., *Dartington Hall* (Clarendon Press, Oxford, 1970)

Freeman, B., *The Yeomanry of Devon 1794-1927* (St Catherine's Press, 1927))

Gilbert, M., *First World War* (Weidenfeld & Nicolson, 1988)

Harris, H., *Devon's Century of Change* (Peninsula Press, 1998)

Hattersley, R., *Borrowed Time: The Story of Britain Between the Wars* (Abacus, 2009)

Hemming, J., *A Devon House: The History of Poltimore* (Intellect, Bristol, 2002)

Hetherington, Sir Hector, *The University College at Exeter 1920-1925* (University of Exeter, 1963)

Jenkin, A.K.H, *Mines of Devon: The Southern Area* (David & Charles, Newton Abbot, 1974)

Keating, J., *A Child for Keeps: the History of Adoption in England 1918-45* (Palgrove/Macmillan, 2008)

Kelly's Directory of Devonshire 1913, 1914, 1919, 1923, 1935

Kirby, A., *In the Cause of Liberty: Exeter Trades Council 1890-1990* (Sparkler Books, Exeter, 1990)

Lane, S.H.N., *Notes on the Public Administration of of Education in Torquay during the 25 years ended 30 April 1929* (Torquay Education Authority, c1929)

Lauder, R.A., *Vanished Houses of North Devon* (R.A.Lauder, 1981)

Lauder, R.A., *Vanished Houses of South Devon* (North Devon Books, 1997)

Lauder, R.A., *Devon Families* (Halsgrove, Wellington, 2002)

Lethbridge, H.J., *Torquay & Paignton: The Making of a Modern Resort* (Phillimore, 2003)

Loughlin, T., *Shell-Shock & Medical Culture in First World War Britain* (Cambridge, 2017 online version)

Lowndes, G.A.N., *The Silent Social Revolution: The Expansion of Public Education in England & Wales 1895-1965* (Oxford, 1969)

Maggs, C.G., *Devonshire Railways* (Halsgrove, Wellington, 2010)

Morgan, N.J. & Pritchard, A., *Power & Politics at the Seaside: The Development of Devon's Resorts in the Twentieth Century* (University of Exeter, 1999)

Nicolson, J., *The Great Silence 1918-1920: Living in the Shadow of the Great War* (John Murray, 2009)

O'Brien, P., *Havoc: The Auxiliaries in Ireland's War of Independence* (Collins, 2017)

Orme, N., (ed.) *Unity & Variety: A History of the Church in Devon & Cornwall* (University of Exeter, 1991)

Overy, R., *The Morbid Age: Britain and the Crisis of Civilisation,1919-1939* (Penguin, 2010)

Parker, D.H., *The People of Devon in the First World War* (The History Press, Stroud, 2013)

Parker, D.H., *Exeter: Remembering 1914-18* (The History Press, Stroud, 2014)

Parker, D.H., *Edwardian Devon 1900-1914* (The History Press, Stroud, 2016)

Parratt, C., *More than Mere Amusement, Working Class Women's Leisure in England 1750-1914* (North Eastern University Press, USA, 2001)

Payne, F.J., *The History of Torbay Hospital 1844-1980* (Devonshire Press, Torquay, c1980)

Perrin, R., *Agriculture in Depression, 1870-1940* (Cambridge University Press, 1995)

Pugh, M., *We Danced All Night: A Social History of Britain between the Wars* (Vintage, 2009)

Radford, J.P. & Tipper, A., *Starcross: Out of the Mainstream* (G.Allan Roeher Institute, Toronto, 1988)

Renwick, C., *Bread for All: The Origins of the Welfare State* (Penguin, 2018)

Sampson, M., *A History of Tiverton* (Tiverton War Memorial Trust, 2004)

Seaman, L.C.B., *Post-Victorian Britain: 1902-1951* (Methuen/University Paperback, 1970)

Simon, B., *Education & the Labour Movement 1870-1920* (Lawrence & Wishart, 1965)

Simon, B., *The Politics of Educational Reform 1920-1940* (Lawrence & Wishart, 1978)

Snell, F.J., *Devonshire: Historical, Descriptive, Biographical* (Wm Mates & Co., 1907)

Stephenson, J. A., *Teignmouth Grammar School: The First Fifty Years,* privately printed, 1970)

Sutton, C.M., *Axminster Hospital 1886-1986* (Privately published, 1986)

Thompson, W. H., *Devon: A Survey: Coast, Moors & Rivers* (University of London, 1932)

Tropp, A., *The School Teachers* (Heinemann, 1957)

Trump, H.J., *Westcountry Harbour: The Port of Teignmouth* (Brunswick Press, Teignmouth, 1976)

Van der Kiste, J., *Plymouth: History & Guide* (The History Press, Stroud 2009)

Walling, R.A.J., *The Story of Plymouth* (Westaway, Plymouth, 1950)

Walsh, E.S., *Kilkenny: In Time of Revolution 1900-23* (Merrion, Co Kildare, 2018)

Whetham, E. H., *The Agrarian History of England & Wales, Volume VIII, 1914-39* (Cambridge University Press, 1978)

Whitfeld, H., *Plymouth & Devonport in Times of War & Peace* (E. Chapple, Plymouth, 1900)

Young, M., *The Elmhirsts of Dartington* (Dartington Hall Trust, 1996)

Articles

Brayshay, M., 'Heathcoat's Industrial Housing in Tiverton, Devon' in *Southern History* 13, 82-104, (1992)

Caldwell, J., 'The History of Dean Clarke's Hospital'; in *Rep.Trans. Devon. Ass.* 104, 174-192, (1972)

Creighton, O., Cunningham, P. & French, H., 'Peopling polite landscapes: community and heritage at Poltimore, Devon' in *Landscape History* Vol 34.2, 61-86, (2013)

Hanna, E., 'Veterans' Associations: GB & Ireland' in *International Encyclopaedia of the First World War Online* (2015)

Heath, A.J.K., 'The Palestine Police Force under the Mandate' in *Police Journal* 1928.78-88, (1928)

Howkins, A. & Verdon N., 'The state and the farm worker: the evolution of the minimum wage in agriculture in England & Wales, 1909-24' in *Agricultural History Review*, 57, II, 257-274, (2009)

Jackson, A.J.H., 'Managing Decline: The Economy of the Powderham Estate in Devon, 1870-1939' in *Rep.Trans. Devon. Ass.*128, 197-215, (1996)

Neville, J., 'Challenge, Conformity and Casework in Interwar England: the first women councillors in Devon' in *Women's History Review*, 22, 6, 971-994, 2013

Penning-Rowsell, E.C., 'Who 'Betrayed' Whom? Power and Politics in the 1920/21 Agricultural

Crisis' in *Agricultural History Review*, 45, II, 176-194, (1997)

Porter, J.H., 'Devon and the General Strike, 1926' in *International Review of Social History*, 23,3,333-356, (1978)

Rothery, M. (2007) 'The wealth of the English landed gentry 1870-1935' in *Agricultural History Review* 55, II, pp251-268)

Rubinstein, W.D., 'Britain's elites in the Inter-War period 1918-39' in *Contemporary British History*, 12, 1, 1-18 (1998).

Sheail, J., 'The White Paper, *Agricultural Policy*, of 1926: its context and significance' in *Agricultural History Review*, 58, II, 236-254, (2010)

Woodcock, G., 'The Town and the General Strike' in *Tavistock's Yesterdays*, Vol 1, 49-51, (1985)

Devon & Exeter Institution, Exeter

Exeter City Council, *The Opening of the 2,000th Post-War Municipal House* (City Council, 1937)

Holladay, R., *Ravenswood School: Some Memories of its first 27 years* (privately published, 2017)

Meredith Davies, L., *Report by the County Medical Officer on the General Condition, Accommodation and Future Use of Institutions handed over to the County Council in Pursuance of the Local Government Act, 1929* (Devon County Council, c1930)

Sturman, J. & Barnes, S., *Willingly to School: A History of Newtown School & its Community* (privately published, no date)

Devon Heritage Centre, Exeter

Devon County Council and Committee Minutes (bound volumes) including War Agricultural Committee, War Pensions Committee, Agricultural Committee, Agricultural Education Committee, Care of the Mentally Defective Committee, Child Welfare Committee, Education Committee, Finance Committee, General Purposes Committee, Special Expenditure Committee

1260F/O/HA/33-59	Royal Devon & Exeter Hospital, Annual Reports 1919-1929
1262M/FH42	Earl Fortescue's memoirs
1262M/O/O/LD/112 & 134	WWI Red Cross & VAD Files/inc Fortescue correspondence
1262M/O/O/LD/113 & 148	Lord Lieutenancy Files (WWI and aftermath)
1987A/PR18-21	Lustleigh Parish Magazines 1918-21
2269C/EFL2	Beer C of E School logbook
5631A/M12, 13, 16	City of Exeter Medical Officer of Health's Annual Reports 1920, 1922, 1925
DPR53	Printed research paper related to Seale-Hayne Hospital entitled *Shell Shocked: The evolving management of Post-Traumatic Stress Disorder in World War One* (anon, 2016)
PLU Honiton 5-6	Board of Guardians Minute Book 1919-28
PLU Okehampton 40-41	Board of Guardians Minute Book 1918-24
PLU Tiverton 1-2	Board of Guardians Minute Book 1920-26
PLU Totnes 104	Workhouse Masters' Report Book 1920-22

Teignmouth Museum

Alfred Best's diary

Brook Street Girls' School Logbook

Exeter Road Boys' School Logbook

Pamphlets published by Teign Heritage
    Prince, P.D., *The Riviera Cinema, Teignmouth* (2006)
    Saunders, K.A., *Teignmouth's Haldon Aerodrome* (2006)
    Thomas, S.F., *A History of Teign Corinthian Yacht Club* (2006)

Paper on Miss Katherine Anson Cartwright

Soldier's demobilisation information booklet and forms

Teignmouth Hospital file

Torquay Library (Local Studies)

Torquay Medical Officer of Health's Annual Reports for 1913 and 1925

Websites

www.britishempire.co.uk/article/plymouth.htm

wwww.cairogang.com/cause-of-death/killed-in-action

www.canadianbritishhomechildren.weebly.com

www.childrenshomes.org.uk/list/Devon.shtml

www.colonelstephenssociety.co.uk

www.dreadnoughtproject.org/tfs/index.php/Francis_Hugh_Sandford

www.encyclodepia.1914-1918-online.net (Veterans' Associations articles by Emma Hanna and Julia Eichenberg)

www.exeterlocalhistorysociety.co.uk/2018-08-08-dr-lovely

www.gracesguides.couk/1930_Road_Traffic_Act

www.grecianarchive.exeter.ac.uk

www.greensonscreen.co.uk/argylehistory

www.historicengland.org.uk/listing/Youlston_Park

www.jacobinmag.com/2018/11/remembrance-day-november-11-soldiers-red-poppy (article 'Comrades at War' by Marcus Barnett and David Broder)

www.landedfamilies.blogspot.com/Bailey of Lee Abbey

www.legendarydartmoor.co.uk/manatonchurch

www.msubs.co.uk/crew/vc-winners/sandford

www.nationalgeographic.com/history/Spanish_Flu

www.oldplymouth.uk

www.policehistory.com/tudor

www.stagebeauty.net/Daisy_Markham

www.theauxiliaries.com/men-alphabetical

www.theirishrevolution.ie/1920

www.wikipedia.org/wiki/Harold_St_Maur

www.wikipedia.org/wiki/Plymouth_City_Airport

Index

Acland, Sir (13th Bart) Arthur
    And land sale 88
Acland, Mrs Frances 54, 56
Acland, Francis (later 14th Bart) 25, 72, 93, 96
    Acland family 27, 94
Acland-Troyte, Lieut Colonel Gilbert (Huntsham) 92, 94, 96, 103
Acts of Parliament
    1832, 1867 & 1884 Representation of the People Acts 86
    1902 Education Act 129, 130
    1911 National Insurance Act 109
    1913 Mental Deficiency Act 131
    1914 Defence of the Realm Act 8
    1914 Government of Ireland Act 14
    1918 Education Act 128, 130, 131, 132, 134, 146
    1918 Maternity & Child Welfare Act 118
    1918 & 1928 Representation of the People Acts 53, 146
    1919 Church of England 'Enabling Act' 48
    1919 Housing & Town Planning Act 68
    1920 Agricultural Act 102-103
    1923 and 1924 Housing Acts 71
Addison, Christopher (Minister of Health) 68, 69, 71, 125, 137
Adkins, Dr (County Medical Officer) 69, 116, 118, 119, 121, 125, 135, 137
Agriculture
    Board of Agriculture condemns Devon 104
    Changes and problems 85-87
    Declining political support 96, 102, 103
    Farm prices fluctuate 89
    Harvest Festivals 100, 101
    Milk controversy 102
    Ploughing matches 100
    Shows 98, 104
    Subsidy dispute 102-103
    Successes 104
    Wage disputes 102
Aircraft 60, 74
    Displays 74-75
Alliance of Honour 50
Amory (Heathcoat Amory) family (Knightshayes) 38, 67, 72, 92, 94, 121, 132
Andrew, Miss Clara 37, 54, 119
Appeals tribunals 40
Appledore 16, 108
Armistice (see also Peace Treaty) 8-9, 18
    Armistice Days 16
Arnold, Rifleman (Exeter) 18
Ashburton 13, 42, 64, 69, 76, 110, 143
Ashreigney 101
Ashton, Lieutenant (Bradworthy) 18
Astor, Nancy, Lady 55
Austro-Hungarian Empire 8, 11
Auton, Acting Captain Gilbert (Broadclyst) 20

Axminster 17, 71, 77, 79, 111, 125

Babbacombe 22
Baldwin, Stanley
    Speech at Bradfield 96
Bale, Dr Rosa (Plymouth) 52
Balls, County/Hunt 96
Bampton 8, 15, 17, 26, 76, 90
    Fair 99
Bannatyne family (Haldon House) 89
Barnardo's Home
    And emigration 121
Barnstaple 9, 12, 16, 17, 19, 24, 26, 28, 37, 38, 52, 63, 65, 72, 76, 77, 89, 98, 109, 115, 117
    Education in 42, 72, 132, 133, 137, 139, 141, 142, 143, 145, 146, 147
    Employment in 40, 41, 42, 43, 44, 45
    Fair 98-99
    Housing 68, 70
    Workhouse 123, 125
Battlefield tours 17
Bazeley, Mrs Harry
    (Chair of Bideford Hospital Committee) 54
Beatty, Admiral Sir David (Earl in 1919) 24, 29, 60
Beer 19, 22, 27, 65, 140, 141
Betteridge, Lieutenant Robert (Totnes) 15
Bickersteth, Rev. H.L. (Tavistock) 45
Bickleigh 77, 90
Bideford 13, 16, 24, 31, 38, 43, 45, 50, 52, 76, 77, 79, 108, 109, 122
    Schools 131, 136-137, 142, 143
Birch, Able Seaman William (Dawlish) 18
Birdwood, General Sir William 23
Bishopsteignton 108, 113, 136
Black Torrington 12, 98
Boards of Guardians 9, 15, 21, 46, 122-125
    'Scattered Homes' 9, 122, 123
    Workhouses 9, 109, 122, 123, 124, 125
Boasley Cross 137
Bolshevikism/Communism 8, 13, 14, 24, 41, 42, 50, 53, 55-56, 137, 141-142
Bovey Tracey 12, 31, 85, 87, 90, 111, 115
Bow 77
Bowler, Rev. J.W. (Exeter) 50
Boy Scouts 11, 17, 25, 93
Bradninch 18
Bradworthy 18
Brampford Speke 16
Braunton 51, 143
British Empire/Empire Day 9, 15, 32, 141-142
Brixham 11, 22, 26, 42, 76, 77, 85
Broadclyst 16, 18, 20, 25, 27, 31
Broadhembury 27
Broster, Sister Annie (Heavitree) 32
Buckfastleigh 17, 71, 110
Bucknall, Rev. Jack 49-50

The People of Devon 1918–1930

Budleigh Salterton 11, 13, 74, 77, 130
Buller, Dame Georgiana 38-39, 121
Buller, General Sir Redvers 8, 39
Bulley, Sergeant Major (Exeter St Thomas) 19
Burlescombe 46
Burnett, Sir Napier (Obstetrician) 118-119

Cable, Sir Ernest (Baron in 1921) 87
    Lady Cable 13
Calmady-Hamlyn, Miss Mary 56, 94
    And Women's Land Army 37
Carew, Sir Walter (Haccombe) 90-91, 94
Carnivals 99,
    Hospital 112, 113, 114, 117
Cartwright, Miss Katherine Anson (Teignmouth) 53-54, 56
Castle Drogo 91
Cave, Sir Charles 71, 89, 121, 138
    Edward Cave 93, 94
Cecil, Right Rev. Lord William (Bishop of Exeter) 8, 11, 15, 45, 46, 53, 120, 124, 142
    Lady Florence Cecil 38, 96, 138
    Daughter's wedding 94
Chadwick, Rev. Samuel (Exeter) 50
Chagford 26-27, 108
Champernowne, Arthur Melville (Dartington) 88
Cheriton Bishop 16
Children (see also Education)
    At celebrations/commemorations 8, 9, 16, 17, 25, 28
    Crippled 121
    Employment/Juvenile Employment Centres 132
    Maternity and Child Welfare Clinics 117-119, 132
    Nurseries/Nursery Education 132
    Pauper 123
    Schools 128-148
    School Health Service 130-131, 134-135
Christmas 9, 12, 36, 77, 122
Chudleigh 87, 142, 143
Chudleigh Knighton 27, 108
Chudleigh, Lord Clifford of 52
Chudley, Petty Officer Albert (Newton Abbot) 14
Chulmleigh 26, 100, 110
Church Reform League 48
Churchill, Winston 10
Churston Ferrers 28, 76
Churston, Lady (Denise Orme) 138
Classey, Rev. H.G. (Plymtree) 50
Clergy/services 9, 13, 17, 22, 26, 32, 45-52, 100, 111, 113
    And strikers 44
    And social/moral decay 48-49, 50, 64, 66
Clinton, 21st Baron 27, 87, 89-90, 92, 96, 138
    Lady Clinton 94, 95, 96, 121
Clovelly 11, 64
Cobham, Alan (Sir) 74, 75
Coleford 77
Coleridge, Miss Betty (Salston Manor) 93
    Coleridge family 94, 111
Coltman, Rev. E.W. 51
Colyton 25, 26
    Grammar School 94, 141, 143, 144

Comrades of the Great War 24-26
    Merges with British Legion 24
Conscientious Objectors 13, 45
Cooke, Rev. H.R. (Torquay) 22
Copp, Corporal A.J. (Exeter) 19
Corkery Dr (School Medical Officer)
    And eugenics 120
Cornwood 77, 136
Crediton 11, 16, 17, 23, 27, 37, 38, 69, 70, 77, 125, 143, 146
Cudmore, Lance Corporal (Gt Torrington) 19
Cullompton 11, 18, 25, 26, 41, 70

Daniells, Lance Corporal (Bradninch) 18
Dark, William (Barnstaple) 19
Dartmoor 28, 64, 76, 77, 115
    Mining on 85
Dartmouth 40, 42, 72, 76, 108, 110, 144
Davies, Rev. J Morley (Braunton) 51
Davis, Major J.S.C. (VAD Director) 36, 37, 38, 39
Davy, Sir Henry & Lady 38, 120
Dawlish 11, 12, 16, 17, 18, 42, 64, 69, 110
Demobilisation 10-11, 13
    problems of 10
Denbury 18
Devon County Council 41-42, 79, 92, 118, 129, 130, 133,
    And agriculture 104-105
    Education Committee 53, 120, 130, 132, 135, 137, 138-139, 140-141
    Schools close 136
    School Health Service 135
Devon County Teachers' Association 135, 136, 137, 139
Devon, Earl(s) of 27, 46, 86, 136, 138
    Sell Alphington estate 89
Devonport 8, 13, 130, 133
    Dockyard 61, 76
Devonshire Regiment 13-14, 25, 30-31, 36
    Bols, Major General Sir Louis (CO) 25
    Bois-des-Buttes honours 22, 29
    Devonians in Russia 14, 32
    Devonians in Ireland 14-15
Drake, Rev. H.M. (Paignton) 44
Drewe family 91, 94, 96
Dunlop, Dr (Torquay School Medical Officer) 118, 134-135
Dunn, Lance Corporal (Dawlish) 11
Dunsford 79

Edgington, Rev. Cyril (Church Army) 50
Education 31-32, 128-148 (see also various towns)
    Board of Education 121
    'Dual System' 129
    Elementary schools 129, 130-131, 133-136, 137-138
    Fisher, Herbert (Pres. Board of Education) 130, 132, 147
    Girls 9, 130, 146
    Reorganisation at eleven 138-139, 142
    Scholarships 140-141, 144-145
    Schools of Art, Science & Technology 42, 132-133, 137
    School Health Service 130-131, 134-135

Schools, historic types of 128-130
Secondary schools 129-130, 143-146
Elections, Parliamentary 55-56
Elmhirst, Leonard & Dorothy (Dartington) 75, 88-89
Employment/Unemployment 41, 42-43
Escot & Kennaway family 11, 138
Estates, complete/partial sales of
    Bassett 89
    Bradfield 88
    Carew 90-91
    Chittlehamholt 87
    Court Hall 90
    Culm Davy 89
    Dartington 88
    Ebberley 87
    Haldon 89
    Halwill Manor 89
    Holley 89
    Iddesleigh 88
    Lee Abbey 87
    Lindridge 87
    Pickwell Manor 89
    Pitt House 87
    Poltimore 90
    Rockbeare 87
    Shute 89
    Sidbury Manor 89
    Stevenstone 89-90
    Stoodleigh 90
    Stover 90
    Stowford 89
    Stuckeridge 90
    Tawstock 88
    Upcott 89
    Wear House 89
    Willesleigh House 87
    Yarner 87
    Youlston Park 88
Exbourne 97
Exeter 8, 11, 12, 15, 16, 18, 19, 20, 24, 25, 32, 37, 40, 43, 50, 55, 63, 66, 72, 73, 74, 76, 77, 89, 98. 102, 117, 121
    ANZAC award 23
    County and city war memorials 28-30
    Education 32, 128-129, 130, 132, 133, 134, 140, 141, 142, 143, 144, 146-147
    Hospitals in 19, 20, 28, 36, 37, 38, 39, 94, 109-110, 111, 114-115, 116
    Housing 67, 68, 69-70, 71-72
    Influenza 108, 109
    Mayors of 10, 11, 17, 22, 25, 38
    Railways 76, 77, 98
    Royal Albert Memorial College 134, 146-148
    Tourists in 64-65
    Women's Local Government Society meeting 54
    Workhouse 109, 122, 125
    Unemployment in 42-43, 45
Exeter Cathedral 8, 15, 30, 31, 38, 42
    Very Rev. Dr Henry Gamble (Dean) 38, 47, 48
    Mrs Gamble 47, 56
Exeter, Diocese of
    And Education 138
    And inter-war issues 45-50
    And National Mission 46-47
    Association for the Care of Friendless Girls 47, 119-120
    Clergy-laity relations 47-48
    Outings 100
Exminster 15, 27, 89, 143
Exmouth 9, 19, 20, 22, 32, 36, 43, 50, 53, 64, 73, 76, 77, 100, 144
Fairs 98-101
Faithfull, Miss Lilian 9
Feniton 16
Ferguson-Davie, Sir William 38, 94, 121
    And land sale 88
Films 66-67
Fortescue, Earl (Lord Lieutenant) 11, 22, 25, 27, 29, 30, 37, 38, 39, 41, 92, 112, 118, 140
    Countess Fortescue 37, 38, 39, 94, 120
    Lady Susan Fortescue 94
France 7, 13, 30
Free Churches 50
Fremington 38, 138
Fulford family (Fulford) 92-3
Fursdon, Miss Cicely (Fursdon) 93
    Fursdon family 94

Geddes, Sir Eric ('Geddes Axe') 136
Germany 8, 11
Giles, Richard (Holsworthy) 19
Girl Guides 17, 25, 93
Goodleigh 15
Gush, Corporal (Beer) 22
Gould, Lieutenant Ronald (Exeter) 14

Haig, Field Marshal Sir Douglas (Earl in 1919) 24
Halberton 12, 26, 101
Halford, Lieut (RFC) (Crediton) 11
Halwill 43, 77
    Harris of Halwill Manor 89
Hambleden, Viscount & Viscountess (Bovey House) 93, 111
Hambleton, Henry Lieutenant (Exminster) 15
Hammond, Miss Katherine Penrose (Ilfracombe) 53
Harris, Rev. W. Gabriel (Walkhampton) 47
Harvey-Endacott, Lance Corporal (Denbury) 18
Hatherleigh 8, 49, 80, 97,
    Carnival/Fair 98, 99, 100
Hatt, Lieutenant Harold (Tiverton) 19
Heddon Mill 79
Hedges, Albert (Exeter) 19
Hemyock 12
High Bickington 95
Holsworthy 11, 19, 77,
    Fair 99
Honiton 26, 32, 43, 54, 68, 119, 125, 129
Hooper, Constable Charles (Exeter) 22
Horrabridge 77
Horses 81, 98
Horwood 32
Hospitals 7, 9, 19, 25, 29-30, 36, 37, 38, 109-117

Cancer treatment 116
Cottage hospitals 110-112
Cripples 121
Fund raising 109-117, 121
North Devon Infirmary 36, 94, 112, 113
Royal Devon & Exeter 20, 28, 38, 94, 109-110, 114-115, 116
Seale-Hayne 20-21
TB Hospitals 115, 116
Torbay 113-114
War Emergency Hospitals close 36-37
Workhouse infirmaries 109, 125
Hotels 61-62, 66
Housing 67-72, 104
Hudson, Rev. H. Rosson Hudson 132
Hunt, Sergeant Fred (Exeter) 18
Hunting, and its opponents 98
Huntsham 32
Hurst, Dr Arthur 20-21

Iddesleigh, 2nd Earl of (land sale) 88
Ilfracombe 16, 17, 43, 64, 65, 66, 74, 77, 100, 130, 143
Ilsington 85
India 13, 14, 19
Influenza 8, 18, 19, 108-109
Instow 38, 65
Irish Civil War
    Devonians in 14-15

Jackson, Private (Budleigh Salterton) 11
Jazz 67
Jewell, Mrs (Barnstaple councillor) 54
Jones, Major General Sir Robert (surgeon) 121
Jordain, Lieutenant (Brixham) 22

Kekewich family, Peamore 27, 47, 52, 94, 96
Kempthorne, Right Rev. John 46
Kendall, Sergeant (Exeter) 11
Kenn 89, 98
Kennford 26
Kentisbury 32
Kenton 12, 27
Kingsbridge 70, 76, 143
Kingswear 76
Kirkwood, Major John (Yeo Vale) 15

Lambert, George (Liberal MP) 70, 92, 96
Lamplugh, Rev. R.C.L. (Bartnstaple) 44
Lane Davies, Rev. J.G. (Babbacombe) 22
Langtree School 137
Lazenby, Miss Katherine 27, 56, 132
League of Nations 26
Lethaby, Gunner Jack (North Molton) 19
Lewis, Captain Arthur (Goodleigh) 15
Littlehempston 32
Living, Robert (philanthropist) 121
Lloyd George, David 14, 40, 54, 67, 86, 130
    Speech at Killerton 96
Lockyer, Sergeant Major (Exmouth) 19
Loddiswell 15

Lopes, Sir Henry (Maristow) 92
Lovely, Dr Charles 69-70
Lucas, Lieutenant Ernest (Shaldon) 15
Lynmouth/Linton 121, 142

Magistrates 19, 46, 120
    First female JPs 56-57
Manaton (and ejection of rector) 48
Marker 'Squire' (Coombe) 93
Martin, Lance Corporal (Milton Damerell) 18
Marwood 136
Matthews, Nurse Mary (Plymouth) 25
May, Major General Sir Edward & Lady 96, 138
Mayoress of Exeter's Depot 7, 9, 11, 14, 23, 36
Medals/Medal ceremonies 14, 20, 22,
    Confiscation of 20
    Fraudulent use of 22
    Awards to Red Cross & Hospital staff 39-40
Meeth 77, 85
Mesopotamia/Middle East 7, 13, 18, 19, 30
Mildmay, Colonel Francis (Baron in 1922) 27, 41, 96, 111
    Mrs (Lady) Mildmay 38, 56, 111
Miller, Lance Corporal James (Exeter) 20
Milton Damerell 18
Mingo, Lance Corporal (Topsham) 18
Montgomery, Miss Jessie (Exeter) 53
Morchard Bishop 28, 140
Moretonhampstead 17, 43, 64, 71, 76, 77, 100, 108, 111
Morwelham 137-138
Motor vehicles/Motorists 44, 64, 65, 77-82
    Anti-social behaviour 81
    Cars, prices 78
    Lorries 77
    Motorcycles 81-82
    Offences and penalties 79-80
Mount Edgcumbe 5th Earl of
    Sells Devon estates 89
Murch, Private (Cullompton)

Newman, Sir George (Chief Medical Officer) 121, 137
Newman, Sir Robert (Mamhead) 92, 94, 96, 124, 146
Newton Abbot 14, 15, 16, 17, 19, 24, 25, 28, 31, 43, 44, 49, 65, 79, 85, 89, 90, 108,
    Education 132, 133, 136, 137, 138, 143
    Housing 70, 71
    Opposition to tank trophy 23
    Railway 76, 77
    Sport 72, 73
    Workhouse 109, 122-123, 124, 125
Nonconformists 50-52, 100
North Devon Yeomanry 30
North Molton 19, 85
North Tawton 17, 27
Northampton, 6th Marquis of (sells Devon estates) 87-88
Northcote, Lady Rosamund 81
Norton, Gunner C.E. 20

Oakford 28
Ogwell 133-134
Okehampton 8, 16, 40, 44, 64, 77, 78, 89, 109, 125, 130,

Index

141, 143, 145
    Carnival/Fair 98, 99
    Hospital 111-112
O'Leary VC, Lieutenant Michael 20
Ottery St Mary 25, 77, 110-111, 143
Owen, Sir James 8, 20, 29, 37, 40, 121
    Lady Owen 37, 121

Page, Nurse Doris (Exmouth) 32
Pageants, Armistice/Victory 12, 13
Paignton 22, 23, 42, 44, 67, 70, 72, 73, 76, 108, 137
Parkham 11
Payhembury 99
Peace Treaty/Peace Day 15
    Celebrations 15-17
Pearce, Sergeant Major George (South Molton) 22
Peek, Captain Roger (Rousdon/Loddiswell) 15
Peek, Lady (Widworthy Court) 56, 96, 121
Perkins, Private (Exeter) 18
Peto, Basil (MP Barnstaple) 138
Petrockstowe 77, 85
Phillips, Mrs Juanita Maxwell (mayor of Honiton) 54, 55, 95, 119
Pike, Charles (Exmouth) 19
Pilton 31, 43, 65
Plymouth 13, 14, 25, 43, 44, 52, 55, 57, 67, 72, 77, 99, 108, 111, 117
    Airport near 74
    Education in 129, 130, 131, 132, 134, 143, 146, 148
    Housing 68-69, 70, 71, 72
    Port 76
    Quarries near 85, 86
    Railways 76, 77, 98
    Workhouse 109, 125
Plympton 125, 144
Pole, Sir Frederick de la (Shute) 25, 94
Pole-Carew, Sir John (Anthony & Shute) 89
Police 79, 80, 119-120
    Hostility to women officers 57
Poltimore, 4th Baron 90
Poole, Frederick (Exeter) 19
Poor Law (see Boards of Guardians)
Ports 76
Portsmouth, 7th Earl of 38, 92,
    8th Earl 92, 94, 140
Powderham 73, 136
Prices 62-64
Prince of Wales 24-25
Prisoners of War 11, 38
Prouse, Miss Dorothy (Exeter) 108
Public Health 69, 71
Pyworthy 31

Quicke family (Newton St Cyres) 31, 94

Railways 41, 42, 43, 64, 65-66, 76-77, 86
    New Halwill-Torrington line 43, 77, 123
Red Cross 18, 38, 39, 56, 57, 94, 114
    Awards to staff 39-40
Refugees 36, 37-38

Religion 8-9, 52
    Services 8-9, 15
    Clergys' views 8-9
Restorick, Frank (Beer) 19
Rhodes, Lance Corporal (Totnes) 11
Rice, Nurse Olive (Newton Abbot) 19
Rivers, Sergeant George (South Molton) 22
Roads 77-82
    Accidents 79-80
    Hazards and complaints 77-79
    Improvements 79
Rowcroft, Lieutenant Frederick 19
Rowcroft, Mrs Ella (Torquay) 45, 113
Royal Navy
    Warships in Torbay 60-61
Rumbold, Lieut Colonel Sydney (Exeter/Torquay) 20
Runciman, Mrs Hilda
    and 1929 Tavistock election 55-56
Rural life (see also Agriculture & Education)
    Hunting 98
    Self contained 96, 98
    Shows and Fairs 98-100
    Social events 101
    Outings 100-101
Rushby, Rev. W. (Torquay) 44
Russia, 13

St Aubyn, John Molesworth (Tetcott) 93
St Aubyn, Lady Molesworth 96
St Maur, Harold (Stover) 90
Sage VC, Private Thomas (Tiverton) 23
Salvation Army 17, 50
Sampford Peverell 78
Sandford 18, 88, 112
Sandford VC, Lieutenant Richard, and Captain Francis Sandford DSO 30
Sclater, Major General Sir Henry 22
Seaton 13, 65, 77
Seale-Hayne (Newton Abbot),
    As war hospital 20-21
    As agricultural college 104-105
Servicemen
    Demobilisation 10-11
    Receptions for 11-12
Shaldon 15
Shapland, Lance Corporal (Sandford) 18
Shell shock 20-21, 110
Shelley, Sir John & Lady (Shobrooke) 38, 92, 96
    Commander Shelley's wedding 94
Shirwell 134
Shobrooke 28
Sidbury 28
Sidmouth 15, 32, 52, 65, 73, 77, 118
Sidmouth, Viscount & Viscountess 94, 96, 138
Somerset, 15th Duke of (sells Devon estates) 89
    Seymour family 94, 121
South Molton 16, 22, 26, 38, 70, 98, 108, 125
Sowton 31
Special constables 40
Splatt, Miss Edith (Exeter) 55, 119

Sport Athletics 101
  Bowls 73, 74
  Cricket 72, 101
  Football 64, 72, 73, 101, 140
  Golf 65
  Rugby 64, 72
  Sailing 73
  Swimming 64, 73
  Tennis 65, 73
Spurrell, Kate Miss (Totnes) 55
Starcross 12,
  Western Counties Institution 131
Stevenstone House 89
Stewart Brigadier Sir Hugh (Ministry of Labour) 10
Stirk, Dr (Exeter Medical Officer) 119
Stoddart, Vice Admiral Archibald (Teignmouth) 24
Stoodleigh Court (becomes school) 90, 128, 129
Street, Corporal (Exeter) 19
Strikes 40-41, 42, 43-44, 48
Strode family 39, 86-87

Talaton 'Club' 101
Tavistock 8, 15, 16, 17, 19, 22, 25, 40, 43, 44, 45, 49, 55-56, 64, 71, 85, 125
  Duke of Bedford's land sale 87
  Education 131, 133, 139-140, 142, 143
  Fair 99
  Hospital 112-113
  Railway 76, 77
Teignmouth 11-12, 22, 24, 44, 52, 53, 64, 72, 76,
  Haldon airfield/shows 75
  Hospital 113
  Schools 141, 143, 145
Throckmorton, Sir Robert (Molland) 93
Tindall, Nurse Mary (Sidmouth) 32
Tithes 46
Tiverton 8, 11, 12, 17, 19, 22-23, 27, 44, 51, 64, 67, 71, 72, 76, 81, 82, 90, 98, 108, 118, 122
  Education 131, 132, 136, 137, 139, 140, 142, 143-144, 146
  Hospital 115-116, 117
  Paupers/Workhouse 109, 123-124, 125
Topsham 18, 73
Torquay 10, 16, 17, 23, 43, 44, 61, 72, 73, 76, 115, 118
  Colonel Charles Burn MP 41
  Comrades of the Great War 24
  Education 42, 132, 136, 137, 139, 143
  Housing 68, 70, 71, 72
  New Zealand flag award 23
  School Health Service 134-135
  Torbay curates awarded MCs 22
  Torbay Hospital 113-114
  War Hospital & Depot 36-37, 38, 39
Torrington (Great) 19, 32, 43, 68, 77, 125
  Fair 99-100
Totnes 11, 15, 22, 31-32, 41, 42, 50, 76, 108, 109, 118, 125, 133, 143
Tourism/Tourists 60, 64-66
Trefusis, the Hon. Mrs Eva 56

Trefusis, Right Rev. Robert (Bishop of Crediton) 8, 29, 45, 46, 48
Trelawney-Ross, Rev. W.E. (Paignton) 22
Trophies, Town 22-23
Trusham 32
Tucker, Private (Exeter) 11
Tudor, Lieut General Sir Henry 15

Uffculme 8, 123
Uplowman 31

Venn, Private (Tiverton) 19
Vicary, Arthur (Beer) 19
Vicary, Miss Eleanor (Newton Abbot) 57
Vlieland, Mrs Alice (Exeter) 54, 55, 119
Voluntary Aid Detachments (VADs) 7, 9, 36, 38, 56, 57, 94, 111, 121
Voluntary Nursing Association 37, 38, 57, 94, 117-118

Walkhampton 47
Walrond family (Bradfield) 88, 94, 96
Walter, Corporal (Totnes) 11
Walters, Rev. T.C. (Highweek, Newton Abbot) 49
War memorials 25, 26-32
Warren, Private (Tiverton) 11
Watermouth Castle (Mrs Penn Curzon) 39, 89
Weeks, Charles (Tavistock) 19
West, William (Exeter) 19
West Hill 26
Westward Ho! 77
Whimple 16, 26
Whittome, Lieutenant Arthur (Tavistock) 15
Willey, Nurse Olive (Exmouth) 32

William II, Kaiser 8, 17
Williams, Captain George (Exeter) 19
Wills, Sir Edward Chaning 38, 94, 110, 113, 114
Winkleigh 77, 87, 103
Withycombe 31
Women, Appointed JPs 56-57
  Attitudes to 9,
  Awards to 39-40
  Devon Education Committee members 53
  Headteachers 146
  Local councillors/mayors 53-55
  Mothers and babies 117-119
  Nurses 32
Women's Institutes 94-95
Woodbury 16
Wrey (Bouchier Wrey) family 88, 92

Young Men's Christian Association 26, 50, 53, 57, 66